Best Newspaper Writing 1986

The Poynter Institute also publishes:
Best Newspaper Writing 1985
Best Newspaper Writing 1984
Best Newspaper Writing 1983
The Adversary Press
Believing the News
Making Sense of the News

Best Newspaper Writing 1979-1982 are now
out of print.

BEST NEWSPAPER WRITING 1986

Edited by Don Fry

Winners: The American Society of Newspaper Editors Competition

Copies of *Best Newspaper Writing 1986* are available for
$7.95 each from The Poynter Institute. 1983-1985 editions are
also available, as well as the Ethics Seminar transcript series.
Some discounts apply. Please write for details.

For Roy Peter Clark,
who started all this....

About this series

AUGUST 1986

If newspapers are a first rough draft of history, as one editor has said, then this book is devoted to the notion that such instant histories should be marked by literary grace as well as by factual reliability.

This is Volume VIII of *Best Newspaper Writing,* which increasingly since 1979 has been bought by students, teachers, and professionals as an indispensable text on clear, effective, and graceful use of the language.

As in past years, *Best Newspaper Writing 1986* is a joint venture of the American Society of Newspaper Editors and The Poynter Institute for Media Studies of St. Petersburg, Florida. The first six editions of *Best Newspaper Writing* were edited by Dr. Roy Peter Clark, an associate director of the Institute and director of its Writing Center. Starting with the seventh edition last year, Clark was joined in the editing process by his colleague Dr. Donald K. Fry, also an associate director of the Institute. For this year's edition, Fry conducted the interviews with the winning writers and edited the book with counsel from Clark.

In 1977, the ASNE made better newspaper writing one of its principal long-range goals. The following year it inaugurated a contest to select the best writing in several categories from papers in the U.S. and Canada and to reward the writers with $1,000 prizes. The Institute volunteered to spread the gospel of good writing by publishing the winning entries along with Clark's notes, commentaries, and interviews with the winning writers. That was *Best Newspaper Writing 1979,* which is now sold out and becoming a collector's item.

Each year the winners are chosen by a panel of ASNE editors that meets in St. Petersburg for several days to screen nearly 500 entries in four categories. The 1986 categories were deadline and non-deadline writing, commentary, and editorial writing.

Fourteen editors, under the chairmanship of Anthony Day, editorial page editor of the *Los Angeles Times,* participated in judging the 1986 entries. They are:

John Carroll, *Lexington* (Ky.) *Herald-Leader*

Don E. Carter, formerly of Knight-Ridder Newspapers

James Clendinen, formerly of the *Tampa Tribune*

Michael Gartner, Gannett Company

William Hosokawa, *Rocky Mountain News*

David Laventhol, *Newsday,* New York

Ross MacKenzie, *The Richmond* (Va.) *News Leader*

Patrick McCauley, *The Huntsville* (Ala.) *Times*

Eugene Patterson, *St. Petersburg Times*

Don Shoemaker, *The Miami Herald*

Claude Sitton, *The News & Observer,* Raleigh, N.C.

Richard Smyser, *The Oak Ridger,* Oak Ridge, Tenn.

Joseph Sterne, *The Sun,* Baltimore, Md.

Frederick Taylor, *The Wall Street Journal*

Dr. Clark was one of the first newspaper writing coaches and has been a national leader in the growing movement to make American newspapers more readable, more interesting, and more accurate. Trained as a Chaucer scholar at the State University of New York, he came to the *St. Petersburg Times* in 1977 on leave from the English faculty at Auburn University for what was supposed to be a one-year sabbatical as a newsroom writing coach. The one year turned into two, the coach turned into a staff writer, and then he joined The Poynter Institute (then known as Modern Media Institute) to direct its Writing Center. He and Fry conduct frequent writing seminars for newspaper professionals and for advanced liberal arts students seeking careers in journalism. They also work with high school students, including many minority students, college journalism teachers, high school newspaper advisors and their student editors. At a time when many despair that "kids just can't write anymore," Clark has developed a pilot program for fourth- and fifth-graders which has had remarkable success in teaching elementary school children not only to write well—but to love writing.

The Institute has four centers: Writing, Graphics and Design, Management, and Ethics, each with its own faculty.

Beginning in 1985, Clark was joined on the faculty of the Writing Center by Fry, who had been a mentor and colleague at the State University of New York at Stony Brook. Fry, a graduate of Duke University and the University of California at Berkeley, is a distinguished scholar of early English and also an outstanding teacher of contemporary writing. He is a writing coach and consultant to many newspapers, a frequent lecturer at several universities, and has testified as an expert witness on the precise meanings of words.

Founded in 1975 by the late Nelson Poynter, chairman of the *St. Petersburg Times* and its Washington affiliate, *Congressional Quarterly,* the Institute was bequeathed controlling stock in the Times Publishing Co. in 1978. It invests its dividends in projects such as this book, its four teaching centers, and other educational and research projects, all of which seek the same goal: to raise levels of excellence in newspapers and the communications media generally.

Robert J. Haiman, President
The Poynter Institute

Acknowledgments

Atlanta *Constitution* and Tom Teepen
Baltimore *Evening Sun* and Carl Schoettler
Baltimore *Sun* and Roger Simon
Newsday and Les Payne
St. Paul Pioneer Press-Dispatch and John Camp
St. Petersburg Times, David Finkel and Larry King
San Diego *Tribune* and Jonathan Freedman
The Wall Street Journal and Daniel Paul Henninger
The Washington Post, Bradley Graham and
    Kenneth Ikenberry

*We wish to thank the following people for their
generous assistance in producing this volume: Jo Cates,
Institute Librarian, for consultation on the bibliography;
Roy Peter Clark, Joyce Olson, and Cary Waulk of the
Institute staff; Walter Dorsett, Daryl Frazell, Cyndy
Rymer, Adelaide Sullivan, and Jim Tyrrell; and of
course, the authors and their editors, especially Ralph
Bennett, Doug Hennes, Jim Hoge, John Linthicum, and
Paul Tash. Special thanks to Billie Keirstead, whose
unblinking eye for quality makes this series possible.*

Book design by Billie M. Keirstead
Portraits by Jack Barrett
Cover by Sally Wern Comport

Contents

Introduction

Journalistic folklore says you win the Pulitzer Prize for snazzy reporting and the ASNE award for pure writing. The five winners of the 1986 American Society of Newspaper Editors Distinguished Writing Awards know better. They report like demons, and they write like angels.

Each one takes us deep inside real human beings caught in extraordinary situations. They teach us about people and the world and ourselves in believable ways. We praise their literary grace, but we admire their determination to make us look at the truth, whether we like that truth or not.

* * *

JOHN CAMP won the ASNE award for non-deadline writing *and* the Pulitzer by taking us inside the Benson family, three generations of Swedish farmers in southwestern Minnesota. Camp, a feature writer with the *St. Paul Pioneer Press-Dispatch*, wrote a five-part series entitled "Life on the Land: An American Farm Family."

Camp's newsroom team decided their farm coverage was in a rut. According to Doug Hennes, the Metro editor, "We were doing too many number stories and not enough people stories." So Camp and a photographer, Joe Rossi, spent six months visiting and working with the Bensons, an extremely articulate and attractive family. Camp and Rossi hoed beans with Sally-Anne Benson for three days to capture scenes like this one:

> "Just down to there—you can see the end. Four more rounds, maybe."
> "Two hours?"
> "I don't think I can do it two more hours."

"How about this?... We get some Hare Krishnas and tell them the thistles are the manifestation of evil, and they could dance through the fields with their hoes, hari-hari, rama-rama...."

And passers-by, had there been any, would have seen two large dust-covered men and a small, tired woman doing an impromptu Hare Krishna dance with hoes, in a blazing sun in the Benson soybean field, not far from the Iowa line, in southwestern Minnesota.

Camp characterizes David Benson as a "Prairie Intellectual," and just lets him talk, as in this segment:

A hoe, for the Bensons, is a philosophical statement.

"The soil has been here since the glaciers left, and you could grow just about anything on it," Benson said. "Since we've started farming it, we haven't done it any good. We send a lot of it right down to the Gulf of Mexico every year, pour all kinds of chemicals on it. Who knows what we'll wind up doing to it?

"There's an alternative to all that. If you're willing to take a little less, you can get along without all the fertilizers and the Lasso and Bigfoot (herbicides). It means you've got to do handwork, but that's OK, too—you build up a relationship with the land by working on it. You put so much work into a piece of land, and you start getting protective. That's got to be good for it, in the long run."

Camp shows us the farm, but always with people at the focal points, as in this description of baling:

Baling means long, lingering hours of twilight as the solstice approaches. Old,

weathered gray wood in the hay rack. Warm
water from glass jars, and never enough of
it. Hay cuts on forearms. Twine grooves in
the pads of fingers. Sweat-soaked leather
gloves. T-shirts sticking to the back and
chest. Dry lips. The sun carving at the eyes.
Arms leaden and aching with fire.

Metro editor Doug Hennes comments: "John
is a very good observer. As he walks in a door,
he picks up things. When he writes, it all comes
back. And he puts you in that story. He puts you
on the farm."

Routine news coverage focuses on the typical
farmer, that is, the failing farmer; but Camp
casts his characters against type. David Benson
talks like a philosopher or an economist, and his
family succeeds without dustbowl heroics. Camp
has chosen a real participant in the backbreaking routine of farm work, but one who can explain the farmers' mentality. At the end of his
series, we feel we know the Bensons, and through
them, the typical farmers who labor around
them, and not just in southwestern Minnesota.

* * *

BRADLEY GRAHAM writes about people in
a more immediate crisis, struggling to deal with
the volcanic eruption and flooding at Armero,
Colombia. He won the ASNE deadline writing
award for his coverage of the disaster, which occurred six weeks after he had arrived as South
American bureau chief for *The Washington Post*.

Graham had to reconstruct events no one had
seen, such as the eruption far away in the night,
and to gather accounts from the survivors:

The stories they recounted had haunting
similarities—about awakening in their
homes before midnight to cries of alarm and
a heavy rain of ash, about grabbing children
and the elderly, then fleeing to the streets,
about finding nowhere to run as the
Lagunilla River, normally just a tributary

of the valley's main Magdalena River, turned into a raging mass of liquid earth....

Hortensia Oliveros, 19 years old and eight months pregnant, saw the rushing water sweep their 11-month-old child out of her husband's arms. In the panic, she heard her husband shout to her to grab a branch, but that was the last she heard of him. She ended up near a road outside of Armero, screaming for someone to help her.

Graham shows the disaster through many eyes: President Betancur declaring a national emergency, a pilot blinded while flying overhead, a geologist explaining volcanos on television, a passing scavenger wearing a Christmas tree on his head, and the desperate rescuers. Everyone remembers Omayra Sanchez, the little girl we watched dying slowly on world television:

She would wrap her arms around the neck of a rescue worker standing in the water in front of her and try, with all her might, to tear herself free of whatever was keeping her feet pinned down. But she could not budge.

Workers dug around her, lifting out huge blocks of broken concrete. Rescuers feared that rising water would drown the girl if they couldn't get her out soon. Her head was just above the water line.

Watching the desperate attempts to save the girl, Alferez, the Red Cross chief, shook his head in despair.

"This makes one feel useless," he said. "What can we do?"

Graham reports and writes in a larger political context than one little village, with real people and their governments in mind. He advises: "In covering a story like this, you have to be conscious of the developing issues and themes, so you can weave them through your coverage.

I could see early that blame was going to become an issue that would survive the actual tragedy itself." We see the growing controversy through the eyes of the officials and rescuers at the scene, but we never lose that scene in the abstractions of government:

> Traces of ruined lives lay strewn across an area about 70 acres wide, where a raging river of mud and stone swept over this town. Today, Armero resembled a giant junkyard bathed in brown ooze.

* * *

ROGER SIMON of the *Baltimore Sun* probes beneath easy answers and attitudes. He won his second ASNE commentary prize for five columns celebrating the new citizenship of a young Russian defector, peeling away revisionist pieties about Nagasaki, exploring the resilience of a 13-year-old victim of the MOVE bombing in Philadelphia, setting the record straight on South African public relations, and burlesquing Yuppie pretensions toward woodburning and wine.

Simon writes with informed annoyance, based on solid reporting, usually taking a tack against fashionable opinion, as in this section summarizing the issue in Walter Polovchak's struggle to remain in the U.S.:

> Though the legal fighting was complicated, to me it was always a simple story, a simple question: Was America still a place of refuge? Was America still a place where the oppressed could come and be free?
>
> Many people said no. A *New York Times* editorial said those who supported Walter were demonstrating "shallow chauvinism."
>
> As one who has spent a good part of his career criticizing the things wrong with this country, it never seemed to me that praising the liberties offered here was either shallow or chauvinistic.

Noting the wallowing in guilt on the 40th anniversary of the Nagasaki bomb, Simon juxtaposes the Japanese attack on Pearl Harbor:

> I know what some will say. That this is the anniversary of Hiroshima and Nagasaki, not Pearl Harbor, and that is why there has been so little linkage, so little thought.
>
> But that is the trouble with these anniversary frenzies. They view history as isolated incidents rather than as a continous flow of events....
>
> Let us ask ourselves what we were doing in World War II and whom we were fighting.

Simon sees events in the world as linked, but our perception of them as flawed by "so little thought." And Simon's thought inevitably returns to American verities: patriotism, honor, history as lesson, basic decencies between people, and witty wariness toward phonies. The lightest piece of the five presents a firewood salesman taking advantage of urban status seekers. An invented Simon unsuccessfully tries to speak the woodsman's lingo, finally delivering a putdown in the form of a wine question. The supposed bumpkin replies: "Wahl, it really don't make me no never mind,...but Ah'd go with a Cote du Rhone or mebbe even a Nuit St.-Georges—less'n you think that'd be a mite sassy." Under the skin, under regional and class dialects, we're all Americans, and Simon says so without shame, indeed with pride.

* * *

JONATHAN FREEDMAN of the *San Diego Tribune* won the ASNE prize for editorials characterized by an unflinching moral vision, powerful rhythms of argument, and certainty of tone. He writes about illegal aliens abused by their own people while crossing the Mexican border, and illegal aliens abused by our own peo-

ple while working here in America. He explicates
the irrationality of skimping on prenatal care,
only to spend fortunes later on damaged babies.
And he takes us on a hair-raising tour of a gay
bathhouse, followed by a disturbingly similar
tour of an AIDS clinic in a hospital.

Freedman redefines the treatment of illegal
aliens as a form of apartheid, and shows us how
our self-absorption keeps us looking elsewhere.
He allows us no illusions about who should do
what to change this American version of
apartheid:

> Apartheid is racist wherever it exists. It
> is inhuman in South Africa and inhuman
> in southern California. It destroys the moral
> fabric of our society and leaves a legacy of
> discrimination and suffering.
>
> But we are blind to it. We point our
> finger at South Africans and feel self-
> satisfied at our enlightened society. While
> the waiters bring us fresh strawberries
> picked by illegal aliens living in ravines
> and hootches. Here. Today.

When I suggested in an interview that we
name the first-person plural pronoun in that last
paragraph "the implicating we," Freedman
responded, "It's the democratic we." Like Roger
Simon, he reminds us how easily we suspend
basic American values when it suits our immediate self-interest. He reminds us of those
values as he describes the Canyon of the Dead,

> ...a ravine running parallel to the interna-
> tional boundary, on U.S. territory, less than
> a mile east of the most heavily used border
> gate in the world. The aliens who enter
> America with visas enter a world of rights
> and freedoms.
>
> But the way through the Canyon of the
> Dead is the path to an illegal world, of
> manhunts and attacks by bandits, of ghet-

tos and exploitation. An apartheid world without rights and freedoms for illegal aliens working in the land of liberty.

Freedman cuts through the veneer of civil rights and government inaction in clear calls for action, as in the ending of his piece on AIDS, which began with a short drive to see whether the health department had posted warnings:

> But bathhouses are businesses posing as clubs, where darkened rooms become cubicles of death. If gays were being forced into cubicles and injected with a deadly serum to wipe them out, we would protest and halt it. But here the cubicles of death are tolerated, while the virus decimates the gay community and threatens people outside.
>
> The gay community must act now to close the bathhouses voluntarily. If the bathhouses won't close, the health and fire departments should shut them down.

Jonathan Freedman pries up the edges of our certainties, and shows us the complicity beneath, not just in San Diego, but here. Today.

* * *

While the four writers above excel at getting inside a family, a situation, or ourselves, DAVID FINKEL of the *St. Petersburg Times* takes us inside individuals, *and* inside families, situations, and ourselves. He won the ASNE non-deadline prize for five profiles of a disgraced harbor pilot, a circus fat man and his tormentors, a family struggling to keep their murderess stepmother in prison, five schizophrenics trying to silence the voices in their heads, and a father who shot his 3-year-old daughter while she lay comatose.

Finkel's interviewing skills and human insight put a window on the minds of his subjects, as in this lead to the story on schizophrenics:

Nighttime is the best time for Charles London Keys. At night, the 32-year-old Pinellas County resident sleeps in peace. While the fan in his room whirs, he's lost in dreams. When the cars go past his open window, he doesn't hear them.

Then he wakes up.

Then, instead of whirring, the fan says things like, "You're a fool for ice cream, Charles London Keys." Then, the cars going by say, "You can't tell Aretha Franklin how to sing a song."

The circus fat man, T.J. Albert Jackson, refused Finkel's usual extensive interviews, so Finkel joined the crowd around him. He let the onlookers do his questioning, and their questions became the story:

"How much do you weigh?"

"Eight hundred and ninety-one pounds."

"Gawd! How many meals do you eat a day?"

"Three."

"What—three *cows*?"

Go ahead. Laugh. He won't mind. He'll even laugh with you, slapping his hand on his knee and chuckling so hard that his belly's shaking. You'll have to excuse him, though, if his eyes seem to cloud over, but truthfully, he's heard your joke before. About a thousand times before.

Finkel's editor, Paul Tash, recalls the "adolescent hoo-hah going on in the newsroom when we saw that picture of him" before the assignment, and how the story made him "feel both voyeuristic and ashamed of being voyeuristic."

Finkel regards the story about Charles Griffith, who shot his daughter, as one of his most difficult. This story pulls the reader's sympathies and empathies in several directions at once, as

Finkel focuses on one character after another, trapped in their inability to deal with the paradoxes of their lives and roles. Griffith held nurses at gunpoint while he induced a fatal overdose of Valium into his daughter's gastronomy tube. One tense hour later,

> [Nurse Goskey] was listening, but not looking, when he brought the gun close to Joy's heart and fired.
>
> "I hear a shot," she said. "I turn around. I smell smoke. He has the gun in his right hand. He's standing over his child, right at the crib, near her chest area. He moves up again, closer, bends down a little bit.... Bang! I saw it, and I heard it."
>
> He straightened up. Goskey stood absolutely still. He turned toward her. She looked at his face: "It looked very sad, very depressed." She watched as he knelt, put the gun on the floor, and pushed it away from him. She heard people running down the hall. He did, too.
>
> He yelled, "Don't touch my baby! Don't come near my baby! Don't let them hurt my baby!"

* * *

All five of the ASNE winners remind us of the most basic principle of newswriting: reveal the character of human beings by telling stories about them.

Don Fry
May 1986

Best Newspaper Writing 1986

John Camp
Non-Deadline Writing

JOHN CAMP, 31, grew up in Cedar Rapids, Iowa, and received a B.A. in American studies and an M.A. in journalism from the University of Iowa. He started at the *Kings Journal* in southeast Missouri, and worked for seven years at *The Miami Herald*. He then became a reporter and eventually a columnist at the *St. Paul Pioneer Press*. He has just become a "self-assigned project writer." He was nominated for the Pulitzer Prize in 1980 for a story about Indian culture. His five-part series reprinted here won the Pulitzer for 1986 in feature writing.

Work holds farm family together

MAY 12, 1985

What is it like being a farmer today?

Most of the stories we have written have dealt with the financial plight of farmers and government efforts to help them. We have covered protests and auctions, and we have analyzed foreclosures and price supports.

But we felt we were missing something. We wanted to find out why farmers chose this difficult and often unrewarding lifestyle.

Out of that concern comes "Life on the Land: An American Farm Family." Over the next six months, columnist John Camp and photographer Joe Rossi will tell you about David and Sally-Anne Benson, who run a 160-acre farm near Worthington.

Today's article introduces you to the Bensons. We hope it, and the other articles to follow, give you a better understanding of why farming is so important to the livelihood—and the character— of America.

—The Editors

David Benson sits on the seat of the manure wagon, behind the twin black draft horses, reins in his hands, and he says this:

"Machinery can be intoxicating. You sit there on top of a huge tractor, rolling across those fields, and you feel like God. It's an amazing feeling, and a real one, and I think some people get so they don't feel complete without it.

"That's one of the reasons they keep buying bigger and bigger tractors, these enormous four-wheel-drives tearing up and down the fields. Tearing up and down. They are incredibly expensive machines, they'll run you $16 an hour in fuel alone, and you can do in one day what used to take you three or four—but then the question arises, are you doing anything useful on the three or four you saved? You buy this gigantic machine with its incredible capability, and all of a sudden, you're done.

"And you start thinking, 'My God, if I bought another 600 acres I could do that, too.' So you buy it, and then you find if you only had a bigger machine, you could buy even more. At the end of it, you're doing 2,000 acres on this fantastic Star Wars machinery and you're so far in debt that if anything goes wrong—and I mean if they stop eating soy sauce in Ireland—you lose the whole works, including the place you started with.

"And it's not the same as losing in the city. These people are going around asking, 'Jeez, what did I do wrong? They said this was the American way, you try to get bigger and take a few risks, but nobody ever told me that if I lose they were going to take away everything, my whole way of life and my children's way of life and our whole culture and the whole neighborhood and just stomp us right into the ground.'

"My God, you know, people are bulldozing farmsteads so they can plant corn where the houses used to be because there's nobody to live in these houses any more. That's happening."

David Benson. He has horses, but he's not a back-to-the-land dabbler, not an amateur, not a dilettante—he has a couple of tractors, and a barn full of machinery. But he finds a use for horses. He likes them.

And unlike a lot of farmers in Minnesota, he's making it. Making it small, but he's making it.

Go down to Worthington. Get off Interstate 90, off the state highway, off the blacktopped county road, and finally go down the gravel track and into the farm lane, listening to the power lines sing and the cottonwoods moan in the everlasting wind, watching a red-orange pickup a mile away as it crawls like a ladybug along a parallel road between freshly plowed fields, leaving behind a rising plume of gravel dust, crawling toward the silos and rooftops that mark the Iowa line....

A MAILBOX ON A POST

The landscape is not quite flat—it's a landscape of tilted planes, fields tipped this way or that, almost all showing the fertile loam of recent plowing. The black fields dominate the countryside, interrupted here and there by woodlots, by pasturage where lambs play in the fading sunlight, by red-brick or purple-steel silos, Grant Wood barns and Sears, Roebuck sheds, and by the farmhouses.

There's a turn-of-the-century farmhouse here. Gray with white trim, it could be any one of a thousand prairie homes. There's a single rural-route mailbox on a post across the road from the end of the driveway. It says "Benson" on the side, but the paint has been scoured by the wind and the name is almost illegible.

There is a tire swing hung from a cottonwood with a yellow rope, and a kid named Anton kicking a black-and-white soccer ball in the driveway.

The walk to the porch is guarded by lilacs and lilies of the valley and a patch of violets. A tortoiseshell cat named Yin lounges on the porch, watchfully making way for visitors; a familial tiger-striper named Yang watches from the side yard. Just before the porch is a strip of iron set in a concrete block: a boot scraper, and well-used.

The door swings open and Sally-Anne Benson is there, navy sweatshirt, blue jeans, tan work boots.

"Hi," she says, "Come in. David is still in the field, with the oats."

From behind her come the kitchen smells of fresh bread and noodles and sauce, and blonde Heather is turning to go up the stairs to her bedroom.

"We're going over to Grandpa's to do the chores," Sally-Anne says to Heather.

These are some of the Bensons. The Bensons in this house are David, 38, and Sally-Anne, 35, husband and wife, and their children, Heather, 11, and Anton, 8. Sally-Anne is small with thin wrists and curly brown hair, blue-gray eyes, a quick smile, and a tendency to bubble when she's had a few glasses of white wine. She answers to the nickname "Sag" or "Sago" which is an acronym of her maiden name, Sally-Anne Greeley. David has a red walrus mustache and the beginning of crow's-feet at the corners of his eyes, smile lines at his mouth, and a storyteller's laugh. The children are blonde, blonder than seems real, or even possible.

RHYTHM OF WORK BLISSFUL

The Bensons in the white house up the road and around the corner on the blacktop are Gus and Bertha Benson, David's parents.

Gus, 82, is mostly retired, though on this day he's been fanning oats—cleaning the oats to be used as seed—for the planting. He has white hair combed straight back, a white stubble on his pink face, and powerful, heavy hands. Bertha is 75. Her hair is a steel brown-gray, she wears plastic-rimmed glasses, and after 56 years of farming, she still can't watch when chickens are butchered. She can pick them, the hens who make the fatal mistake of not laying, but she can't watch them topped with a corn knife.

David and Sally-Anne do the bulk of the heavy farm work now. Gus particularly likes to work with the beef cattle, and Bertha keeps house and recently has taken up weaving and rug-making, and cans and freezes produce during the summer; last year she got in 100 quarts of applesauce. Heather and Anton have their chores. Together they live on 160 acres of the best land God ever made.

And they work it hard. They have the crops, the cattle, a growing flock of sheep, chickens, geese, and a boxful of tiny turkeys on the back porch.

The day started with David getting up at 6:15 a.m. and apologizing for it. "Boy, I got up earlier, but I just couldn't.... Oh, boy, I just laid back down and the next thing I knew, it was after 6...."

He's planting oats, and has been hard at it for the previous two days, sitting up on top of the John Deere, first disking, then chisel-plowing a small patch of compacted ground, then hooking up a grain drill to seed the oats.

"You sit up there, going back and forth, when you're disking, and your mind goes on automatic pilot," he said. "You can think of anything, and sooner or later, you do. It's a liberating experience, really. You put in maybe 400 hours a year on a tractor, and you spend a good part of it just...thinking. It's even better when you're working with the horses, because everything moves fairly slowly and you don't have the tractor engine, so it's quiet. There's a rhythm to it. It's almost...blissful, is that the word?"

THE LAND COMES FIRST

At noon, Sally-Anne brings out lunch, cheese sandwiches and fresh milk from Bluma, the milk cow, and homemade bread and a chunk of cake. David climbs stiffly off the tractor and drops down into the roadside ditch and leans back into last year's tall brown grass, out of the eternal prairie wind.

"It's just going so well, going so well," he says, looking across the barbed-wire fence toward the field. "Just need to get it in, this is beautiful weather, but I wish the wind would lay off."

He looks up at the faultless blue sky. "And we could use some rain, use some rain. Sure. We sure could."

He lies in the ditch eating, his face covered with dust, alternately eating and explaining: "We'll grow beans and corn and oats and alfalfa for hay, and the alfalfa puts nitrogen back in the soil; of course, we won't grow all those at once, we'll rotate through. You've got to be strict about it, you can't decide just to knock off a little extra here and there, or you'll kill it, the land."

He's almost apologetic about the chisel plow. "Normally we don't need it, but last year we brought in some heavy earth-moving equipment to build that terrace down there, and it compacted the ground enough that disking won't do it."

He needed the terrace to correct a drainage problem. "If you don't build water structures, you're going to get wash ditches, and that's another way you can kill it," he says.

Kill the land. The nightmare. The land must be cared for, the Bensons say. But the land is in trouble right now. Neither David nor Sally-Anne Benson would be considered solemn, but David will sit in his dining room chair after supper, leaning his elbows on the strawberry-patch oilcloth that covers the table, and talk like this:

"The strength of the Midwest culture was that it had a people who were developing an interest in the land, and in developing a community that had some continuity to it. Without that, we have an ethereal culture that just isn't satisfying to most people, and can't be—a people who don't really know what they want.

"We are living in the middle of one of the largest areas of fertile land on the planet. Normally you'd think that people would go to a place like that. Would *want* to live there, to form a good rooted culture, where you could form your own ties to the land and to the neighborhood and even to those people you just see driving by, but whose whole lives you know and they know yours...."

The connections between the people, the land, the crops, the food, the neighborhood, the community—they're impossible to put a hand on, but they are real. Much of its connecting web can be explained in stories of times past, of incidents that somehow hallow a particular patch of ground or even make it a place of humor, or sadness, or dread.

Gus and Bertha sit at their dining room table, at what their children call the home place, and remember it.

"Spring is always the moving time for farmers," says Bertha. "We bought this place in 1938, and we moved here in the spring of 1939, from Stanton, Nebraska. That's where Gus was born, in Stanton, and two of our children—the other two were born here. Gladys and Shirley and Marilyn and David, 17 years apart, the four of them, and we enjoyed every one...

"When we moved here, we couldn't tell what color the house was, it was so bad, but we were more concerned about the land. When we bought it, the land cost $95 an acre, and we were trembling and afraid, because we thought if we did something wrong, we could lose it and lose everything we saved."

They had been married in Nebraska in 1929, and spent the next 10 years as renters, building up a working capital of $3,000. It all went into the new place in Minnesota.

"We moved up here because it was dry in Nebraska for so many years, you couldn't farm. We came up here on a trip and we thought it was so beautiful in Minnesota, so beautiful," Bertha says.

UNFREEZING THE CAR

And it was cold, and windy, and the life was rough. They laugh about it now, Bertha and Gus, but at the time...

"When Marilyn was born, it was so cold I had to start a fire with corn cobs in a pan, and put it under the engine to get it warmed up so we could start it," Gus recalls. "She was ready for the hospital, 4 in the morning, and I can still remember the cold...."

"And remember, when we got electricity...."

"Oh, yes, when we got the electricity," says Bertha. "That was in, when, 1948?"

"1948, that's when it was."

"I remember," says Bertha, a glow in her face, "we got an electrician from Dundee to do the house, all the way from Dundee because all the other electricians were busy. The whole neighborhood went on at the same time. We were one of the last, because we were so close to the Iowa border, we were like in a corner. But I remember how the lights came on, and we sat with all the lights all evening, sat with the light on us....

"The electricity is the best thing for farm wives. Before that we took soft water from the cistern, and regular hard water from the well in a pail. I think I could go back to that way of living, except that I want my hot water. Hot water is the most wonderful thing!"

"Oh, we had a wedding here, too," says Gus.

"One of Shirley's girls, Christina" says Bertha, "they had their wedding in the yard, and dancing in the corn crib, and a hay ride in the afternoon."

"They decorated the corn crib," says Gus, "they cleaned it out and decorated it and danced in there."

"We never thought David would come back," Gus says suddenly. "We thought we'd be the last. We thought he would be an engineer. He was living in San Francisco, and one day he called and said, 'Don't sell the farm, we might come back.'"

David and Sally-Anne have their memories too, some of their courtship in Sally-Anne's hometown of Lexington, Mass., and some of San Francisco, where they spent some time when they were in their early 20s, and many, now, of their 14 years on the farm.

MEMORIES GREW FAST

Of walking the beans. Of haying time. Of rebuilding the aging machinery. Of David on the John Deere, dragging a plow, Sally-Anne on the David Brown 990 with the disk, the wind whistling across them both, the sun beating down....

Sally-Anne, laughing: "You remember at a party putting those chickens asleep?"

David: "Nothing like it. Hypnotizing chickens. We had one asleep for three or four minutes I think, just stretched stone cold out on the ground.... A rooster.

"By the way," he says to Sally-Anne, "do you see we've got another transvestite rooster coming along?"

"Oh, I saw that, he's getting big, too, he's almost as aggressive as the top one...."

"Well, not that bad...."

David explains: "We decided to get rid of all our roosters. We ate them, every one, or thought so. Then all of a sudden, here comes this chicken out of the flock. I mean, we thought all along he was a hen, but he starts getting bigger and growing some wattles and pretty soon he's crowing all over the place. He was hiding in there, pretending to be a hen. Now we've got another one coming out of the closet, he's getting bigger....

"I remember when we were kids, we used to chase the chickens down—chickens have got pretty good speed over the short haul, and have pretty good moves. Anyway, you'd get a rock and just chuck it at them, and every once in a while you'd lay it right alongside their heads, just throwing it at them on the run.

"And then you'd be hiding out behind the corncrib, because it'd drop over and you were sure it was dead. But it never was. It'd always get up and walk around like nothing happened. I'm not sure you can hurt chickens, to tell you the truth.

"No kid should grow up without chickens; chickens have got to be good for you...."

SOME MEMORIES DIFFICULT

Some of the memories are funny, like the chickens. Some are not.

Sally-Anne: "One time we had this horse, named Belle, and that year there was an unusual mold that grew on the corn stalk, and Belle ate some of it. It turns out that it destroys your muscle control. She couldn't control the way she moved...like polio in people. Anyway, we had the vet out, and he said that's what it was.

"There was nothing we could do, and David had to shoot her. David got the gun and brought her out of the barn, and kept backing away from her so he could get a clean shot and she kept going to him, kept trying to walk up to him, because she trusted him and she didn't know what was wrong with her..."

Sally-Anne shivers as she tells the story. "I didn't want to watch. It was just awful, but finally he got back and shot her. The vet said there was nothing wrong with the meat, so David and a friend skinned her and butchered her...it was still pretty bad, but then, after a while, another friend came over and said 'Ah, Taco Bell, huh?' And that made it better, somehow. God, it was awful."

A farm of 160 acres can't really support six people, and the Bensons know it. They talk about buying more land, of going into debt, the very experience they saw drag down so many of their neighbors.

In the meantime, Sally-Anne teaches at the Worthington Montessori school in the mornings, and David does casual work as a mechanic. Sally-Anne brags that he can fix most things, especially Volvos. "If you live anyplace around Worthington and own a Volvo, you probably know him," she said.

The life suits them. More land would be nice, but the spectre of debt is overpowering. The Bensons, for now, have no debt—they don't even need spring operating loans. Between grain sales, auto mechanics, and Sally-Anne's job, they are self-supporting and self-financed. They're proud of their ability to survive, but there is no sense of victory when they see a neighbor fail.

Instead, there is a sense of loss. It's their community evaporating, the Bensons' along with everyone else's.

"I don't know," says Dave. "Maybe what we need is some kind of creative financing like they do for home mortgages. Some kind of rent-share ʳogram where younger farmers can have a ˒ance, can move into these homesteads and take ˒m over and work them like they should be.

"And if they fail anyway? Well, at least we tried. If we don't try, we're going to kill it, the land."

Strong stuff, deeply felt; but it's hard to stay solemn for too long at the Bensons.

"When are you coming back?" they ask the visitors at the table. "Three or four weeks? Gee, that'd be just about right time for haying."

Sure would like to see you for haying, yes indeed, they say. Bring a hat. Bring gloves. Bring beer. Love to have you.

Observations and questions

1) John Camp begins a five-part series with a barely-introduced character who speaks five long paragraphs. What sort of signals has he just sent to his reader?

2) Where does Camp's lead end? I would nominate the eighth paragraph, just after the clause "...but he's making it." How does he hold his reader through such an unconventionally long lead?

3) The 10th paragraph ("The landscape is not quite flat...") sets the scene with increasingly close focus, from "landscape" to "Sears, Roebuck sheds." Think about this technique in terms of a zoom lens.

4) Camp introduces the cast of characters in the 18th and 19th paragraphs ("These are some of the Bensons."). What factors do we weigh in deciding whether to introduce all our characters at once as opposed to one at a time?

5) In paragraph 24, Camp uses technical terms such as "disking," "chisel-plowing," and "grain drill." We might expect his St. Paul audience to recognize these terms, but the specificity gained may come at the price of losing some readers. How would you make such decisions?

6) David Benson does not speak like any farmer I know. Should Camp have explained Benson's high-style conversation early?

7) But Gus and Bertha do sound like farmers. Think about the dialogue Camp presents in the

middle of this story in terms of the interplay of voices.

8) Camp unifies the piece with talk about the issues of expansion and debt at both ends. What other unifying devices does he use?

9) The final paragraph has no quotation marks around it. Who speaks and to whom?

Sweat, toil all in a day's work

JUNE 30, 1985

Making hay.

A scorching sun, south wind, the sweet smell of fresh-cut alfalfa mixed with gravel dust thrown up by passing cars and the scent of diesel fuel; down on the farm, south of Worthington, staring dry-mouth and aching through the shimmering heat waves toward the gleaming white grain elevators of the town—the town with its beckoning bar, the cold beers, and the air conditioning—that stands a mile farther south on the Iowa line.

Wherever farm people get together, the farm crisis dominates serious talk. But talk is not the real material of the spring and early summer on a farm. Talk may dominate a prairie winter, when the planting loans are in doubt. With the crops in the ground, the spring and summer are for work.

"Man can't save himself," said the hard-sweating Calvinist who stopped at the Benson farm to throw hay. "Work can't be redemptive in itself, but it's an honor. It's not given to everyone to have the honor of good work."

Hay is the first crop in the barn. The initial cutting comes around the first week of June.

"Hay is the crop where you get your heart broken most often," David Benson said as he stood on the edge of the farmyard, nibbling at the bottom of his reddish-blond mustache and squinting over an alfalfa field south and east of the house. Benson's face was caked with dust, with heavier lines in the crow's-feet around his eyes.

"After you cut it, you need at least two or three days of good hot weather to dry it out, and the drier you can get it on the ground, the better off you are. This time of year, though, you get these evening thunderstorms. You get a good day to swath, get it down, and then watch the clouds building up and the rain coming in. It can break your heart."

While a day or two of rain won't completely ruin fresh-cut hay, sometimes the rains last longer than that. Benson recalled a time a few years ago when he and his family were eager to take a vacation trip, but had to get the hay in first.

"We cut it early because we wanted to get away. We even baled it a little green. So we got out of here just as everybody else was swathing.

"When we left, everybody had hay down and drying. When we came back, like a couple of weeks later, it was still out there in the fields. A rainy spell hit, and they couldn't get it in. A lot of people lost the whole first crop—it was worthless by the time the rain stopped. It was laying out there looking like sludge."

SWATHING TIME

This year Benson began swathing early in the first week of June, chugging remorselessly through the alfalfa field while purple martins darted around the swather, gobbling the insects set into flight by the passing machine.

A 20-mile-an-hour wind and a blistering sun dried the fresh-cut alfalfa as efficiently as if it had been shoveled into an oven; and the aroma of the cooking hay spread softly across the landscape.

With the swathing done, the Bensons watched the sky anxiously, the puffy white clouds popping up in the west, born of the afternoon's rising humidity. Nothing came of them; the days stayed dry.

"This is good hay. This might be the best hay we've ever had on the first cutting. Usually the first cutting is kind of tall and stemmy and coarse, but this is very good hay," Benson said as he turned piles of hay with his foot during an exploratory trip through the main field.

The swathing is hot and tiring, but the baling is the real back-breaker. The baler is pulled by a David Brown 990 tractor, with Benson's wife Sally-Anne in the driver's seat. The hay rack—hay wagon—is towed behind the baler. The baler scoops off the long rows and carries the hay into a chute where it is packed by a hydraulic ram and tied into bales by a device too crazy to describe. As the ram packs more and more hay into the chute, newly tied bales are expelled from the rear of the baler, to be grabbed and stacked on the rack.

"You've got to stack the bales just this way," Benson told a helper, laying out a pattern along the back of the rack. "If you do it right, you can stack them six high and everything will stay on the rack."

He is sweating profusely now, swinging a hay hook in one hand, grabbing the baling twines with the other, stacking the bales into a head-high wall as they pop out of the machine every 30 seconds or so. The hay is abrasive, and nicks the forearms and lightly-clothed chests with dozens of tiny pin-prick cuts; sweat gets into the cuts and a characteristic hay rash develops.

"It's a good thing we moved that hay around in the barn this morning," Benson said as he piled the bales. "That's just the kind of warm-up you need when you're our age. When you're 16 and in good shape, it seems like you can throw all day. You get older, you need something you can start slow with."

* * *

There are six Bensons on the farm now. Gus, 82, and Bertha, 75, own it and are semi-retired; their son David, 38, and his wife, Sally-Anne, 35, are both management and principal labor; David's and Sally-Anne's two children, Heather, 11, and Anton, 8, do the chores.

As in most farm families, everybody works.

With the school in recess for the summer, the two children are expected to do several hours' work each morning, and one or two more in the late afternoon.

They are still children; their work isn't heavy, but is considered necessary both for its intrinsic instructional value as well as product.

The children's morning jobs may vary, anything from house or field work to such special jobs as sanding and lacquering a firewood box to trapping gophers in the oat field.

EVERYBODY WORKS

"David said he would give us a dollar each," Anton said confidently as he and his sister picked their way through the oats toward a stick that marked the gopher trap. "After we trap all these, we're going to go see if the neighbors need help with theirs."

The problem with pocket gophers is that they leave behind mounds of dirt, six or eight inches high, up to two feet in diameter, as they tunnel. Besides destroying small amounts of the crop, the mounds harden in the sunlight, and can damage farm machinery at the harvest.

A gopher tends to work in one direction, leaving behind a series of increasingly fresher mounds. By following the trail of mounds, the trapper will soon arrive at the freshest. He looks for an indentation on the side of the mound, which is the dirt-blocked mouth of the newest tunnel.

Carefully digging out the tunnel with his hand, the trapper may set any of several kinds of traps in the tunnel itself, with a holding chain leading to the outside, where it is firmly staked into the ground.

The open hole is then covered with a piece of wood, a shingle, or newspapers, the edges carefully sealed with dirt to prevent any light leakage. If it's all done right, the gopher will walk right into the trap.

"We got one," Anton said breathlessly as he dug around the hole with a spade. It was their first.

"Pull it out, pull it out," urged Heather. "Is it dead?"

"No, no, it's not dead," said Anton, "it's moving."

The fuzzy, dirt-brown, nearly blind gopher squirmed feebly in the trap. "We've got to kill it."

Nobody wanted to kill it. The children's eyes eventually fell on a friend who said, finally, "OK. Give me the shovel." The gopher died with a quick thrust of the shovel's edge against the back of its neck.

"Poor thing," said Heather.

"Let's show Dad," said Anton. The gopher was placed on the lid of an oil can and taken home for the reward.

"Poor thing," Heather said again, on the way back to the farm house.

The children's evenings are less dramatic, carrying water and feed to the animals, collecting eggs from the chicken house.

The worst of their spring jobs, hands down, is walking the corn, and later, walking the beans. They start in mid- to late June, and carry into July. It's a job for the entire family and any friends and relatives who want to volunteer. It's a tough one.

A TOUGH ROW

"Walking (the corn) isn't done much any more," said Sally-Anne. Sally-Anne is also known as Sago, an acronym of her maiden name, Sally-Anne Greeley.

"You can get rid of most of the weeds with chemical herbicides, but we don't want to get into that. We used some when we first came back, when the thistles had just about taken over, but when we got them down (to a tolerable level), we just started walking them."

The principal piece of farm machinery involved in walking the corn—and the beans, of course—is a sharp hoe. The idea is to walk along a row of knee-high corn and root out the waterweed and the creeping jenny and the nightshade and especially the Canadian thistle.

The posture is head-down; on a sunny day, the derivation of the term "redneck" becomes painfully clear. As row fades into row, with hits on the water bottle at the end of each round, an ache grows just below the shoulder blade and in the back just above the pelvis. And the thistle seems to grow thicker as the hours wear on, and the hands become tender and ripe with burning scarlet sore spots.

"You can sacrifice a corn to get a thistle," Sally-Anne said, "but try not to do it too often."

"Oops," said one of the walkers.

"A fine obituary for a corn plant," said another. "Oops."

"The thistles are growing right up against the corn, I can't believe it."

"Pull that creeping jenny. If you let it go, it can climb right up a corn plant and choke it."

"Tell us about that Rodney Dangerfield movie you saw on Home Box Office...."

"How many rounds do we have left?"

"You know, walking the beans isn't all that bad," Sally-Anne said late one afternoon, as she sat at her dining room table drinking tea. "At this time of year, David's in the field so much that I hardly get to see him, and then he's so tired and dirty he just wants to wash up, eat, and go to bed...when you're walking the beans, you can go along together, and talk about things."

She smiled and the lines around her eyes crinkled. "The only problem is that you usually run out of talking before you run out of beans."

Anton twits his father: "Why don't we get one of those big tractors and a tank and just spray them down with Lasso (herbicide)," he asks, fully aware of his father's antagonism for solutions built on lethal chemistry and brute horsepower.

Walking the corn, and the beans, has the status of a Midwestern myth; the Bensons possess a record by Iowa/Minnesota folksinger Greg Brown, a man whose reputation is swelling through the cornbelt countryside, mostly because of songs like "Walking the Beans."

"It's a mile-long row, that's a lot of room to grow,
    *For the nightshade and the thistle and that
miserable so-and-so. Two miles around, more like
10 I think*
    *I would just put all four up, but I gotta have
a drink. Bandana on my head and a hoe in my
hand,*
    *People are afraid of hell and now I under-
stand, I can picture some devil from that land
below,*
    *And he's pushing pigweed up from under in
the row."*

"I think he's walked beans," said Sally-Anne.

* * *

His shoulders straining under the dark-blue
cowboy shirt, the Rev. Ronald Lammers swung
fresh bales off the battered hay rack and threw
them onto a ladder-like elevator, which carried
them up to the loft in Gus Benson's barn; a good
quarter-hour's work for a man of Calvinist con-
victions, and a pleasure to see the undoubted sin-
ners higher in the barn sweating to keep up with
him.

Midmorning, the sun glowing evilly through
a haze of humidity. The farm buildings farther
south shimmer above the fields of corn, oats, and
alfalfa, patches of broken color against the haze.

A short round of haying has already been
completed this morning, Lammers driving into
the farmyard as the tractor and hay rack rolled
in from the other direction, just in time to be
recruited to throw bales. As a Christian Re-
formed minister, Lammers presides over a white
clapboard church at Bigelow, a church whose
shrinking congregation reflects the emptying of
the great Minnesota prairie farmlands.

"When I started, eight years ago, there were
22 families (in the congregation), and now we're
down to 14. The way it's supposed to work, you
have a turnover. The older people die as the
younger people marry and have children. Now
the younger people marry and move away. They
just vanish from the landscape," Lammers said

later, when the hay was safely in the barn. With
the sun and the heat and the heavy lifting, the
breaks are frequent: the workers need the time
to put water back in their bodies.

And it's cool at the picnic table under the
trees in Gus Benson's back yard. Bertha Benson's
garden is doing fine, just there beside the picnic
table, lettuce and beets and tomatoes growing
cheerfully in the good black dirt. Most of them
look cheerful, anyway, aside from one or two that
were trampled the night before when a horse got
loose and paid the garden an impromptu visit.
Evidence of the visit remains in a soil-enriching
pile at one corner of the vegetable plot.

Lammers is a soft-spoken, serious, graying
man. At 41, he is a thesis away from a master's
degree in the Old Testament from the respected
Calvin Theological Seminary in Grand Rapids,
Mich. He pushed his black plastic glasses back
up his nose with an index finger and said quietly that our national farm debate doesn't seem to
consider the morality of the new situation.

"One thing that's never talked about is
justice. We have all these arguments between the
left and the right about who's got the better idea
to get the economic pumps working, but nobody
talks about justice. The final worth of a nation
isn't determined by how much money its people
make, but whether they are just. People who
dedicate themselves to injustice," said the
Calvinist, "will inevitably perish. Those who
strive for justice will endure."

GOOD NEIGHBORS

Their mutual interest in the farm issue is
part of the cement in the relationship between
the Calvinist minister and the Bensons. None of
the Bensons belong to Lammers' congregation—
Bertha takes the children to Indian Lake Baptist Church, and David describes himself and
Sally-Anne as "sort of Quaking Unitarians. I
have an interest in the Quakers and we've met
with the Unitarians."

The minister and the farmers met in the most prosaic of ways. A car owned by a church deacon broke down in Lammers' yard, and the deacon called David Benson to fix it.

"I found out what a good mechanic I had in my own backyard, so to speak, and we started trading labor. I'd do some work on the farm and he'd work on my car, and that's how we got to be friends. We talk about everything; we talk about what's happening with the farms. It's something that worries us both," Lammers said.

"I'd seen him around for years, but never said anything to him. Then once we said a few things, we found out what an interesting guy he was, and we never stopped talking," said David.

They talk, but their approach to politics and life seems radically different, although it shares a deep sincerity.

David Benson talks of a relative, human morality, a complex mix of manners and tradition and economic pressures. Ronald Lammers approaches the problem through the revealed word of God.

Benson is profoundly concerned with the disappearance of the small farm and the rise of giant agribusiness enterprises, issues so complex he sometimes finds it difficult to express the dangers of the phenomenon and the urgency of a resolution. Lammers uses David Benson's language in a general discussion of the topic, but has no trouble finding fluent expression of the troubles.

Because, he said, it has all been discussed before, and with the greatest of eloquence.

"Woe unto them that join house to house, that lay field to field, till there be no place, that they may be placed alone in the midst of the earth," said Lammers. "That's Isaiah 5. He was talking about the Near East, but he was talking about this place, too. We're changing from a farm culture to a plantation culture, and the people working them will soon be peons. That's injustice. And squeezing people off ancestral lands, that's not only injustice, that's the stuff from which revolutions are made."

As Lammers ponders the problem of the farm, the younger Bensons disappear around the big red barn, headed for the corn field with hoes over their shoulders.

VALUE OF WORK

"There are parts of the world where five acres will support a family. What does it mean when you live out here, in the richest earth God ever made, and 1,000 acres might not support a family, no matter how hard they work?" Lammers asked. "Work has always been an honor, work is an honor. But what does it mean when people can't work hard enough to live? When they just can't do it? You know, in (biblical) Israel, the people failed to husband the land. That was what Isaiah was talking about. Eventually the whole land was blown away with the wind. If we don't listen to Isaiah, it could happen here."

Work may not be enough. But the Bensons work:

Sally-Anne Benson chopping Canadian thistles in the hot sun, her face glowing fiery red with heat, despite the woven straw hat; David Benson rolling the cultivator down the endless rows of new beans, five hours with barely a stop, the hot wind blowing the dust and grit into his eyes and ears and teeth; Heather Benson, laying out the table, putting together a quick dinner because her parents are late in from the field, and she knows they'll be tired almost to sickness; Anton Benson, pulling a full round of evening chores while his parents work on in the long lingering twilight of the summer solstice.

Working on the Benson farm, just off Nobles County Road 4, nine miles south of Worthington, a mile north of the Iowa line, out on the prairie in Minnesota.

Observations and questions

1) The first two sentences are fragments, little spurts of imagery. Discuss this sentence strategy and how the second paragraph serves as a table of contents for the whole piece.

2) Camp sets up his quotations, especially the longer ones, without much apparatus, often with no introductions or attributions. Think about the gains and losses of such a technique in terms of the reader's comprehension.

3) Paragraph 19 lists all the Bensons again. Camp says, "I felt I had to introduce everybody at least briefly every time" because the pieces appeared more than a month apart. Do you agree with that decision? What other means might he have found to review the cast for the reader?

4) Camp devotes 13 paragraphs to the children killing a gopher. What does this section add to his story? What would you lose if you shortened it?

5) The middle of this piece captures the backbreaking, repetitive nature of farm work, which Camp and his photographer reported by hoeing along with the farmers for three days! Discuss the trade off of empathy versus the danger of getting too close to a subject. Or breaking your back.

6) The Reverend Lammers adds a new viewpoint to the ongoing debates in these pieces. Discuss how Camp incorporates thought without making it look too much like thought, or boring the reader.

7) Camp ends with another sentence fragment. Why?

Farm squeezes out last drops of summer

AUGUST 25, 1985

When Bertha Benson stands with her hands in the soapy water of the kitchen sink and looks out through the east window, she can see down across the salad garden and sweet corn patch, across the steel-colored pond and the deep-green alfalfa and cornfields to the next farm home, where her son, David, and his family live.

There's a tree belt around David's house, old cottonwoods mostly, and an aging orange-brick silo behind it. Early in the morning, after her husband, Gus, has gone out to the barn and Bertha is cleaning up the breakfast dishes, she can see the sun climbing over the cottonwoods around David's house.

"In January when the days get longer, I say to Gus when he comes back in, 'Oh, you should see the sun over David's house; already it's over the trees. Spring is coming.'

"You know, in the bottom of winter, the sun is so far down, it seems to stay down forever. Then it jumps. One day it's down, and the next day you can see it's higher. Spring is coming."

In the summer—right now, in August—the sun is slipping down the sky again, hiding behind the trees and the orange-brick silo as the season slides inexorably into autumn. Bertha Benson, gray-haired, bespectacled, measures it all through the east window over the kitchen sink.

There are six people and two houses on the Benson farm, nine miles out of Worthington on the prairie in southwestern Minnesota. There are Gus and Bertha, the elders, in the main house; their son, David, and his wife, Sally-Anne, in a second house; and David's and Sally-Anne's children, Heather and Anton.

Three generations, split evenly between male and female; two houses, and many windows.

Bertha's kitchen window discloses private places—the garden, the pond, the fields. The front room window is sharply different. It faces west, looking over public places, the driveway, at the shop where David runs his Volvo repair service.

"You know what I saw from this window... really, I didn't see it, that was the scary thing," Bertha said with her soft Scandinavian vowels, fingertips poised thoughtfully on her cheek.

"It was when David and Sally had just come back to farm. There was a big storm. A famous storm, so many people were killed. The telephone was out—we used to say that you could tell when a storm was coming, because the phone would go out—and David was over here for chores. Sally was at their house, with Heather, who was just born.

"The snow was so thick you couldn't see anything. David wanted to walk back to his house because we couldn't call on the phone. He didn't want to leave Sally there alone with the baby. So he walked back, and I ran to my window to see him go.

"I couldn't see him. There was nothing out there. Only snow. We couldn't get out of the house after that. We didn't know for two days that he had made it home...."

This is summer, a good distance yet from the first lashing winter winds. The David outside the west window is another one: the summer David, laughing and talking and pounding on an orange '73 Volvo while a friend lies on the ground and strips a large black number on the side.

"Ninety-nine," said Bertha. "Is that a lucky number?" She peered out the west window and shook her head. "I wish they wouldn't do it; I hope nobody gets hurt. I won't go. If I went, I would sit with my hands over my eyes."

She is talking about an automobile race. That night.

* * *

This is a good week at the Benson farm. The field work is light—the second cutting of hay is already in, though the family will spend a few hours pulling weeds from the soybean fields. The work that *must* be done is...fun: freezing corn, canning peaches and tomatoes, squeezing cider from early apples, making applesauce.

Rebuilding the car.

The car is a rusted-out, stripped-down Volvo. The engine isn't too bad, and the transmission works after a fashion, though it has no reverse gear.

"When you throw it in reverse, it's like the shifter fell in a hole," David said.

But it's a machine granted beauty by circumstance. The Nobles County Fair has announced an Enduro Race, 250 laps on a quarter-mile black-dirt track, where speeds approach and sometimes exceed 45 mph. This is the car for it, this broken-down orange Volvo, now dubbed the *General Ole* (pronounced Oh-Lee) with the Swedish flag on the roof.

The flag is for Volvo and Benson and Rolf Carlson, a Worthington psychotherapist who kicked in $50 to have the tires put on new rims. He gets credit in black paint, on the front fender: Tires by Rolf, Ph.D. David takes credit on the back fender: Benson Volvo. Bob Yeske, an auto body man from the town of Bigelow, provides race-crew experience and mechanical backup.

The driver is a Hollander, the bearded Bigelow building contractor Marvin DeVries, who in his younger days drove sprint cars on the local racing circuit. Marv is supposed to get "Marvelous Marvin" in script letters under the driver's side window. As it works out, there's never time to do the painting, and Marv settles for the ride and lets the credit go....

That's the week: freezing, canning, the Enduro Race, with a brief timeout for Heather's 12th birthday.

* * *

If the spring and first weeks of summer are times for the fields—for the plowing, planting, cultivating, walking the beans and corn, haymaking—the late high summer is the time for the kitchen.

Vegetables are ripening in the gardens, the trees are heavy with big, blushing, tart apples, the groceries advertise unbeatable deals on long-season produce from Georgia and California. It's the time for the pressure cookers, for the freezer bags, for the Ball and Kerr jars whose lids go *dink* when they seal....

The corn is one thing.

It starts with David and Sally-Anne down in the sweet corn patch behind Gus and Bertha's place, where the tassels are so laden with pollen that walking through the patch is like breathing water. The day is hot, and loud country-western music blares from a battered radio hidden in the middle of the patch at the end of a 150-foot extension cord.

"We've done tests," David said, tongue in cheek, "Country-western keeps the 'coons out of the corn patch better than anything else."

"Even better than Duran Duran?"

"Yeah, even better," he said solemnly. He turned and looked down the patch where his wife was thrashing through the corn. Everybody calls Sally-Anne "Sago"—Sag-Oh—an acronym of her maiden name, Sally-Anne Greeley.

"I think Sago is going crazy," David said. He raised his voice. "Jeez, Sago, I think we've got enough...Sago, stop...." He dropped his voice again. "When she gets the bit in her teeth, it's hard to stop her. We could be doing this until midnight if we don't get her out of here."

The ears of sweet corn are fat, but the kernels are the pale, pearly yellow-white that almost sing of sugar; nothing with the telltale fullness or the dark-dried silk escaped Sago's grocery sacks.

"Look at it all, we've got to get it before it goes bad," she said with chin-out determination, snatching an ear off another stalk. A line of sweat glistened on her upper lip and her cheeks were dappled with pollen.

"Sago, we've got enough, we've got too much, oh boy," David pleaded. "Sago...."

After a while: "OK. I'm done."

The corn is shucked on the picnic table behind the house, the pile of clean corn growing quickly, the shuckers—Bertha, David, Sago, and the kids—calling attention to special prizes: "Oh, look at this one—oh, that's a good one. Let's keep that one out...."

Sago and Bertha moved inside before the shucking was done and got the kettles ready. Gus used a whetstone to put a fine edge on a set of paring knives. When the last of the corn was clean, David carried it inside and Sago began feeding it into the kettles of boiling water.

"Five minutes," said Bertha. "If you go longer, I think you get a taste of the cob."

The work was done assembly-line fashion. Sago blanched the corn, David and Gus cut it from the steaming cobs, and Bertha packed it into one-pint freezer bags. The corn sometimes popped off in individual kernels, sometimes in slabs the size of a middle and ring finger held together. Most of the slabs are packed; others are passed around for instant consumption.

"Twenty-five pints," Bertha announced when they finished, a smile like a quarter-moon lighting up the bottom of her face. "Big pints. Sometimes three cups in a sack. That's good."

That's just the corn. Not all of it, but some of it. And there's more: tomatoes, peaches, beans; it's produced all week in the steamy kitchen, Bertha Benson, director.

* * *

With the canning done, and the crew gone on to other things, Bertha sat in her front room and talked about the canning and the work of her life and pronounced herself satisfied.

"I enjoy the housework—I especially enjoy the baking. Sometimes I'd get so carried away with the baking that I'd forget to do the other things....

"It was not just work in the house that women used to do. We had chickens, and I took care of the chickens and sold the eggs. We used to have hundreds of chickens, 400 one time. The worst was carrying water from the windmill to the chicken house. The girls (her three daughters) used to say they have long arms from carrying water.

"Separating milk was my job, and the older girls would help. I was happy when that ended, but you know, you give up things, too...the milk truck would come and take the milk and drop off some butter, and one time one of the younger girls asked me where butter comes from....

"Sometimes I would help in the fields, but only in a pinch. That was Gus's job, he did the field work, and he took care of the tractor, the machinery. I did the housework, and took care of the children, though Gus is handy around the house and makes a good oatmeal...."

* * *

Sally-Anne Greeley Benson also loves the farm life, though she grew up in New England as the daughter of an official of the Massachusetts Institute of Technology.

"Bertha made it a lot easier. She wasn't born on a farm, either. Farming isn't something you *just do.* You have to know an awful lot and she taught me an awful lot," she said.

Sago is not, however, satisfied to divide the life she shares with David Benson into housework and fieldwork, women's work and men's work.

"When David grew up, he was expected to help his father with the farm work. He had older sisters to help his mother with the housework. So, he didn't do housework. He didn't know how to do housework." She smiled: "He's a lot better now than when we first came here."

Sago sat at her table behind a cup of hot cider she had just "nuked" in the microwave. She had made the cider herself, the day before.

"There's a lot of housework that just plain isn't fun. It's drudgery. Most fieldwork is at least a little bit fun. You're outside, you're working hard, you might feel like it's killing you, but you can feel like it's really important. Housework doesn't always feel like that," she said.

Sago works in the fields more than Bertha ever did. She routinely does disking and chisel-plowing, and runs the haybaler. She says matter-of-factly that she can drive anything from motor-cycles and cars to trucks and tractors.

Her dislike for some types of housework—which she does anyway—is not a matter of unhappiness.

"It has to be done," she said. "You can look at David when he comes in and his face is all white and exhausted and he just about falls in bed, and you go ahead and do it (housework). It's really all a matter of adjustments, back and forth. One of the really good things about David is that he adjusts. That's really good."

Bertha's work has impressed her with the routine of the seasons, as she sees them through the kitchen window. Sago has no window in her kitchen. She remembers listening...

"I remember I was pregnant with Heather, it was the first part of August. David had cut across the fields on a moped to do some chores, and I heard this voice. It was, 'Sago, Sago,' real-ly low, and quiet—and then I realized it was David, and I knew, I knew, we had some serious business. He'd hit a fence post that was laying down in tall grass and went over and broke his collar bone. He could barely walk back, and he could barely get his breath to call me, and I went running out.... I can remember that, 'Sago, Sago.'"

* * *

Race day started clear and cool. Sago and the kids picked apples at a friend's home—they have no apple trees of their own—while David worked on the Volvo—painting, bracing, figuring tactics.

At noon, the family broke off work for Heather's birthday party. Heather smiled shy-ly as the family gathered around the dining room table, clasped hands, sang a grace song and "Happy Birthday."

Heather opened her gifts—she seemed particularly pleased by a calendar featuring American Impressionist paintings. And it was back to work, David on the Volvo, Sago with the apples.

The Bensons are in possession of an ancient hand-powered apple press. The press is a machine—two machines, actually—of almost sublime simplicity and efficiency. The first part grinds whole apples to a juicy pulp, and the second, a screw press, squeezes the apple juice from the pulp.

The press produces a torrent of cinnamon-colored cider, which Sago caught in an ice cream bucket and transferred to plastic milk jugs. Halfway through the cider run she got cups from the house and took a long draught of cider. She swallowed, caught her breath, her cheeks sucked in. "Wooo, that is...tart. That is *good.*"

In the distance, from up near the other house, there was a burst of noise, a popcorn sound, like old thunder or a distant light machine-gun fire.

"That's the car; they're running it," she said.

The county fair. Pole barns and cattle judging, the smell of manure and new-mown grass, gasoline fume and oil smoke, sandy hot dogs and a thousand gallon jugs of air-aging mustard.

Long rows of clouds rolling in on the grounds as *The Car* is backed off the transporter. The car is ugly. The doors are chained shut, there is only one seat inside if you don't count the one strapped vertically onto the driver's door as padding, and there is no glass at all. No headlights, tail lights, or windows. In place of the windshield is a wire screen, which supposedly will stop the bigger mud clods thrown off the track.

"What do you think the average value of these cars is?" David was asked, as the Benson crew looked over the competition.

He shrugged. "About $150," he said.

"The thing about an Enduro Race," explained the driver, Marvelous Marvin De Vries, "is keeping the car alive. If you can make it through the first hour, you should make it all the way. But in those first few laps, you can go out like this." He snapped his fingers.

The track was a muddy quarter-mile oval with a low bank at the turns. The floodlit infield swarmed with drivers and pit crew, dressed in cowboy shirts and cowboy hats and cowboy boots or running shoes, and billed hats and striped bib overalls and heavy-soled boots, or some combination of those. The exceptions are a half-dozen drivers like Marvin, who wear white drivers' jumpsuits with red piping.

The pre-race ceremonies are quick: a crew meeting, the raising of the colors by a veterans' group color guard—the flag has 48 stars, but it's a perfectly good flag—and the cars begin rolling onto the track.

Nothing is new. Nothing is clean. The auto bodies look like hammered brass ashtrays. Fifty-eight cars start the race. Three finish. The 55 cars that die do so in a variety of colorful ways—some blow engines, some catch fire, some shred tires, some lose drive shafts, some are wrecked, some disappear over the low bank and never return. One is abandoned in midtrack, and the remaining cars drive around it for 150 laps or so.

The *General Ole* lasts about 20 minutes.

"He's running on a flat," David shouts. "The left front is gone." Sago is tense, standing on a stack of tires, turning, turning, as the Volvo goes around.

Under track rules, repairs can be done only if the race is stopped to clear the track. There is no guarantee it will happen—you could only wait and hope. The Bensons turn and turn, and finally the tire comes apart and tangles the axle so badly the rim begins to drag. It's the end. Marv sadly bounces the *General Ole* onto the infield, and a moment later, as he walks away, another car smashes into it, crushing the right front fender and ripping open the radiator.

Later, with the track quiet, the pit crew pushed the mortally wounded Volvo back on the transporter and passed around the Bud Lites.

"You know what," said Marvelous Marv. "We've got to do this again."

"Hey, it was a good time, wasn't it?" asked David.

And Sago is laughing.

* * *

During the race, while Marv was running on the rim, Heather and Anton sat in the grandstand with friends. As her younger and more demonstrative brother did everything but handstands, Heather sat tensely quiet, watching intently.

Of all the Bensons, she is the quietest. From the infield, her shy smile flashed out across the track once or twice, alive under her blue Volvo cap. When the crisis came, she stood to watch. That was all.

What about Heather? She would like to live on a farm, she said, like her mother and grandmother. But there are other things, too. She doesn't know.

Earlier on race day, she would briefly put on an inexpensive pair of pearl earrings she had gotten as a gift.

"Oh, Heather, you look so grown up," said Sago, pushing out her bottom lip. And Heather did look grown up, just for an instant.

At the birthday table, the family had linked hands for the grace song:

"The silver rain, the shining sun, the fields where scarlet poppies run," the three women sang, a complex of alto voices from three generations, *"and all the ripples of the wheat are in the bread that we do eat....*

"So, when we sit to every meal, with thankful hearts we always feel, that we're eating rain and sun, and fields where scarlet poppies run."

Heather has a west-facing window in her bedroom, with a view over the checkerboard prairie toward the horizon with its glorious prairie sunsets. It's a good place, she said, to sit and look out at things.

Observations and questions

1) Camp says, "It seemed to me that the women did so much work on the farm that I ought to include something that focuses on women." How does he differentiate the women's roles from the men's, and how does he show the similarities?

2) What is a section on a car race at the county fair doing in a story on women?

3) Notice how Camp uses scenes of women looking out of windows to unify this piece. He regards this technique as "just a little bit contrived." Do you?

4) In the scene where David tries to get Sago to quit canning corn, note the images and gestures. Discuss some of the effects Camp achieves with great economy here.

5) Camp credits his photographer Joe Rossi with the detail of the 48-star flag during the race scene. Is this flag a symbol or just a flag? Or both?

6) The last section focuses on the daughter Heather. Notice how it bridges from the race scene back to the windows motif. Do you find this ending effective? Why?

Delayed harvest puts farmers at razor's edge.

OCTOBER 20, 1985

It was Monday noon, the 14th of October, Columbus Day—a day of high clouds, cool winds, and fractured sunshine.

Blackbirds gathered on roadside power lines, flocking for the arduous trip south. Skunks traffic-flattened on the road wore their long, opulent winter fur. And on the rich prairie farmland around Worthington, Minn., it was a day of waiting.

David Benson, 38, drove an aging Volvo northwest along a tar road toward the KRSW radio tower. The road ran through an ocean of soybeans and corn, over flat prairie creeks, past small herds of black-and-white Holsteins grazing their still-green pastures.

Benson did a running commentary on the grain fields—on their cleanliness, soil types, productivity. He pointed out patches of weeds whose seeds had been planted in otherwise clean fields by flowing water. He was intent in his judgments: Benson operates a small farm near Bigelow, Minn., nine miles south of Worthington. He grows beans and corn as cash crops, and hay for 39 head of beef cattle, six work horses, a pony, 14 sheep, and an aging milk cow named Bluma.

On this day, almost nothing was moving in the fields—in his fields, or any other. The beans were dark brown and full, the corn a light, bright tan, with heavy ears hanging down from the stalks. Here and there, on the edges of the cornfields, brilliant yellow kernels flashed from split-open husks.

"Everything is, ohhh, man, everything is beautiful, and that's what could break your heart," Benson said. Crow's-feet deepened at the corners of his eyes as he peered at the sun-dappled landscape. "You look out there, and you could cry. You can feel the mood of the whole county: it's getting lower every day. Lower and darker. If we get some snow, ohhh, man, that would do it. That would kill us."

This year's harvest in southwestern Minnesota could be substantial if the farmers could get at the crops. So far, they hadn't been able to. Fall work was more than a month behind.

"For all practical purposes, the harvest hasn't started," said Gene Lutteke, manager of the grain elevator at Bigelow.

HARVEST A MONTH LATE

"A few years back, I did a spot of work for a man who was having a little trouble with cancer," said another man, who came out of a country Standard station to pump gas. "I remember we were all done, cleaned up, and I put the last of the machinery away on the 17th of October. This year, he hasn't even been out in the field yet."

The problem is water. Too much water. The soybeans have never had a chance to dry out, and the very process of picking them would destroy them. They are so soft they can be eaten like fresh peas.

The corn is tougher, closer to picking, but still too wet.

"I can pick a bit of it, maybe, in the next couple of days, if we don't get any more rain," Benson said. "I can pick it and grind it and feed it right away. I just can't crib it. But the corn isn't worth much this year anyway, and a snowstorm or two won't wipe it out. It's the beans that could break your heart."

The night before, Benson stood on the edge of a 60-acre soybean field, and counted his metaphorical chickens.

"We'll get, ohh, gosh, at least 30 bushels to the acre, and maybe a little more. They look great, don't they? Even if the price stays right

where it is, that's $150 an acre, that's almost
$9,000 sitting right there. If we get a snowstorm
or a sleet storm, it'll pull them right down and
we won't get a thing. And it's getting so late in
the year, we could get snow. We could get some
sleet. Boy, it would break your heart."

In one short spell of drier weather, Benson
managed to cut some hay, but the rains returned
before he could bale it. With much more rain, it
would be gone. Sludge, he calls it.

"I love that last cutting of hay because all
the swallows turn out, diving around the tractor. They eat all the bugs they can find before
they head south," Benson said. "It's like working in a field full of big butterflies. It's absolutely delightful. This year I was out there by
myself—the swallows'd all gone south before I
had a chance to do the final cutting. I really
missed seeing them."

The weather has been the main topic in the
Worthington area since the second week of
August.

FARM WORK ONLY PART OF IT

"I've never seen anything like this fall: in all
my years, nothing like this," said Gus Benson,
83, David's father. "It seems like it rained every
day—it didn't, but it never got dry, that's for
sure."

And this Columbus Day was yet another day
when no field work could be done. It was clear
enough, and a fine drying wind was blowing. But
it had rained again only two days before, further
saturating the soggy countryside.

The condition of the fields was no excuse for
idleness, however. Like more and more small-
farmer families, the Benson family puts together
an annual income with a pastiche of part-time
jobs and farming.

One of Benson's part-time jobs involves work
as a repairman for local radio stations, climbing
the towers that soar hundreds of feet over the
patchwork prairie.

It's a job that his wife, Sally-Anne, doesn't like, won't talk about, and doesn't want to hear about. When David gets a climbing job, her normally cheerful face turns grim, and it hangs in the background of her mind until he's back on the ground.

Both reactions—David's willingness to climb, and Sally-Anne's unhappiness with the work—run in the family. David's father, Gus, never had much fear of heights, either. When Gus was young, he did a good deal of farm windmill repair, and *his* wife, David's mother, Bertha, didn't want to hear about that, either.

"There's our tower over there," David said, pointing through the Volvo's mud-spattered windshield.

The tower is on a low hill near Chandler, Minn., surrounded by cornfields. From a distance, it looks like a short piece of red-and-white thread dangling from the clouds.

"We have to fix a beacon," Benson explained. "Some kids climbed up there one night and broke it. It's going to cost somebody, ohh, better than $1,000 for a new light and the work. The insurance company, I guess."

He really isn't afraid of the open height?

PAID SIGHT-SEEING TRIP

"Not really. You're working on the inside of the tower," he said, with his tongue in cheek. "If you fell, it wouldn't be the height that killed you. It'd be hitting all those support bars on the way down. You'd kill yourself falling 15 feet in there, so 700 feet won't make any difference."

The work is at the 280-foot level.

"Those kids had to be nuts to climb up there at night," a friend said standing at the base of the tower and peering straight up the slender steel structure. A prairie wind rustled through the surrounding corn field and hummed across the tower's support cables. "You're a little weird yourself, David."

"It makes a change," he said. "And it's beautiful up there—boy, you can see for miles. You can see over to Blue Mound, over to the ridge where South Dakota starts. You can see down to Worthington...."

Benson works with rudimentary equipment: blocks taken from barn hoists, a kid's pack full of tools worn backward on the chest. He wears an insulated jumpsuit as protection against the wind, and replaces his farmer-standard billed cap with a woolen watch cap.

"It can get cold," he said, just before he started up the tower. It took 20 minutes to climb the 280 feet to the broken light, and four hours to complete the repairs. Benson gets $25 an hour for the job.

"It's a handy kind of work to do, if you're a farmer and don't mind working up high," he said when he got down. "You can earn a quick $100 cash money for three or four hours' work. It comes in handy."

As soon as he was back on the ground, he called Sally-Anne to let her know.

JOBS HERE AND THERE HELP

To an outsider, grain farm work appears to be sporadic. There's plowing, planting, cultivating, and harvesting, each in a separate compartment of weeks. It looks different to a farmer. To a farmer, there's never enough time for the work to get done.

"It's hard to make a living with straight farming, especially with prices like they are now," Benson said. "But if you're going to farm, you can't have a regular job, even part-time, because you need such big blocks of time off. So you get a lot of little jobs."

To keep the Benson farm going, Sally-Anne (whose nickname is Sago) teaches half-days at a Worthington Montessori school, while David fixes cars in the farm shop, climbs radio towers, and trades work on various kinds of agricultural and construction equipment—he has a strong local reputation as a diesel mechanic and specialist in Volvos and Volkswagen Rabbits.

They also keep costs down by producing and preparing most of their own food. And David, of course, keeps the family cars running.

"There's always something to do. Sometimes I think, you know, after the kids are grown, Sago and I ought to take a long sabbatical somewhere," Benson said late on a rainy Saturday night in the farm's shop.

Sago's old car was on its last legs, so David had driven to the Twin Cities where he located a diesel Volkswagen Rabbit with a good body and interior, and a blown engine. He happened to have another Rabbit with a cracked block, that he'd bought for parts, and now he was making one machine from the two.

THE MONEY'S NOT ALL GRAVY

"In our best year, I guess we pulled in, gross, about $26,000, including Sago's money. But then, when you're running a farm, you have expenses, just like you do in any business. So the $26,000 wasn't all for groceries. We get away a little cheaper than most guys because we can substitute labor where most of them use chemicals—cheap labor is one of the advantages of an extended family. And I think our equipment is sized better for the farm than most people's....

"But you get very tired when you get into the cities and you hear people say, 'Aw, the good farmers are making it,' or 'It's the farmer's own fault,' and you know how hard you work, and how hard your neighbors work, and you aren't making anything....

"I'm not going to say that some farmers didn't get greedy when things were looking good and got in over their heads buying land. But that's not all of it. Look at soybean prices. That one field we were in. If I get those beans off, and sell them right now, we'll get maybe $9,000 or a little less. If I could sell them for the *average* price we got last year, they'd go for $12,500.

Same crop. Same expenses, or even a little higher—and we get 25 or 30 percent less, off a price that wasn't that good to begin with. It gets real tough."

Benson's case is stated on a half-page of blue-and-white charts in the *Worthington Daily Globe*'s Saturday "Farm Report."

The charts include bar graphs, which are particularly interesting for one striking aspect—the graphs for current corn and soybean prices don't have any bars on them. That's because the prices have fallen below the bottom level of the graph.

Instead of rescaling the graphs, the newspaper, to call attention to the problems of farmers, simply prints the current price of the crops where the bars should be. On Friday, Oct. 11, corn stood at $2.15 a bushel at Worthington; last year's average was $2.90. Soybeans stood at $4.67, Worthington bid. Last year's average was $6.90. That's down 30 percent.

As Benson works under a trouble light to fit the replacement head on the newer Rabbit, he talks both economics and social history: the problems of making a living while preserving the land, the false assumptions of economy-of-scale theories, the uses of labor as a replacement for foreign oil, the philosophical reasons for maintaining national agricultural population.

A HOUSE FULL OF BOOKS

Although it embarrasses him when friends call him a "Prairie Intellectual," that's precisely what he is. Sago, too. In the north bedroom of the old farmhouse, where they live with their children, Heather and Anton, there are 1,000 books or more. There are an even dozen works by Lewis Mumford, a half-dozen by Thorstein Veblen. There are books by Ayn Rand and Alan Watts, Barry Goldwater and Hunter S. Thompson, Upton Sinclair and Tom Wolfe.

They have *The Golden Bough* by Sir James George Frazer and *The Journey to Ixtlan* by Carlos Casteneda; *The Female Eunuch* by Ger-

maine Greer and *The Courage to Be* by Paul
Tillich. There are works by Nietzsche and Balzac
and Chekhov and Whitman and Emerson and
Kafka and Tolstoy and St. Thomas Aquinas, all
in paperback glory. They also own a tattered copy
of *The Exorcist* by William Peter Blatty, and Benson said, "My God, don't write *that* down," when
the book was mentioned.

On a rainy Saturday night, with auto grease
covering his hands, a battered green-and-white
billed hat perched on his reddish hair, the driz-
zle graying-out background noise, he mixed those
writers in casual conversation as he fit together
the rebuilt car. And he talked about Charles
Dickens' *Great Expectations.*

REPAIRS GO ON BACK BURNER

A road company of the Guthrie Theater of
Minneapolis was to present a dramatized version
of the Dickens novel Sunday night at the
Memorial Auditorium in Worthington. He wants
to go...but he'd like to work on the car, too.

"I have to admit I like Sunday nights in the
shop," he said. "It's quiet. You can think about
things. It's nice to see an engine go together—I
really like that. I don't know. You think Sago
would let me out of the Dickens thing?"

No. Sago won't. The following night, the
whole family, except Gus, is scrubbed and seated
in the balcony. David entered a mild protest—
"Listen, Sag, I could get that car going for you."
But she shook her head and he went along.

Afterward he said, "I'm glad I went, though
I kind of wanted to work on the car." Kidded
again about his Prairie Intellectual status (how
he might have lost it if he hadn't attended the
Guthrie production), he asked: "I wonder how
much of being a Prairie Intellectual means doing what your wife tells you?"

MANY HANG ON HOPEFULLY

And that, for the most part, has been the late
summer and fall on the Benson farm. Rain, odd
jobs, a growing tension over the harvest delays.

"People are in bad shape," Benson said. "The countryside is being depopulated. Too many people just can't make a living anymore. There are too many people who are supporting their farming habit by working other jobs, and they're saying to themselves, 'If we just quit farming, we'd have more money.'

"Now, if on top of it all we have a real crop disaster, if we get a snowstorm that beats down the beans before we can get them out—that'll finish a lot more people. There must be thousands of people sitting on a razor's edge, and that would be the end of them."

The growing nervousness about the harvest is allayed a bit by visits from family and friends: over the weekend, one of David's older sisters, Marilyn Beckstrom, a minister with the United Church of Christ, came down to Gus Benson's house for a visit. She brought a friend, Bob Shoemake, a Methodist minister, and Shoemake's parents, Earl and Vivian Shoemake of Paducah, Ky. Earl Shoemake is a Baptist minister.

Bob Shoemake, a longtime friend, came equipped with a pair of barber shears and scissors. He promised David a free haircut and a professional shave in return for an oil change. After dinner, accompanied by a good deal of hilarity, he kept his promise in Gus Benson's kitchen.

"Another advantage of an extended family," Benson said around a hot towel.

And later: "Your family keeps you going; everybody moans and groans, but nobody says they want to do anything different."

Even later one night, he stood in the side yard of his house with his 9-year-old son, Anton, and picked out the Big Dipper, the Little Dipper, the North Star, the Pleiades, and other constellations in a sky that looked like black velvet touched by sugar.

"Look at the Milky Way," he said, his face turned up, his finger tracing the grains of stars across the sky. "You can't see anything like this in the city; you just can't do it. It looks like you could fall right into it."

WHAT'S THE WEATHER

Things turn quickly on the farm.

Benson climbed the radio tower last Monday, and the fields were soggy. But the day was dry, and so was Tuesday. So Tuesday, he sneaked out, picked the end rows of the corn fields, taking in a single wagonload of corn. It was still wet, but fine for grinding. And he turned over the hay he'd cut before the last rain...and Tuesday night he and Sago baled it, Sago on the tractor and David throwing the bales on the hay rack.

Wednesday was dry again. Humid, but no rain. Thursday was the same. Friday, two days ago, he picked the end rows of the bean fields.

"We got the field open, but the beans are still wet," Sago said by phone late Friday. "If the weather holds, we might get in Sunday. We hate to work Sunday, but if the weather holds...."

If the weather holds, the Bensons are out there this minute, bringing in the big cash crop. It'll be a good one.

If the weather holds.

Observations and questions

1) This story concerns weather seen from the farmer's point of view. Read through, noticing how Camp weaves the weather imagery around the various characters.

2) In paragraph 16 ("I love that last cutting of hay..."), David speaks in lyric terms, as Camp does occasionally, especially in landscape scenes. Discuss how Camp uses such language without seeming "arty."

3) In the middle section on climbing the 280-foot tower, Camp gives the reader no sensation of danger. What could he add to make the reader experience the height? Should he try for such an effect?

4) Camp keeps reminding us of Sally's nickname "Sago." Does the long-term series require repetitive elements that might tire the reader?

5) David's role as the "Prairie Intellectual" first appears in part four. Would the series profit from introducing this theme earlier? Would Benson's speech seem more real if the author had told us earlier about his bookishness?

Three generations of love and work

DECEMBER 8, 1985

The November landscape was brown and black and tan, spotted with stark clusters of leafless trees, dark evergreen windbreaks, and here and there a glint of silver from a frozen pond. It was a rough, grainy Middle Ages landscape painted in bleak northern earth colors by Pieter Bruegel the Elder, and revealed by John Deere.

But a winter storm was prowling down to the south, over Iowa somewhere, and the fast-talking television weathermen said the border country was in for it. Anyone who must go on the road should carry blankets and a source of heat. If the car goes into a ditch, stay with it.

Along the Minnesota-Iowa border, farmers pushed their tractors and looked to the south. The sky was an edgeless slab of mean gray cloud that obliterated any hint of the sun. The prairie wind, whipping in from the northeast, cut your face like splinters of broken glass.

Time was trickling away. Snowflakes in the air, one here, one there, like ghosts of summer fireflies. Every time you looked up, there were more of them. At mid-morning, the grain elevator at Bigelow, Minn., three miles to the south, had been sharp on the horizon. By mid-afternoon, it was hidden by the falling snow.

On the west side of an unmarked gravel road, a combine was broken down with no more than a dozen rows of corn still standing in the field. The John Deere service man crouched at the front of the machine, his back hunched against the wind, trying to wring a last mile out of the 1985 harvest.

On the east side of the road, David Benson pulled his corn picker out of the field and stopped.

It wasn't riding right. It had a tired sag. He had been having trouble with cornstalks wrapping into the picking gears, but this was something else. He climbed down from the tractor to look.

"Oh man, look at that," he said to a friend. "It just gave out." He pointed at a main support strut in the picker's frame. The quarter-inch-thick steel strut was twisted and folded like a piece of fabric. Benson's picker is old; he bought it for $92 at a spring auction.

"It's going to take time, take too much time," he said, looking south. "The corn is good. I bet we're getting 90 to 100 bushels an acre. Boy, I'd like to get it out."

The cure for the corn picker was simple but time-consuming. Tow it carefully back to the farm shop, straighten the folded strut with a winch, and reinforce it by welding in a couple of pieces of angle iron.

But with winter coming in, other tasks were pressing—the barn to close up, two wagons of corn to unload, animals to move. Night comes early. By 6 p.m., it's too dark to work.

Across the road, the neighbor was working again, snow squalls whipping around his ungainly green combine. The prairie was flat enough, and the neighbor's corn was tall enough, that a man on the road couldn't see beyond it. There was only the wall of corn, and the sky. But as the combine chopped the last rows, the countryside beyond it became visible, as though the machine were pushing back a theater curtain.

* * *

The year went like this:

Spring came early. The oats were in by the first week of April, and the corn and soybeans by early May. The first cutting of hay came shortly afterwards, and it was a good one, "maybe the best first cutting we've ever had," Benson said. The cutting and baling of hay was followed by hand-hoeing the beans and corn, a long stretch of hot, back-breaking work that extended into the heart of the summer.

In mid-July, the second cutting of hay came, and when that was done, the oats were ready. They were out by the end of the month. Then came the rains. From the second week of August through early October, the fields were too wet to work. The last cutting of hay was lost, and the soybean harvest was delayed a month.

The beans finally were harvested at the end of October, and the yield was mediocre. Then more waiting as the moisture left the slower-drying corn. When the corn eventually was picked, the yield was as high as it ever had been.

But prices were low all year and dropped even more through the harvest season. More farmers than ever quit the land. The Bensons held on.

That was the year by the calendar, also a market year, a year you could summarize and graph, a year with a mean, a mode, and a median, a year squeezed into this block of type. A year that says nothing of the faces, the names, the smells and the sounds, the feel of the work.

FARM YEAR, POKER ARE ALIKE

A farm year knits together personalities and opportunities, market prices and snowstorms, machines and philosophical tendencies that produce different quantities and qualities of oats and corn and soybeans and alfalfa.

It's an accumulation of quick conversations behind hot waiting tractors, of grunts and warm drinking water exchanged on 100-degree days on hay racks, of equipment breakdowns and apple picking, of kitchen smells and dim, cool milkings in the bottom of the barn, of country music blaring from the corn patch to repel the raccoons, of nights so dark and so far from city lights that the Milky Way looks like Manhattan.

A farm year is like a poker game. A poker game is not simply a matter of who won and lost—knowing the game is knowing how the cards were played, the tension, the bluffs, the hard decisions, the bets.

A year on the farm is a playing of cards, each card an individual, yet each related, each card a memory and simultaneously a new day, cards that are played out in hands that are always familiar and always subtly different.

* * *

David Benson is a large man with blue eyes that turn down at the outside edges. He has a walrus mustache and an unruly mop of blondish hair, smile lines in his cheeks, and crow's-feet at his eyes.

He has what friends teasingly call an act. With intellectuals, he talks like an intellectual; with other friends, he's full of yups and ain'ts and gol-lies.

It's not an act. His two sides are simply that.

He reads Lewis Mumford and Alan Watts and has a reputation as a fine diesel mechanic and welder. He drives 90 miles on Sundays to a Unitarian church in Sioux City, Iowa, to hear discussions of moral philosophy, and on Sunday nights he rebuilds Volvos and Volkswagens. He reads each night before sleeping, serious works on ecology and feminism, political theory and economics, and he is building a new house.

He climbs hundreds of feet up radio towers to earn extra money by replacing burned-out or damaged beacon lights, and he gives public radio a break on his price for high tower work because he values public radio.

"CAN'T AFFORD A MISTAKE"

Sometimes, sitting around a dinner table, he talks like this:

"The future of farming is in the hands of the older farmers. The financial system we have right now makes it almost impossible for new farmers to get started. The financing terms are so bad that a new farmer, once he buys his land and equipment, can't afford to make a single mistake, ever. If he does, it's all gone. Everybody makes mistakes. Everybody.

"You don't even have to make a mistake. You can do everything the extension people tell you to do, you can do everything the government wants you to do, then we get a new president and he changes something, and everything is up for grabs. Somebody changes the rules, and what used to be a good practice is now a mistake, and you're out of business."

Talk at the kitchen table. Talk and food, food and talk. The two are inextricably tied together. For the Benson families, as with many farm families, the kitchen table is at the center of life.

There are two houses at the Benson farm. One shelters David, 38, and Sally-Anne, 36, and their children, Heather, 12, and Anton, 9. It is about a mile, by road, from the main farmstead, where David's parents, Gus, 83, and Bertha, 76, live. The farm is nine miles south of Worthington and just north of the Iowa line.

The kitchen tables are important in both homes. This is where the plans are made, the reverses are assessed, the stories are told. This is where the talk is.

And the talk, in this bitter year of 1985, often has to do with the agricultural crisis.

"Older farmers, the ones who want to get out and retire, have it in their power to provide more favorable terms for new people coming in," Benson said. "Maybe they could farm shares, maybe just taking a little less money."

OLDER FARMERS "ONLY HOPE"

"You know a bank isn't going to do that—a bank is set up to make as much money as possible. That's what it's for. But an older farmer, who has taken a good living out of the land over the years and wants to retire, maybe he'd be willing to take a little less for moral or philosophical reasons. It might be the only hope we have. We may be at the point we have to depend on altruism to save us, because nothing else works."

The present system of farming frightens all the Bensons, the older Gus and Bertha as well as the younger David and Sally-Anne.

"If you are pushed to the financial wall, you'll take extreme measures to save yourself," David Benson said. "Forget good farm practice—water structures, conservation, and all that. You'll *have* to get the most possible profit every year just to pay off the debt load."

SHORT-TERM VIEW WRONG

"That means you'll soak the place in pesticides, which may be a terrible decision in the long run. You'll soak the soil with fertilizer instead of trying to build it up naturally, which may be a terrible thing in the long run. You'll plow it the fastest way that takes the least amount of fuel—you'll cut every possible corner. And in the long run, you'll destroy the land.

"That's what the system encourages right now. It encourages the absolute shortest possible view of every problem we have. It's an awful thing, and you can already see the result. The countryside is being depopulated. People who can't make it are being forced out. They're losing everything—their farms, their neighborhoods, their way of life, their whole culture."

Why should older farmers take less than a farm is worth?

"There are a couple of good answers," Benson said. "You owe something to the land. It has made you a place to live and work all your lives, so you ought to see that it gets into the right hands—somebody who will take care of it.

"And sometimes, taking less will get you more. Look at all of these old farmers who sold out six years ago for $1,400 an acre and 14 percent interest on contracts-for-deed. Nobody can make those payments. So the guy they sold it to, he just quits. He gives the place back.

"Now the old farmer, who used to be retired, gets back a farm that's worth $750 an acre, if anybody is buying, and it's not in nearly as good shape as it was six years ago. So he never really got that big price, did he? He would have been better off selling it on more reasonable terms, something the guy would have a chance to pay off, than take what looked like all that big money."

The farm, Benson said, is the basic ecological unit on the planet, and should be used to hold the planet together. As the family passes around lamb stew and cranberry bars, he warms to the topic:

"Christianity once came out of work and the land, but it's gotten more theoretical, and I think that's unfortunate. The churches represent the moral leadership of the culture, and I think the effort to save the land, that impulse, might best come from the pulpit. Social sciences? Maybe. But I don't think so. I don't think you can trust social science the way you can trust the instinct to religion...."

The kitchen table is not just a place for philosophy. It's also a place for good stories and good memories that once were bad and now have the warm familiarity of a worn flannel nightshirt.

Sally-Anne seems always conscious of her children, hugging them, talking to them, touching their heads. Her stories are less of farming and economics than of family.

SALLY-ANNE TELLS A FAMILY STORY

"Oh, God, one time Anton swallowed some popcorn the wrong way, it went down into his lungs, and he had trouble breathing," she said. "He just seemed like he couldn't breathe, or he'd just kind of doze off, like he wasn't all there...."

Her hands dance in the air as she tells the story, and the legs of her chair scrape the floor as she becomes more agitated.

"We rushed him into the hospital, and when we got there, he was all right again...and then he started fading out again," she said. "Finally the doctor told us we ought to take him to Children's Hospital in St. Paul. We put him in the car and headed up the highway, 80 miles an hour...."

"A cop stopped us, a highway patrolman," David interrupted, "and I stopped and jumped out of the car...."

Sally-Anne pushed back in, excited by the story. "And the patrolman took one look at David's face and he said, 'You've got trouble, don't you,' and David told him, and he said, 'Go on up the highway, don't worry about the speed limit but keep it under control.'

"So we took off again, and all the way up, nobody bothered us—the patrolman had called ahead and cleared us. And Anton kept fading out, and we'd say, 'C'mon, Anton, c'mon Anton,' and we got up to the hospital and rushed him inside and the doctor took him....

"They took him back to examine him, and came out and said it was popcorn and they could get it out. David and I, we just went out to the car and sat there and cried. We just cried. What a day that was. God, I'll never forget that, Anton fading out, and sitting there in the car...."

The children, both blond and round-faced and blue-eyed, chip in their own stories of snowstorms past, of skating on the farm pond, of doing evening chores, and of social trauma on the school bus.

Bertha talks about her youth in Finland, the memories of war, of bombs and bullets. Gus talks of warming the crankcase of the Ford with a hubcap full of burning corncobs so he could get Bertha to the hospital for the birth of their middle daughter. Bertha tells of the night they got electricity, of her hands bathed in electric lamplight. Gus brags of picking 150 bushels of corn a day, by hand. David tells of riding a motorcycle to San Francisco, where he lived through the final years of the '60s, right there on Haight. Sally-Anne laughs about a hair-raising hitchhiking trip through Canada, just before she and David settled down with farming.

"YOU KNOW WHAT YOU'RE EATING"
The kitchen table also is the place for food.

"One of the best things about living on the farm is that you know what you're eating," Sally-Anne said. "Our kids are going to be healthy."

The Bensons raise all their own meat—beef and lamb and chicken. They milk an aging cow, Bluma, and maintain a chicken house for the eggs. They raise most of their own vegetables, eating fresh in season, and frozen and canned through the winter. They pick apples for sauces and cider. On any given day, the kitchens of Bertha and Sally-Anne are redolent with the odors of fresh bread or pies, meat stews, and vegetables.

"Grandpa (Gus Benson) always figured food was fuel, and he wanted plenty of it," Sally-Anne said. "David grew up that way, too, and it's a necessary thing—sometimes, when it's cold, and you have to work outside, it seems like you can't eat enough to keep yourself going."

Kitchen operations are passed deliberately and carefully down the generations. Heather goes to Bertha's kitchen to learn about apple pies. Together, they build a pie from scratch, an extended process that involves discussion of all the reasons for each different action and ingredient.

"What about nutmeg?"

"Just a little. Here. Just shake it on, just a touch.... But plenty of butter. The more butter the better it is. So never skimp on butter...."

"And you roll this?"

"You pinch it, here. That seals it up, and it makes it look nice...."

* * *

The farm year began in late spring. The entire world seemed composed of different shades and tints of green. The air was soft and humid and still. The only breeze was artificial, born of the motion of the hayrack, and, at that, not enough to ruffle the hair on a forearm. In the shade of the windbreak, it was almost cool. As the tractor moved out the front gate past the mailbox, crunching over the gravel shoulder, sunlight fell on the bare necks and lightly clothed shoulders, and heat prickled on the skin.

"You gotta make hay while the sun shines," Sally-Anne Benson said cheerfully, swinging her legs off the rack as her husband, David, towed it out to the west field with the David Brown tractor.

Sally-Anne Benson's nickname is Sago, an acronym of her maiden name, Sally-Anne Greeley, with the "o" tagged on for reasons of euphony. She is a small woman, 5 feet tall, 105 pounds, and pretty. She is a teacher (mornings only) at a Worthington Montessori school, the mother of Heather and Anton Benson, a good cook, an enthusiastic dancer, a maker and drinker of apple cider, a milker of cows and a doer of any number of other things, including a frequent driver of tractors. She drives at haymaking.

"You have to keep the moisture down, so you wait late enough in the morning to get the dew off," she said. "You mostly won't get out much before 10 or 11. A hot day with the sun shining and a good wind will really dry the hay out."

FIRST CUTTING OF HAY A GOOD ONE

In the field, David and Sally-Anne traded places, David hopping on the rack while she drove the tractor over windrows of hot yellow hay.

If haying was a card, it would be the queen of diamonds—a sweetness with a definite edge to it. Hay is the first crop of the year, the first payback.

And the first cutting of hay on the Benson farm was a good one. It was baled and stacked while the sun shined and the daily temperature climbed over 100 degrees.

The drying alfalfa smells like ginger and something else, a sweet, fat odor riding the silky summer breezes with gravel dust and gasoline fumes, riding into the elbow-out side windows of dusty old automobiles.

Baling means long, lingering hours of twilight as the solstice approaches. Old, weathered gray wood in the hay rack. Warm water from glass jars, and never enough of it. Hay cuts on forearms. Twine grooves in the pads of fingers. Sweat-soaked leather gloves. T-shirts sticking to the back and chest. Dry lips. The sun carving at the eyes. Arms leaden and aching with fire.

Baling is noise. A baler is a strange, violent piece of machinery. Trailed behind a tractor, it picks up pre-cut and dried windrows of hay—alfalfa, mostly—smashes and pounds them into a bale, ties the bale with twine, and ejects the bale from an upward-slanting chute that just touches the front edge of the hayrack.

A hayrack is the open wagon pulled behind the baler. You stand at the front edge of the rack, knees bent to absorb the shock of the bumpy ride, hands protected by leather gloves which are sweat-soaked in minutes, and when the bale comes up, you reach out with the stronger arm, snag the twine with your fingers, lift and grunt, balance the bale on your out-thrust hips, take three or four quick steps to the back of the rack, and push the bale onto the stack.

And go back for another.

"Like this. Stack it like this. That'll tie it together," David Benson shouted as the first bales pushed over the lip of the rack.

There is a pattern to stacking, as Benson demonstrated. The first bale is set all the way to the back, with its long side parallel to the side of the rack. The rest of the bales are placed with their long sides parallel to the back of the rack. The pattern is reversed on the next level, so the bales always cross each other from one level to the next.

"We're going to be stacking these up over our heads, so you want to tie them together like that—so the whole pile doesn't fall off on the road back to the barn. It gives you just that little bit of stability," Benson said.

The work was hard and unremitting. The stackers took turns grabbing, swinging and stacking, the baler hammering all the while, Sago half-turned in her tractor seat as it rolled up and down the field.

When the rack was full, it was towed back to the barn. The bales were swung off the rack and onto an elevator, a piece of machinery that looks like a cross between a conveyor belt and an escalator. It's even noisier than the baler.

"You guys unload the rack, and we'll go up to the top and stack," Benson said. The men on the bottom began pulling bales off the rack and dropping them onto the elevator. Up in the loft, the bales popped off much the same way they had popped out of the baler. Benson and a friend hooked and grunted and lifted, as they had on the rack, and carried the bales as far back and high in the barn as possible.

HEAT WEIGHS IN THE LUNGS

The barn, in its own way, is as bad as the field. Balers are exposed to the fierce, slicing sunlight, but in the barn the heat is close, dense and heavy, sitting in the lungs like soup.

"When I was 16, a friend and I hired out all over to bale," Benson said. "We could throw bales all day. Boy, were we in shape. Baling will do that for you. It takes a little longer after 35."

"You ought to start a spa for yuppies," Benson was told. "The Benson Hay Plan—$150 a day, good meals, guaranteed to whip the body into shape in only 14 days."

"You'd have to be able to stand yuppies for 14 days."

"A major drawback."

"Not more than 30 bales left, now."

"You said that 30 bales ago."

"Yeah, but I was lying then."

* * *

Early summer.

"Remember," David Benson asked, "going out there with the hoes and chopping the weeds out?"

The Bensons have hoes. A lot of hoes, kept sharp with a grinder, one for every member of the family, for cousins and sisters and out-of-town visitors.

A hoe, for the Bensons, is a philosophical statement.

"The soil has been here since the glaciers left, and you could grow just about anything on it," Benson said. "Since we've started farming it, we haven't done it any good. We send a lot of it right down to the Gulf of Mexico every year, pour all kinds of chemicals on it. Who knows what we'll wind up doing to it?

"There's an alternative to all that. If you're willing to take a little less, you can get along without all the fertilizers and the Lasso and Bigfoot (herbicides). It means you've got to do handwork, but that's OK, too—you build up a relationship with the land by working on it. You put so much work into a piece of land, and you start getting protective. That's got to be good for it, in the long run."

Hoeing is one of the bad jobs of the farm year. It's not particularly hard work, like haying, nor does it take much skill, as plowing does. It's hard in a different way. It demands attention, but lacks drama. The work is constant, but there is little sense of progress.

The principal villain in the soybean field is the Canadian thistle, a tall, tough bristly plant that crowds beans and chokes combines. It grows in shapeless patches that pay little attention to the order of bean rows.

The individual thistles seem to grow best near the stems of corn or beans. The thistles have to be hooked out with the hoe, rather than simply attacked with brute force.

HOEING THE BEAN FIELD IS "THE WORST"

"This has got to be the worst," Sally-Anne Benson said, halfway through a round of hoeing in the bean field. A thistle patch trailed across the rows in front of her. She was sweating hard, her face brown and unhappy in the hot summer sun. Two friends were working with her, and they both stopped.

"I thought you said it wasn't that bad," said one, leaning on his hoe.

"I keep forgetting," she said.

The Bensons have relatives and friends in the Twin Cities who come down with their families to help. "It's a family get-together, and it's a good chance for David and I to talk," Sally-Anne said one night at the kitchen table.

"Most of the time, he's on the tractor and I'm doing something else, or I'm on the tractor and he's doing something else, or I'm at the house and he's in the field, or I'm at school and he's in the shop. This is one thing we do together, at least."

But not on this day. The relatives had not come down yet. David was cultivating the corn with the tractor, and the bean field stood there, demanding attention, its thistles spreading and sprouting with great glee.

"This," Sally-Anne said, "is the worst."

At the end of each round of hoeing (a round is one trip up and down the length of the field), Sally-Anne drank water from the gallon glass jugs left at the ends of the rows. Her face glowed with heat and dehydration.

"Maybe you're too small to do this," a friend told her.

"Why?"

"Your body's surface area is a lot bigger compared to your weight than with larger people. Maybe you dehydrate a lot more than we do."

"I don't know. It sure is hot."

"How many more rows?"

"Just down to there—you can see the end. Four more rounds, maybe."

"Two hours?"

"I don't think I can do it two more hours."

"How about this? See, you set up a Benson Academy of Performing Arts and you apply for a grant from the arts council, and then you hire a bunch of starving artists from the cities, and give them hoes and tell them that this is a performance of life and death and they are out here to kill. Maybe we could tape it and run it on public TV."

"How about this? We get some Hare Krishnas and tell them the thistles are the manifestation of evil, and they could dance through the fields with their hoes, hari-hari, rama-rama...."

And passers-by, had there been any, would have seen two large dust-covered men and a small, tired woman doing an impromptu Hare Krishna dance with hoes, in a blazing sun in the Benson soybean field, not far from the Iowa line, in southwestern Minnesota.

* * *

Autumn.

If a playing card were chosen to represent the 1985 soybean harvest, it would be what? The ace of hearts? A warm card, a card of the highest level. Soybeans are the cash crop, the money crop, the crop that will decide how the year goes. Even a small crop is a pleasure to harvest.

David Benson, the worry lines etched around his eyes, stood at the edge of his field, plucked a few pods, shelled out the small, yellow soybeans, and popped them into his mouth.

"Soft. They're so soft, they're mushy," he said. "Run these beans through a combine and you'd lose them, you'd just mash them up."

The trouble began in early August.

"Rain came just about the second week of August—right after I bought that Deutz (tractor)," he said. "I remember we only used it once, and after that, it was always too wet to get in the fields. The rain was OK at first. We already had the oats out, and the second cutting of hay, and the corn needed a touch of wet weather. But it never stopped. It just kept going. Here it is the middle of October, and we're usually finishing up everything, just about now. We haven't been able to get in the fields. We haven't even touched the beans."

At the house, Gus Benson, from his easy chair next to the kitchen table, said, "I've never seen anything like it in 83 years. It's never been this wet and this late."

"It's getting cold," David said. "If we get snow, it'll drag the beans right onto the ground. You can't combine that way. We'd lose the crop. That's $9,000 in beans in that one field down there, and it'd be gone just like pfffft.

"It happened one time to us—not snow, but hail. I remember, we ran up and stood in the doorway and watched the hail come down and take the beans right out. Took them right out. I tried to get in and combine, but there wasn't any point in it. We'd get a few beans, but it cost us more in fuel than we were getting out. Of course, nothing's ever a total loss—I plowed those beans under, and next year that soil was terrific. Beans make good manure; it's the kind of manure you wish you could afford to put on the land, build it up."

WEATHER TURNS DRY

Two weeks later, everything changed. The rains broke and the weather turned dry.

By Monday, Oct. 28, the harvest was on. It was a Monday of the full moon. Not the harvest moon of September, but the hunter's moon.

To a man traveling down Highway 60, the major diagonal roadway from Mankato to the southwest corner of Minnesota, the hunter's moon was like a lamp flying along the edge of the road, illuminating the landscape.

On other trips, on other days, the landscape had been still. The windbreaks around the farmhouses, as seen in the moonlight, had looked like vast ships in a dark ocean anchorage, their blue mercury-vapor yardlights serving as warning lights at the peak of unseen mainmasts.

And all of the small towns had gone to sleep early. Lake Crystal, Madelia, St. James, Butterfield, Mountain Lake, Bingham Lake, Windom, Heron Lake, Brewster—all strung out on

Highway 60 like rosary beads, and all asleep by
11 p.m. Farmers' hours.

But different farmers' hours were kept
beneath this hunter's moon. The landscape was
alive with combines that crawled and clawed
their way through endless miles of rust-brown
soybeans. Grain trucks roared down side roads
and onto the highway, the elevators were lit and
working hard, and locomotives maneuvered
grain cars onto elevator sidings.

The towns were awake. The Dairy Queens
and groceries were open. Clusters of dusty, tired
men in work shirts and pinstriped bib overalls
gathered around the back of pickup trucks, their
smiles flashing in the electric light. The harvest.
A month late, but coming in.

A TIME FOR FIELDS

Benson got his beans out in a week of hard
work, sitting on top of the combine, churning
through dark, clean fields. Not a time for talking. Just a time for the fields.

A bean combine, like most working farm
equipment, makes no concession to beauty. It's
an ungainly thing, like a giant green stinkbug,
groaning and lurching through the fields, pulling dried bean plants in the front, spewing
shredded leaves and stems from the back. The
pale yellow beans go into an interior tank, to be
dumped later in high-sided wagons.

Some farmers take the beans straight into
the local cooperative elevator. On the Benson
farm, the wagons are towed to the main farmyard
and dumped into storage bins.

"You can't really know what it feels like
unless you've done it. Gosh, it just feels so good
to get them out," Benson said. "Remember going out there with the hoes and chopping the
weeds out? This is the payoff. These beans are
clean. Look at those beans."

Later comes a colder judgment.

"The beans, I'd say, were mediocre," he said.
"I mean, they're all right, but we got maybe 30

bushels an acre, average. We've gotten used to more than that—35, 40 bushels an acre—but that wet weather back in August maybe kept the pods from forming like they usually do. Maybe—I don't know."

Though the crop was only fair, the feeling remains warm.

"I'm glad we got them off," he said. "Gosh, it makes you feel good."

* * *

Closing down the year. Snow whips through Gus Benson's farmyard, and wagons of corn wait to be unloaded.

"We've got to close the big door," David Benson said. "That's always a job."

The "big door" is the huge, drop-down door to the barn's hayloft. Eight feet wide and perhaps 10 feet tall, it hangs upside down beneath its open doorway all through the summer.

To lift it into place, ropes are run from the back of the door to a series of pulleys inside the roof of the barn, then down to the ground floor. A single thumb-thick tow rope emerges from a ground-level door directly beneath the big door. That end of the rope is tied to a pickup truck bumper, and the pickup hauls the door up.

On the first attempt, a side rope broke and the door fell back.

"Gol-darned rope has probably been here since 1938," Benson muttered. Working barehanded to untie the broken rope, and re-tie the new one, was a slow, clumsy task. When he was done, Benson climbed back into the pickup and put it in gear.

"Easy, easy, easy...get the hooks, get the hooks...."

As the door swung up, the light in the barn died and the outside sounds were muffled. The change was anything but subtle, the loft changing from airy balcony to comfortable cave with the creaking swing of the great door. The metallic sound of the catch-hooks confirmed the closing.

CORN IS LAST CROP IN

The closing of the barn is one acknowledgment of winter's approach. The final acknowledgment—the final concession—comes with the corn harvest.

"When the last of the corn is in, that's it," Benson said. "There's all kinds of other stuff you keep doing, but that's it, really. After that, it's getting ready for winter, and waiting for spring."

As the storm came in, Benson towed the broken corn picker back to the shop and left it. There were other tasks to be done—two loads of waiting corn to be unloaded, the house to be converted to its winter configuration.

The high-sided grain wagons were towed under a rack that looked much like a child's swing set without the swings. A winch, run by a tractor's power takeoff, was hooked to the front corners of the wagon. When the winch cable was tightened, the front of the wagon lifted from the ground, and the corn slid through small doors at the back.

Beneath the back of the wagon was the lowest step of the corn elevator, which boosted the corn to the top of the crib, where it was dropped inside. The process was simple, efficient, and noisy.

"The corn is hardly worth growing, if you were going to try to sell it," Benson said as he watched the elevator carry the neat yellow ears into the crib. "We feed most of it, so we're OK. Even if we don't sell the beef, we can always eat it."

As the snowstorm intensified—the television weathermen now were calling it a blizzard—the Bensons began talking about the conversion of their home.

When David and Sally-Anne married, and then later moved back to his parents' farm, they bought an aging house. Although they worked to make it livable, it never had good insulation or modern heating systems.

THE HOUSE NEEDS WINTERIZING

The Bensons heat with wood, kerosene, and sometimes oil; wood is the mainstay. In the spring, the big Ashley woodstove is moved out of the front room to storage. In the fall, it regains its dark, glowering prominence in front of the couch.

"It's always nice to have visitors at a time like this," Benson said cheerfully. "We can use the help moving the stove."

The conversion was quick but heavy. The big old upright piano was pushed and carried from one wall to the next while Sally-Anne ran around with a broom, chanting, "Wait, wait just a minute."

When she was satisfied with the new arrangement of furniture, the Ashley was mounted carefully on cinderblocks and the chimney pipe was fitted carefully on top of it.

Sally-Anne further winterized the house by taping large pieces of transparent plastic over drafty windows. All of the Bensons worked together to shovel snow around the house's foundation to prevent wind from getting beneath the house.

"The hardest part of living here is the winter," Sally-Anne said. "The wind never stops, and when it's 10 below, or 20 below, you feel like it's cutting your face open. It can go on like that for days. You don't go outside except when you absolutely have to. You feel like you're living in a cave."

As the Bensons rearranged the living room for winter, the storm intensified.

"Can you see Bigelow? The lights?" Sally-Anne asked at 9 p.m.

No. There was nothing out there but the suffocating white mill of the storm.

Near dawn, the storm began to weaken. By mid-morning, Bigelow was visible again. Drifts blocked the road outside the house, but David, expecting them, had left a car in a non-drifting area of the road during the night. The Bensons were still mobile.

The next two days were cold. On the third day, the weather turned milder, and Benson thought about the corn again.

"Maybe I could use the bigger tractor and pull the picker through there," he said. He decided to try. Repairs on the picker took two hours, and he pulled it down to the cornfield and through the snow. It worked.

"I figure two hard days and it'll be done," he said with evident pleasure, ice bristling from his mustache, as he towed the first full wagon back to crib. "You see us go through there? She pulled right through." He patted the tractor.

It didn't work quite that way. He spent the rest of the week struggling with the increasingly crusty snow and breakdowns with the picker.

"It's the ice going through it," he said. "It puts a heck of a strain on all the machinery."

But he did finish.

For the work he had done, for all the planting, cultivating, hoeing, the waiting for the rain to stop, the tension of the late fall—for all that, he finished without fanfare, although you almost expected there to be some.

There was not. He pulled the picker over the last rows of corn, through the snow, and drove home.

* * *

On a cold, snowy November day, I climbed the soft steps of baled hay to a place near the peak of the Bensons' big red barn, and made some final notes.

A barn is a place of mysteries. A place of birth and death and endless sweat. A place of hatches up and down, of unexpected turnings and gates and barriers, a place where you can build a castle or a fort or a nest in the bales of hay.

In seven months of reporting on the Benson family and their farm, I had been in and out of the barn 20 or 30 or 40 times. So, on the last day, as I left for the barn, Sally-Anne asked, half teasing, "Going to think?"

I was. When I stepped inside the barn, I found Gus Benson's big hound, Moses, curled up on a bale of hay a few feet from Bluma, the aging milk cow. I stepped over Moses and climbed the steps made by the bales until I reached the peak. Six half-grown barn cats—four tigers and two calicos, the survivors of the summer litters—climbed right along with me, curious about the intrusion.

A barn is basically a large wooden envelope designed to keep the worst of the weather off whatever is stored inside—hay, animals, miscellaneous equipment, and tools. It is not designed to be as weatherproof as a house. Up near the top of the barn, light and snow were filtering in through cracks around the big door, a hole in a windowpane and other places.

The cats stepped carefully around the snow and sat down to watch. And I sat down to think about the year, the faces and names, the things we did, the way the farm looked and felt.

To tell the story of a farm family, over a growing year, is difficult if you are determined to do it honestly. As you accumulate information, you find too many bits that will not fit into a smooth-flowing story—the low cards in the deck, in a way.

But an accumulation of low cards can make a powerful hand—you'd bet the house on four deuces in draw poker. So what do you do with the small bits, the pieces that characterize the land, the people, the work?

In the months of interviewing and writing, I never told how the Bensons fight occasionally, as any sane couple does, and how, when they have a difference of opinion, they call each other "honey" in every other sentence.

Nor did I say much about the killing of animals—the butchering of chickens, the transportation of sheep to the locker, David's comment that the beef cattle "represent a lot of corn and work," or his suggestion that he can maintain a personal relationship with his animals at the same time he quite happily sends them to slaughter.

I never wrote much about Sally-Anne's hunger for seafood or about Heather playing beginner's Bach on the old upright $25 piano.

I never wrote anything about the stock tank used as a swimming pool, about the tire swing in the backyard, about the sweat-inflamed forearm cuts left by haying, about how the handles of the hoes are worn concave by years of use, about how drivers wave to each other when passing on country roads under the assumption they're acquaintances or wouldn't be there.

I never wrote about the peculiar cast of the sun on the prairie at dawn. I never wrote about Gus Benson's hands, which all by themselves look like 50 years of farming—or how the Bensons link hands, big and small, rough and smooth, to say grace before meals.

In a year with the Bensons, I've been writing about the face cards. I could have done as well with the deuces and treys.

Observations and questions

1) This section intertwines the farm year with the simile of a poker game, which Camp explains as an organizing device. Does this comparison illuminate his material, or merely decorate it?

2) The section includes a review of the farm year. Think about the rhythms and cycles of nature, agriculture, and people in this series, and about how Camp has incorporated them into a whole.

3) Camp says that Benson "has what friends teasingly call an act. With intellectuals, he talks like an intellectual; with other friends, he's full of yups and ain'ts and gol-lies." But he never quotes Benson in the second mode. Would the series have been stronger if we had seen more of David's duality? Would he have seemed more real, or less?

4) The narrative part of the series ends with the final harvest and a great storm as the family settles in for a winter of waiting. The final word is "home." Rehearse some alternative endings that might recast the whole series into a different theme.

5) Camp admits that the Bensons, for all their attractiveness, are atypical farmers, even for southern Minnesota. How has he taught us so much about farmers, while using such eccentric models?

6) An editor's headnote to the series says, "We wanted to find out why farmers chose this difficult and often unrewarding lifestyle." Have they succeeded?

7) Camp introduces himself as a character, climbing to the top of the barn to reflect on his series. He tells us regretfully what he had to leave out. Does he undercut himself by stepping to the footlights and spoiling the illusion? Or is he honest about the limits of journalistic form?

A conversation with
John Camp

DON FRY: You won the ASNE award for non-deadline writing, although you're a columnist. Did you start in St. Paul as a columnist?

JOHN CAMP: No, I started as a reporter in 1978. I've been given a lot of freedom since I've been up here. Editors have been very cooperative about that. After a couple of years here, they gave me a column. I'm leaving the column now and going to full-time, self-assigned project writing and news features.

Tell me about this farm project. Whose idea was it? How did it get started?

Well, the genesis of the thing is complicated. I was becoming increasingly interested in the whole farm business, what was happening to farmers, the fact that they were feeling powerless. In the early fall of 1984, I started talking to some people about the possibility of expanding our farm coverage.

Had you been writing columns on farming?

Yes, I had written quite a few columns about specific instances and particular injustices that have happened to individual farmers. Some of the things done to the farmers are just unbelievable, horrifying. And a lot of it is done by the federal government in a bumbling, stupid way that

---

I conducted these interviews over the telephone, except for David Finkel's. I have edited the tapes very heavily for clarity and brevity; in some cases, I have recomposed the questions.

destroys things. It's like watching a giant walk around in a toy shop, just stepping on stuff without knowing it.

So what happened next?

So our managing editor was very interested in the idea, and he got together a working group of people to talk about it, including our graphics editor, the metro editor, and some people who were just interested. In the meantime, one of our photographers, Joe Rossi, kept telling me I had to talk to this farm family down in Worthington.

The Bensons.

The Bensons. And eventually I talked to the Bensons. They were small farmers, they were struggling, and they came from a long tradition of farming that went all the way back to Sweden. But the interesting thing about them was that they were extremely articulate about their problems, and they were very concerned about their neighbors.

When I read your series, I liked the Bensons because they're wonderfully articulate and caring. But did it bother you at all that they don't look like typical farmers? They're terribly hip, with a thousand books in the house.

A lot of farmers are extremely well-educated, extremely hip. David is from a line of Swedish intellectuals. A couple of weeks ago, I stopped in for dinner at their house, and David was reading the poetry of Wallace Berry at the dinner table. He repairs a radio tower for enormously cheap rates just because he likes to get National Public Radio; and he likes PBS.

They're perfect.

They are perfect. They are Minnesota Swedes. The kids are blonde. And they're photogenic. And they do things like jump in the farm stock tanks for swimming pools, jump off the barn roof, and chase chickens with plastic baseball bats.

Tell me how you approached them in the very beginning.

Joe told them we were thinking about doing a story, and asked if they would be interested in talking about it. And they said they would, mostly because they're that sort of people, although they were a little bit nervous about the whole thing. So Joe and I drove down there, and we found David plowing. David hopped down off his tractor, and we all sat down in the ditch by the roadside. We ate our lunches and talked, and by the time we got out of the ditch, the project was on.

Did you live with them, or just go out and visit them?

I did a little of both. Most of the time I stayed at a motel in Worthington. I had to get away from them, because when I write, I like to be a little bit away from things. I would take a lot of my meals with them, and stay with them from the time I got up in the morning until evening.

How long would you spend with them at a time?

The longest I was ever down there was five days in a row. For each of the stories, I went down at least two times and sometimes three. And then in the middle of the summer, I started sleeping on their front-room floor. I got my sleeping bag and stayed over, mostly because I wanted to find out about getting up at 5 a.m.

Did you design the whole series ahead of time, or did it develop?

No, it just developed. When I'm writing longer pieces, I like to have some kind of conceptual framework. And one of the hardest things was coming up with a legitimate framework that wasn't phony. You could probably sit down six months ahead and build one, but I didn't want to do that because I was afraid I'd start jamming stuff into the framework. So I decided that the first piece was just an introduction, like a hand-shake. I was thinking about what they do on a farm, and what they did relentlessly was work, total immersion in work.

You start the first segment like this: "David Benson sits on the seat of the manure wagon, behind the twin black draft horses, reins in his hands, and he says...." And you follow that with a six-paragraph quotation. Do you normally lead with a six-paragraph quotation?

Because this was an introduction, I wanted David talking to you immediately. He sits behind the horses and just starts to roll, almost as if he's talking to himself. I taped substantial parts of it. I looked at this long passage and I thought, "That's terrific, and I've got to put it someplace."

I have a hard time writing leads, and so I sometimes write my leads second. I'll start roll-ing with the story, and then the lead will come to me. But a lead never came to me. I kept look-ing at this part, and that's how it happened.

For a man brought up on the *AP Stylebook*, that's pretty chancy. It violates everything they tell you.

You have to remember that the Iowa Writers Workshop got to me first.

Let's talk about scene setting. Eleven paragraphs in, you write: "The landscape is not quite flat—it's a landscape of tilted

plains, fields tipped this way or that, almost all showing the fertile loam of recent plowing. The black fields dominate the countryside, interrupted here and there by woodlots, by pasturage where lambs play in the fading sunlight, by red-brick or purple-steel silos, Grant Wood barns and Sears, Roebuck sheds, and by the farmhouses." That's so pastoral, we could set it to music.

Sometimes I feel like I'm not qualified to do the work, and so I have to work really hard on some things I'm afraid I'm going to forget, like scene setting. I'm afraid that I'll get so involved with people that I'll forget what the scene is like.

We have these little Radio Shack lap computers, and I would go out and sit in the field with nobody around me. I would look at things, and start trying to characterize them in my mind, and write down on the computer what they actually look like. And a lot of it is just naming things that are out there. Enough people in this country have rural experience, especially here in Minnesota, so that when you simply name things, you touch off these hidden sensory nuggets in their brains.

Did you come from a farm background?

I grew up on acreage outside of Cedar Rapids. If you think about the memory of a hot afternoon when you're mowing the grass with a power gas mower, that smell of gasoline and fresh-mowed grass. It's one of those smells that brings back your childhood so clearly. I'm trying to find things that are already in people's heads and touch them off.

I think it works beautifully. Can we go to part two, "Sweat, toil all in a day's work." Nineteen paragraphs in, you give this summary of the Benson family: "There are six Bensons on the farm now. Gus, 82, and Ber-

tha, 72, own it and are semi-retired; their son David, 38, and his wife, Sally-Anne, 35, are both management and principal labor; David's and Sally-Anne's two children, Heather, 11, and Anton, 8, do the chores." You keep putting that block in, always in different forms. It's a cast of characters, isn't it?

Yes. Since these stories were published a month apart, I felt I had to introduce everybody at least briefly every time, because we're a newspaper and not a novel.

It strikes me as an odd way to introduce them, in a very tight paragraph with lots of names and numbers. I wonder why you did it that way, rather than spreading them out over three or four paragraphs, weaving them across each other.

It's a matter of economy in this particular place, because I'd already introduced them in the previous story. And so I just decided to go with the list.

In the section called "A tough row," you really captured the backbreaking, repetitive nature of farm work. Tell me about the reporting on that part.

The Bensons were happy to have us come down and report because they had us working.

Oh, you were out there with a hoe?

Yes, I was out there with a hoe for hours, and it just killed me. You just feel the water being sucked out of you. Joe was out there hoeing, too. He left his cameras at the edge of the field. Later, we helped them get the hay in.

Did you have any worries about reporters participating in stories?

I usually have a problem with reporter participation, especially when it involves trips, because too often it becomes more trip than reporting. And the stories suffer for it. But in this particular case, I thought that if you really wanted to try to get inside the work, it would help.

There's real empathy here.

Empathy is the key to this kind of work. You almost have to become part of the family. You have to feel what they're doing, because if you just observe from the outside, a lot of it doesn't look like that much.

You can feel the derivation of the word "redneck" when you're working out there. You keep your head down, looking for weeds, and your head begins to pull on your back muscles. At the end of the day, when you're sitting at their kitchen table, putting your observations into the computer, you kind of move around and say, "Well, let me see, this pain must have come from when we did this." It's a physical way of taking notes.

Ouch! Part three, "Farm squeezes out last drops of summer," has all the women looking out windows. Did you choose that image deliberately?

Yes, but now it strikes me as just a little bit contrived.

I don't find it contrived. Women play major roles in this story and the whole series.

Well, they do. It seemed to me that the women did so much work on the farm that I ought to include something that focused on them. A lot of what the women talked about related to looking out windows, and that image just stuck in my head. Bertha was always in the kitchen, and she was always looking out the window, and she was always telling me about the windows.

In the section on the car race, you have this wonderful detail of the flag: "The pre-race ceremonies are quick: a crew meeting, the raising of the colors by a veterans' group color guard—the flag has 48 stars, but it's a perfectly good flag—and the cars begin rolling onto the track." I like that little aside about the flag.

Joe, the photographer, pointed it out. We were standing out there, and he said, "Look at that flag. It's got 48 stars."

It helps to have a second set of eyes out there, doesn't it?

He is more in this story than he'll ever get credit for. He would see things, and he would tell me about them. And he not only has a good photo sense, but also a sense for scenes, almost like a movie.

Did you ever suggest pictures to him?

Yes. I suggested a whole series of pictures that would have been in the series, except we couldn't figure out the layout problems. In the next section, we drove out to the KRSW tower that David was going to climb. Rossi climbed the tower above Benson, 280 feet up this tower, shooting right down it, a magnificent photograph!

That guy's a treasure. In this section, you introduce the idea of David as "Prairie Intellectual." I guess I shouldn't have been so surprised by that description, because he's so articulate. But talk about why you saved this section so late.

It's just more explication of his character. I was up in this little room upstairs where all the books were. But after I spent some time working in that room, the books made their presence felt. I started looking at the titles, and I realized how wide the guy's interests were.

And as you said before, this kind of prairie intellectual isn't all that unusual up there. But in the next section, one thing bothered me, the part about David's dual modes of speaking: "He has what friends teasingly call an act. With intellectuals, he talks like an intellectual; with other friends, he's full of yups and ain'ts and gol-lies. It's not an act. His two sides are simply that." But nothing you quote has "yups and ain'ts and gol-lies."

That's because he was talking to me. Maybe one of the problems with this story is I didn't show him enough talking to grain elevator operators and other farmers. We went up to the grain elevator and talked to the guy about how much water there was in the corn. But I always felt a little strange about pulling out a tape recorder or a notebook and taking down what farmers were saying.

Why? You're a reporter.

Because there's no unobtrusive measure. If you introduce yourself as a reporter, most of the farmers become very reticent. By the time I got finished, I looked pretty much like David, wearing jeans and a blue nylon coat and a billed hat and boots. When I went places with him, people assumed I was a farmer, so I would be in on the full conversation. But if you're introduced as a reporter, all of a sudden you're not one of the boys. And so I didn't show him as much in direct quotation dealing with other farmers as perhaps I should have.

Do you ever try reconstructing conversations from memory?

Not very much. So many things are said in nuances; if you reconstruct, you leave out those things. I think that people are most like themselves in complete quotations. If you reconstruct a longer quotation, most of the time it seems more like you than like the person who spoke it.

In the last part, you devote five paragraphs to a comparison of poker and the farm year. Where did that simile come from?

That was a case of invention. A lot of this material is hard to organize, and so I would look for familiar metaphors. Poker has all these small events throughout the game. All these little decisions accumulate towards the end of the evening. And it struck me that this is the way a farm works. You make all these decisions whose ramifications over the long term might not be particularly visible, although they seem to be the best you can do at the time. Also it's gambling. I'm not sure that came off as well as it should.

I thought it was a very apt simile.

As I go through these things with you, I'm not really sure I'm satisfied with a lot of the images I used. But I like that one.

You should like it. I'm pointing out the good parts.

We're going to come to the bad parts next, right?

No, we're going to talk about the very end, where you speak in the first person and climb to the top of the barn. Why did you decide to drop the reporter's invisibility?

I don't know. I really can't tell you why I did it.

Perhaps it's kind of a "reporter's notebook"?

Well, when you write a story like this, you internalize so much stuff that you can't get into

80 inches. But in the first person you can con-
dense it.

**Well, let me tell you how I took it. You
apologize for all the things you didn't have
time or space to write about. You're saying,
in effect, "All this stuff I've told you is quite
rich, but there's a lot more to it, because of
the depth of these people."**

That was exactly what I was trying to say.
Writing gets you as close to the essence of things
as any abstraction can. Film and television seem
closer, but are actually further away from the
real experience than writing is.

**How does writing come closer to real
experience?**

Writing doesn't fool you with the images of the
things. You're sitting there in front of your television set, watching a program on farms, and you
think you're experiencing a farm, but you're not.
Writing does not pretend that you're experiencing a farm. So you don't have that false image
to deal with first.

So here at the end, I'm saying that writing
is artificial. And I don't want you to feel that,
because you read these articles, you've then ex-
perienced the farm, because you haven't. There
are all these other things that I never seem to
tell you about.

**So it's an act of honesty. You step up to the
footlights and say, "This has all been a show,
you know."**

Let me ask you a question. Have you ever met
Greta Tilley?

**Sure. She's a friend of mine. She was here
at Poynter two weeks ago.**

Well, I think of myself in competition with other reporters. I read her stories, and she makes me very nervous. You can hear footsteps coming up behind you, and you're about to be killed by a free safety. She's very good.

You bet.

In *Best Newspaper Writing 1985*, she talks about how everyone in her newsroom said, "We've got to do that someday." I think that's where all the good stuff comes from. Not from a newsroom situation, but from a couple of people who get together. In our case, the editors knew that we had a big farm crisis out there. And I had a concept. And Rossi had this family.

Then when you get rolling, everybody starts to feel good. Newspaper people feel bad a lot of the time.

Why is that?

Because they feel they're writing the first draft of history, and what they would rather write is the last draft. And what you're doing is temporary. But with a story like this, all of a sudden everybody starts feeling good.

Editors should recognize the fact that reporters, people like Greta Tilley, are out thinking about things. They should point them in the right direction, and let them go. You get writers like Greta Tilley, and you're in fat city. All you have to do is use them right.

That goes for you, too.

Thank you.

Thank you.

David Finkel
Non-Deadline Writing

DAVID FINKEL, 30, was born in Reading, Pennsylvania, and grew up in Pennsylvania, Maryland, New Jersey, and Florida. He was graduated from the University of Florida in 1977 with a bachelor of science degree. He worked briefly for *New Look* magazine before joining the *Tallahassee Democrat*, where he covered the courts beat, including the trial of the serial murderer Ted Bundy. In 1981, he moved to the *St. Petersburg Times* where he writes general assignment pieces around the state of Florida. He has won several awards from Florida press organizations.

For John Lerro, Skyway nightmare never ends

MAY 5, 1985

NEW YORK—On a gray, miserable April day, a man with a beard is limping toward a boat on the East River. He looks cold. He looks lousy. He has tears in his eyes from the wind and a cast on his left hand from punching a wall. Because of the cast, he can't button his jacket, and it's flapping around in the icy wind.

His name is John Lerro. He doesn't want to be here. He would rather be in bed asleep. Or in sun-blessed Florida. Or in the arms of a beautiful woman. Or even eating breakfast. But it is Tuesday. On Tuesdays he has to be on the water by 8 a.m.

So he has awakened before he wanted to, thrown some bran in a bowl, added some raisins and wheat germ he keeps under his bed, watered the mixture down in the bathroom sink, and stumbled into the unwelcoming arms of a new day.

"I feel terrible," he says. He is limping because of multiple sclerosis, and the wind gusts are playing havoc with his balance. He says, "I look like a drunk."

At the dock, six students from the State University of New York's Maritime College are waiting for him. All of them are glad when he arrives. All of them are anxious. Today's the day they're going to learn how to dock a boat.

And Lerro—John Lerro of the Sunshine Skyway Bridge disaster, *the* John Lerro—is going to teach them.

Taking his seat in the boat, he has only one piece of advice to offer. He is the voice of experience, and the students are attentive.

He says, "If you misjudge, you've got hell to pay."

"I'M LIVING LIKE AN ANIMAL"

This Thursday, it will have been five years since Lerro, standing on the bridge of the 608-foot-long freighter *Summit Venture*, felt the sickening sensation of his ship grinding against a support column of the Skyway bridge.

He can still see the bridge collapsing, the cars falling, the Greyhound bus pitching forward and turning upside down. Now he is 42, and there are moments when he doesn't seem eager to make it to 43. Of the accident, he says, "It screwed up my profession, it screwed up my significance, it screwed up everything."

Of his mental state, he says: "Am I p----- off and frustrated? There aren't words in the dictionary."

Of his life: "I'm living like an animal."

He is living on a ship these days, a ship that, believe it or not, is docked beneath a bridge. He doesn't see any irony in this, or in the fact that he is teaching 18-year-olds how to steer boats. He is teaching, he says, because he needed a job, and he is living on the ship because he can't afford a place of his own.

The ship is called the *Empire State*. Once it was a passenger ship, then it carried troops, now it is the teaching ship for the Maritime Academy. It is just over 500 feet long and has several closet-sized cabins. One of them—No. 18, the one next to a room labeled "Slop Sink Locker"—is Lerro's.

The cabin is five steps long, two steps wide. It has a low ceiling, blue walls, and a porthole that Lerro has covered with a dark blanket. Furnishings include a radio tuned to a classical music station, a wheezer of an old TV that someone loaned him when he broke his hand, and a humidifier that is propped on a box and aimed at his pillow.

The humidifier runs constantly. Unless the air is moist, like in Florida, Lerro gets a sore throat. He can't stand the dry air of the North, but he has to be here because of the multiple sclerosis. The heat, he says, wipes him out.

"I think back to my life in Tampa," he says. "It was beautiful. I died and went to heaven. Now I have filth. I touch things, and I'm filthy."

The ship smells of diesel oil. The halls are narrow, the steps are steep. Even in winter, the showers are cold. And when the radio's off, the sounds are of trucks crossing the Throgs Neck, the bridge across the East River connecting the Bronx to Queens.

Like the Skyway, the Throgs Neck is a huge bridge, breathtaking to see, but it is built differently. For one thing, around each support column are fenders to help stave off ships.

"If I had hit that bridge," Lerro says of the Throgs Neck, "nothing would have happened."

He says this in a New York accent. He was born here in the Bronx. His mother was a teacher. His father worked construction. He wanted to be a ballet dancer.

Instead, in 1960, he ended up as a student at the school where he is now teaching. He studied hard, became a merchant marine, married a woman named Sophie, fathered a son named Charles, and spent the next 20 years on ships.

"If I had life to do over again," he says, "I'd be a flute player."

"FORTY MILES OF BAD ROAD"

His career, if not remarkable, was at least well-rounded.

He was a third mate, then second mate, chief mate, and ship's master. He took container ships to Japan, passenger ships to South America, chemical tankers to Europe. Eventually, he became one of the 150 or so pilots qualified to guide a ship through the Panama Canal.

"I had identity," he says. "I had self-assuredness. Forget the bridge. I've done a lot. I've been around the world."

His only problem came on small ships headed directly into the wind. For reasons no one could explain, he would get seasick.

It was a problem easily managed. He began carrying plastic bags with him. "Yes, I felt terrible," he says. "Did I make a mess? Never. And the boatsmen appreciated me for it."

In 1976, he became the first outsider to penetrate the closed world of the Tampa Bay Pilots Association.

For years, the 20 pilots in the association had hand-picked their new members in what Lerro describes as a "good-ole-boy system." Then, in the mid-'70s, the state stepped in, openly advertising a new slot in the trade guild.

Lerro, down in Panama, heard of the job and applied. "I memorized every inch of that channel," he says. "I sat up at night after Panama Canal transits. I took study cards with me." After the Skyway accident, there would be trial testimony that Lerro's bosses in Panama were dissatisfied with his work and were thinking of dismissing him. But Lerro says he wanted the job so he could come back to the United States and settle down.

Starting pay was $500 a month. The job was to guide any ship entering or leaving the Port of Tampa through the curves and turns of the bay's 40-mile-long shipping channel, the one pilots call the toughest in the state.

"Forty miles of bad road," Lerro calls it now.

At first, he felt less than welcome. "I was chosen by the state. I was an outsider. I was an Italian outsider. I was a New York, Italian outsider. I was an ex-Panama Canal, New York, Italian outsider. What I'm saying is they had their reasons."

But the job, he decided, was a dream. "This little man is moving that big thing. You're a very significant person. It was the reason for getting up, the reason to be."

By 1980, Lerro says, he knew the channel as well as any of the other pilots. He was earning $40,000 a year. He had been up and down that channel 800 times. He had piloted 865-foot-long ships, among the longest allowed, and ships carrying a pressurized gas called anhydrous ammonia, which, if spilled, would form a vast, poisonous, explosive cloud.

By majority vote, the pilots decided to promote him from deputy to senior status. It was a big promotion. His salary would instantly increase beyond $100,000. The one hitch was that he had to pay the association the customary initiation fee of $120,000.

In early May, he arranged for a loan, he says, and scheduled the closing for the afternoon of May 9. The only thing he had to do before going to the bank was bring in the *Summit Venture.*

"MAYDAY, MAYDAY, MAYDAY"

Headed to Tampa for a load of phosphate, the freighter sat empty and high at the mouth of the bay. It was nearing daybreak when Lerro approached. As had become his habit, he carried a seasickness bag with him as he jumped from the pilot boat and climped the rope ladder hanging over the freighter's side.

For all practical purposes, once he reached the pilot house, the *Summit Venture* became his.

The trip to the dock was expected to take about four hours. Monitoring the two-way radio, Lerro knew the bay was dotted with showers, some of them bad. At one point, using his radar, he helped direct an outbound vessel lost in a fierce little squall.

Then his storm hit. It was toward 7:30. He was watching the channel, watching the radar, watching the clouds, when out of nowhere, it seemed, blinding rain and darkness engulfed the *Summit Venture.*

It was an impossible storm to figure, Lerro would say later. At first, the winds were out of the southwest. Then, suddenly, they began to swirl, and the rain came from all directions, slanted almost sideways. The drops hit hard enough to sting.

Trapped in this storm, the ship moved up the channel at about 5 mph, past the final buoys before the bridge, into the final turn.

Then, just as suddenly as it had come on, the storm began to clear, revealing a sight that Lerro has yet to get out of his mind.

"At first I saw nothing. And then, way off the starboard side, I saw a piece of the bridge," he says. "I saw a piece of the bridge that I never should have seen from that angle."

Later, Lerro would be asked why he hadn't stopped when the bad weather was building. Or why he didn't veer off and ground the ship in the spoils. "You think that way afterward," he said, "but not before." There had been other storms in his four years, he noted, some of them blinding, all of them navigable.

But this time, as the weather cleared to the south, the bridge appeared where it shouldn't have been. The ship was off the channel's center line by 800 feet. Right then, Lerro says, he knew.

"It was not clear ahead yet, but because of that I did emergency full astern. I ordered both anchors dropped. And just then it cleared dead ahead, and I saw my bow was dead on. That's when I ordered hard port rudder. She was about a ship's length away. That's 600 feet. That ain't enough time to do s----. The ship started turning to the left. Then the flare of the apron on the bow grazed—just grazed—the side of the bridge. That's all I saw. The ship went under the bridge, and then the whole bridge fell down. Then I saw two cars drive off the edge and disappear. Then I grabbed the radio and called, 'Mayday.' "

"Mayday, Mayday, Mayday," he yelled into the microphone. "Mayday, Mayday, Mayday, Coast Guard.

"This is—all the emergency—all the emergency equipment out to the Skyway Bridge. The Skyway Bridge is down. This is a Mayday. Emergency situation. Stop the traffic on that Skyway Bridge!

"People are in the water."

While he stayed on the ship, divers began bringing up the bodies, 35 in all. Only a few had water in their lungs, signifying drowning. Most of the victims had died when their cars fell 150 feet and smacked against the surface of the water.

"One decision," Lerro says, thinking back. "I was so proud of myself as a pilot. I was so proud of my ability."

"WHY DID IT HAPPEN?"

After the funerals came the questions.

Was Lerro at fault? Partially, ruled the National Transportation Safety Board.

Should he become a full-fledged pilot, as had been scheduled before the accident? No, Lerro and the other pilots informally agreed.

Should his piloting license be revoked? No, decided a state hearing examiner.

That decision came eight months after the accident. During that period, Lerro retreated from publicity as much as he could. A few days after the accident, driving toward his home north of Tampa, he stopped at a Catholic church, walked inside, and began crying. "He needed to talk, desperately," remembers Father Tom Cummins, who approached him. "He wanted to know, 'Why did it happen?'"

He tried religion. He tried philosophy. He took comfort in people who stopped by his house and told him to keep faith, that he was a victim, too. But for every one of those, there was someone who would call and threaten him, or cuss him out. "My son, 13 years old then, got a phone call. 'How does it feel to be the son of a murderer?' He was devastated."

In March 1981, two months after the state hearing examiner recommended that Lerro be allowed to keep his license, the state Board of Pilot Commissioners agreed, 7-0.

The decision meant Lerro could return to work on Tampa Bay, and on April 9—11 months to the day after the accident—he was piloting once again.

He remembers his first trip. "The captain was wearing a Mickey Mouse shirt. I'll never

forget that. By the time we got to the bridge, he
knew something was up. He said, 'You're the guy
who hit the bridge.' He said, 'Don't worry. I'm
a born-again Christian. This was meant to be.'
He was very relaxed. He sat there with his
Mickey Mouse shirt, and I kept driving."

At the bridge, he says, he remembers looking up only to see reporters watching over the
edge and helicopters with camera crews hover-
ing just beyond.

He remembers the second trip. "You won't
believe it. You know what it was? An ammonia
ship."

He remembers the rest of the trips that
followed:

"The captain would be looking through
binoculars and say, 'Oh, what happened!' They
didn't know it was me. I'd say, 'Ship hit a bridge.'

" 'What'd they do with the pilot?'

" 'He's still piloting.'

" 'Did many people die?'

" 'Yeah. Thirty-five.'

" 'Oh. Very bad.'

" 'Yeah. It was.' "

"IF NOT FOR THIS JOB..."

Late in 1981, Lerro went to a chiropractor.
He was having trouble climbing the rope ladders
onto ships. He was staggering a bit. He didn't
drink, but people accused him of being drunk.

The chiropractor took a pen and ran it along
the bottom of Lerro's left foot. Involuntarily, his
toes curled upward. The chiropractor sent him
to a neurologist.

The neurologist also ran a pen along his foot.
Again his toes curled. The neurologist asked him
to track a pen with his eyes. His right eye
jumped. "That's right brain damage," the
neurologist said.

Another neurologist said the same thing. So
did another. Without a doubt, they all agreed
Lerro had multiple sclerosis. A chronic nerve condition, it would only get worse.

So on Dec. 24, 1981, a year and a half after
the accident, Lerro stopped piloting. He had no
choice. He couldn't pass the necessary physicals.

He did find work as a third mate on a container ship. But soon into the voyage he had to
fly home because of the multiple sclerosis, which
was growing worse because of stress. Sometimes
he got dizzy. Especially on hot days he could barely get out of bed.

He sold real estate. He tried to write a book.
He spent a lot of time alone. His wife, Sophie,
had become a ship's radio operator and was off
at sea. They weren't getting along anyway. He
began sending out resumes by the dozen.

In response, polite refusals began stacking
up.

Then came the letter from the Maritime
Academy. Yes, they remembered him from his
days as a student. Yes, they were aware of what
had happened to him. Yes, they would be happy
to hire him as an adjunct professor, to teach a
class called Nautical Science 306.

Yes, he could live on the *Empire State*.

In January, he headed north. He was optimistic. "If not for this job, I don't know what
I'd do," he joked. "I can't even rob banks because
you have to be able to run."

There were a lot of new buildings at his old
college, but many things were still the same. The
freshmen still were required to move around
campus in double time. The picture of him on the
rowing team was still hanging. And the Throgs
Neck, built while he was still in school, still
arched supremely over the campus.

Then, one night, all the frustrations welled
up at once, and before he knew it, he had
smashed his left fist into a wall. For a moment,
it felt good. Then the pain came on.

"IN OTHER WORDS, NO ANSWERS"

Sitting in the boat, surrounded by cadets, he
shivers. The wind is strong. The East River is
covered with whitecaps.

"If you misjudge," he warns, "you've got hell to pay."

The object is to dock. The first cadet takes the wheel. "These kids are beautiful," Lerro says. He knows they have been checking out the federal report on his accident from the school library, but he doesn't mind. "I love these kids."

The first student overshoots the dock, then tries to back in, realizing too late there's another boat in the way.

Bump.

Another student takes over and tries to drift in with the wind.

Thunk.

For two hours, it goes like this. The wind gets stronger. There are snow flurries. Finally, Lerro takes the wheel and brings the boat toward the dock. He comes in slowly at a 30-degree angle, swings parallel to the dock, cuts the engines.

"Hey, a pretty good docking!" he says.

"Not bad for an old man," one of the students says.

Class over, they scatter. Limping, Lerro heads back to the *Empire State*. He's having a particularly bad day. The wind is hell to walk against.

"I don't get any balance messages from my feet anymore," he says.

At the ship, he rests. Then, gripping the handrail, he makes his way up the gangway.

"I spent thousands of hours thinking about that day. Thousands of hours. Trying to figure out, Why me? You know what the answer is? Because. Why me? Because. Why the poor souls who died? Because. In other words, no answers."

Out of the wind, he feels better. But the steps leading to his cabin are especially tough.

"Yeah, I feel pretty guilty about it," he says. "I don't feel stupid, but I feel guilty. The weather was bad. I didn't rise above it."

Up the stairs, down the hall, past the slop sink. "I failed at being a pilot, but I'm teaching these kids good stuff."

Dragging his leg, he wobbles to his room. He is through the door and past the closet when he begins to teeter. It's his equilibrium. He is falling. He throws out the arm without the cast, pushes off a wall, falls back the other way, ducks his head, collapses onto his bed.

"Anyway," he says, "it's a miserable existence."

Observations and questions

1) Where does Finkel's lead end? Does this story have a lead?

2) This story appeared as part of a large spread about the fifth anniversary of the Sunshine Skyway Bridge disaster, as familiar in St. Petersburg as the moon landing. Finkel saves the link of Ferro and the disaster until the sixth paragraph, although we might expect this identification higher in traditional news form. Can a reporter rely on the materials surrounding the story to anchor the chief character?

3) Study the language of the opening of this piece. Finkel achieves powerful description with the simplest and shortest words, e.g., *gray, man, beard, boat, cold, tears, wind,* and *hand.*

4) Lerro teaches his class in the shadow of the Throgs Neck Bridge. How does Finkel play this bridge against the Sunshine Skyway Bridge? Notice that Finkel does *not* use the bridges as symbols, an easy and obvious effect.

5) This piece pivots on this quotation: "This little man is moving that big thing. You're a very significant person. It was the reason for getting up, the reason to be." Consider how the imagery and concerns of this quotation run through the entire story.

6) Finkel's long story is divided into segments with short quotations as subheads. This device helps readers follow the narration and keeps them reading. How can editors and writers col-

laborate on the content and placement of
subheads?

7) Finkel organizes this story with complex
chronologies: the day of teaching, Lerro's career,
and the disaster. Study how he helps readers
keep all the time schemes straight.

A murder story

MAY 26, 1985

Her weight's gone up. Gray hairs have sprouted. She's gotten used to flat shoes instead of heels and eggplant-shaped dresses instead of the gowns and furs she used to wear. But after a decade in prison for having her husband killed, Betty Lou Haber, closing in on 50, is still as polite and sweet-sounding as ever.

"There's never a night that I go to bed and don't say my prayers," she said last week. "I just do the best I can."

And that's why Albert Haber's surviving children are worried.

Ten years ago, after a sensational trial in Tampa, Mrs. Haber was convicted of planning the murder of her fourth husband, a well-known department store owner in Tampa and St. Petersburg. Her motive was to seize control of his estate. Her sentence was life in prison with a 25-year minimum before any chance of parole.

Sickened by the murder, Haber's four children took consolation in the thought that their stepmother would be locked up and gone from their lives at least until the year 2000.

But now, because of a little-known Florida law, she could be freed much sooner.

The law was written long before the Legislature mandated minimum sentences in 1972. It says that anyone serving a life sentence who goes 10 years with no discipline problems must be recommended to the clemency board for a possible commutation of sentence.

Several weeks ago, noting her perfect record in spite of her 25-year minimum sentence, the Florida Department of Corrections automatically recommended Mrs. Haber for such a commutation.

"I feel that I've earned it," she said in an interview. "I've waited 10 years for something good to happen."

Her four stepchildren, though, are appalled.

Says Susan Haber Mace, 32, of Brooksville, "You just don't plan a murder and wipe a person off the face of the earth and get out in 10 years. It's not long enough."

Says Frank Haber, 41, of Indian Rocks Beach, "We knew all along she was being good, we just didn't know why."

"PEOPLE WERE SHOCKED"

Albert Haber was killed the night of Jan. 24, 1975. He was 53. When Mrs. Haber, then 39, was arrested three weeks later, no one could believe it.

They had been married almost seven years. They held hands in public. They had known each other for more than 20 years, since Betty Lou, barely an adult, began modeling in ads for Haber's stores, which specialized in women's fashions.

At first they were simply friends. After a dozen years of friendship, romance finally took root. They had their differences. He was 14 years older, she grew up poor in the country. But they also had a lot in common, including failed marriages. Betty Lou was Haber's third mate-for-life; he was her fourth.

A week before their marriage, perhaps sensitive to one more failure, Haber asked Betty Lou to sign a prenuptial agreement that said she could recover nothing from his estate except $1,000 per year for every year of marriage they made it through.

She signed and moved into his five-bedroom, fully carpeted, chandelier-and-mirror-decorated home on Davis Island.

Three years later, he changed his will to leave her one-third of his estate. Four years after that, when he was murdered, she was in one of his two waterfront condominiums on Treasure

Island, chaperoning a slumber party for her daughter.

According to trial testimony and family recollections, Haber was standing in the dark near the kitchen when the man hired to kill him, James Joseph Brandt, hit him on the back of the head with the butt of a rifle. The blow caved in his head but didn't kill him. He collapsed into a wall and fell to the floor.

Then the person who hired Brandt—Mrs. Haber's first-born son, Arnold Jefferson McEver III—began kicking Haber with steel-toe boots.

When the kicks didn't kill him, either, Brandt bent over Haber's quivering figure, propped open his mouth with a piece of wood, put a gun in there, fired once and said, in Latin, "May God have mercy on your soul."

Then, to make it appear as if Haber had interrupted a burglary, he and McEver ransacked the house and fled.

The maid discovered Haber's body the next morning. By nightfall, three of Haber's children, who were living in California at the time, had flown in from San Francisco. At first, they were told their father had been in a bad car accident. But after arriving in Tampa, they were taken into a small room at the airport and told of the murder.

The next morning, Frank Haber, his sister Susan and Betty Lou were allowed into the house. They saw the blood on the walls and cried. Then, Frank remembers, Betty Lou wandered off. He caught up with her in the master bedroom. She was sitting on the bed.

Recalls Frank, "She started babbling, 'Why'd they do this?' " She started hiccoughing. She fell onto the floor and began shaking. He picked her up, carried her in his arms through the house, and drove her to the hospital. At the emergency room, doctors examined her, pronounced her in shock, and admitted her for observation.

"You should have seen her," Susan says now. "She could have won an Academy Award. When she was arrested, people were shocked."

"SHE IS A LADY..."

In exchange for a guaranteed life sentence, Brandt became the prosecution's star witness. He testified that he did the shooting, McEver did the kicking, and Mrs. Haber left open a sliding-glass door before going off to the slumber party so he and McEver could get into the house. Mrs. Haber, he said, wanted her husband "eliminated."

All three were sentenced to life in prison with a 25-year minimum. Brandt went to the prison reception facility at Lake Butler. Four days after he arrived, he was killed by another inmate.

McEver also went to Lake Butler and now is in Polk Correctional Institution.

And Mrs. Haber went to Florida Correctional Institution at Lowell, where she began compiling a spotless record.

She enrolled in an art class. She received a high school equivalency diploma. She took piano lessons. She learned yoga. She joined the church choir.

"She is a lady, is quiet, is respectful, and never presents any problems," it was noted in one of her official progress reports. "She also volunteers to assist the charm teacher," it was noted in another.

She was moved to the women's prison in Broward County and put in the honor dorm. She joined the Jaycees, worked on the prison paper, and helped the chaplain in her spare time.

Moved back to Lowell, she worked keypunch, in the hospital, in the law library. Never was there a complaint. Always she was well groomed.

To prison officials, she was a model inmate. But to Haber's four children, she was making life miserable.

Immediately after her sentencing, she began appealing her conviction, a process that still is nowhere near completion.

And even before her sentencing, she began fighting for her dead husband's estate, arguing that the will Haber wrote entitled her to a one-third share.

Even when the will was thrown out of court because it was shown Mrs. Haber had obtained witnesses' signatures to the document after her husband's death, she argued for her share of the estate anyway because of an old Florida law that says a widow is entitled to a one-third share no matter what.

It took her five years to give up the fight. During that time, with no money from the estate to fall back on, all three of Haber's stores were forced into bankruptcy, and the family business that was begun by Haber's father came to an end.

Then the lawyers began arguing over how much they should be paid for saving the estate. After years of wrangling, they settled on $160,000. That was $20,000 more than the value of Haber's life insurance policy, so the family's Davis Island home has been put up for sale to satisfy liens placed on the property by two lawyers who weren't paid in full.

In addition to their court battles, the Haber children have also had to contend with the problems of their brother, Randy, who fell apart emotionally after his father's murder. Arrested repeatedly over the past 10 years on charges ranging from vagrancy to drunkenness to drug abuse, he is in a Tampa rehabilitation center trying to straighten his life out.

"For the first two years after my father was murdered, there was a numbness in all of us," says Lee Haber, 35, of Lutz.

"I would say for the first eight years, I sort of floated through life," says Susan Haber Mace.

"I hate her inside my heart," Frank Haber says of his stepmother. "I hate her for what she's done to this family."

But as disturbing as all of this has been to the Haber children, inside the prison, Mrs. Haber's perfect record continued.

Finally, last October, as 10 years approached, she received this evaluation:

"Betty's treatment teams over the past nine years have observed that she has coped with her incarceration, as well as the length of her sentence, in an exceptional manner."

LETTERS FOR, LETTERS AGAINST

So she was recommended for a commutation of sentence. Because the minimum-sentence law was passed only 13 years ago, this is the first year such cases have begun colliding en masse with the older law guaranteeing commutation recommendations for good behavior.

This year alone, corrections officials say, they're expecting 116 recommendations. So far, there have been 33, according to Art Wiedinger, the lawyer who handles clemency matters for Gov. Bob Graham.

Of those 33, Wiedinger said, six have been considered by the clemency board. Of the six, he said, four were rejected, one was put on hold, and one was granted. That one changed the minimum 25-year sentence of convicted murderer David Fanning to straight life, which means he is eligible for parole as soon as the parole commission decides to release him.

Mrs. Haber's case is expected to be heard by the clemency board in September. In the meantime, while the parole commission is investigating her, friends have begun writing letters to the clemency board urging her release.

Says one of the letters, from a bank vice president in Tampa, "So many of us really believe the only thing that Betty Lou is guilty of is always being a good mother and dedicated wife."

Says another, a form letter copied and signed by 38 people, "If any prisoner ever deserved consideration for clemency due to their conduct and performance in prison, Betty Lou does."

For Haber's children, the letters are just one more insult. They say they don't care that their stepmother has helped the chaplain or lived in the honor dorm or consistently behaved in a way they never knew her to be. After 10 years of fighting her, they say, they want her in prison at least another 15 years.

So they also are writing letters to the clemency board. Like the letters urging release, theirs are being filed away for consideration. But unlike the others, they stand apart because of their unshielded emotion.

From Frank Haber's letter: "My father was not just killed. The word 'killed' is too antiseptic to describe what he went through the last hour of his life."

From Susan Haber Mace's letter: "I was told he was beaten so bad, he was unrecognizable."

From Frank Haber's: "After dragging us through this mess for 10 years, we feel that Betty Lou has made us into victims, too."

From Susan Mace's: "Justice is our only consolation."

Observations and questions

1) Finkel tells us that "the pieces that I like best are the ones with the most simple sentences in them." Study his simple sentences, and notice how he intersperses them with complicated sentences. What effects does he achieve with such simplicity and variety?

2) Finkel devotes the first two paragraphs to the characterization of Ms. Haber, but the story is about her family, not about her. How do these two paragraphs set up the third one?

3) Finkel has to deal with six people named Haber in this story. How does he help readers keep them apart? Notice how lightly the family members are described.

4) Finkel describes the murder in rather graphic terms. Why?

5) Do you like Betty Lou Haber, the murderess? Study how Finkel manipulates the reader's reactions to her. Why does he seem to want us to like her and dislike her at the same time?

6) Close to the end, Finkel devotes three paragraphs ("So she was recommended...to release him.") to a new wrinkle in Florida's commutation procedures. What would happen if we brought this section higher in the story? How else could Finkel present this factual material?

7) Finkel tells us that he dislikes ending a story with a quotation, yet he ends this one with four of them. Think about this ending in terms of its effect on the reader's opinion. Is Finkel editorializing or just presenting the family's emotions?

Program helps mental patients make it outside

JULY 21, 1985

Nighttime is the best time for Charles London Keys. At night, the 32-year-old Pinellas County resident sleeps in peace. While the fan in his room whirs, he's lost in dreams. When the cars go past his open window, he doesn't hear them.

Then he wakes up.

Then, instead of whirring, the fan says things like, "You're a fool for ice cream, Charles London Keys." Then, the cars going by say, "You can't tell Aretha Franklin how to sing a song."

Without a doubt, it is a strange world that Charles Keys lives in. Imagined voices are constant. Anything with a motor has something to say. Fans whisper. Cars bellow. "Airplanes are the worst," he says. "It's just something that keeps going on all the time."

Odd as all this may seem, Keys is considered a success story among those whose job is to help people deal with the mental illness of schizophrenia. Fifteen years ago, when his voices first began, they were much meaner. "Go kill a police," they urged. Instead, he got help. Now he has the voices under control. He is living in a downtown St. Petersburg boarding house, making his meals, keeping his room straight, and managing his very simple life.

A prime reason for this is a little-known program in Pinellas County called Boley Inc. Started in 1970 as a single, small halfway house, it has grown into a nationally recognized, $4-million-a-year operation with room for 220. Like Keys, who is a graduate of the program, all of the people in Boley are fighting mental and emotional illnesses, but the illnesses aren't severe enough to require hospitalization in a state institution.

The goal at Boley, says executive director Paula Hays, is to return mentally ill people to the streets and neighborhoods of Pinellas County rather than tuck them forever away out of sight. That goes for Charles Keys, and for the woman at Boley who recently smashed her hand through a window when she missed a bus, and for the deaf-mute at Boley who hallucinates like most schizophrenics, but whose hallucinations are acted out in sign language.

OUT OF THE INSTITUTIONS

Up until a decade ago in Florida, few of the people at Boley would have been allowed to remain in the community. Archaic as it now seems, those with serious mental illnesses were routinely sent off to secluded, fence-rimmed institutions such as G. Pierce Wood Memorial Hospital in Arcadia, or Florida State Hospital in Chattahoochee. There they stayed, usually for years, often until death.

That began changing in the 1970s because of several laws and court decisions that grew out of the civil rights movement, including one U.S. Supreme Court decision that said an institutionalized person should be kept in the least-restrictive environment possible.

The decision, out of a lawsuit brought by a patient in Chattahoochee, helped begin Florida's ongoing efforts at what is called deinstitutionalization. The success of the effort is apparent through statistics: in 1975, not including the criminally insane, there were 5,600 people in Florida's mental hospitals. Ten years later, the number has been halved to 2,850.

Similar attempts in other states have produced similar results—with one exception. In many of those states, an apparent backlash is now under way because patients were often returned to their communities long before they were ready. Because of problems resulting from that, "some citizens now want to 'bring back asylums,' " a recent issue of *U.S. News & World*

Report said. "Individuals in California sport 'troll buster' T-shirts belittling the homeless mentally ill...."

Not so in Florida, at least this part of it. "My feeling is we have as close to a perfect situation as possible in Pinellas County," says Paula Hays. "You're not going to hear about a backlash here."

The reason, she says unabashedly, is the program she is in charge of.

Supported mostly through state and county funds, it is a program that can take a person from a few months to a few years to get through. Most of the people come from Horizon Hospital, where they have spent a few days under observation, or from the mental hospital in Arcadia, where they were put until they passed through the crisis that required their hospitalization.

A few are manic-depressives, but most are chronic schizophrenics, an illness said to affect one out of every 100 Americans. Their lives were going along fine until they reached their late teens or early 20s. Then, because of a combination of genetic predisposition and too much stress, they simply fell apart.

Now, many of them hallucinate. Some of them have become almost catatonic. None of them will ever be completely cured, and most have to take some form of tranquilizing medication to keep at all in touch with the ordinary world.

Hays says that with 220 beds, Boley's program is by far the largest in the state and one of the largest in the country. In recent years, it also has gained a reputation as one of the best, and mental-health workers from other states frequently come by to see it.

What they see at first glance can look only so impressive. The activities center that Boley clients spend their days at is new and brightly lit, but the 14 group homes, halfway houses, and supervised apartments they return to at night are old and in need of repair.

As for the clients, at first glance, they don't look much better than the buildings. Clothing is often ill-fitting. Posture is often slumped. Everyone, it seems, nervously chain-smokes.

But the clients, like the buildings, deceive. Inside the buildings is an orderliness that bespeaks a healthy sense of hope. And inside the clients, at the root of everything they're trying to re-establish, is something most people learned long ago, an emerging sense of survival.

SANDRA COFFEY

Sandra Coffey is the amazing seamstress. Five hours a day, five days a week, she sits at a sewing machine at the Boley activities center and turns out insulated-cloth drink coolers like nobody else. She does the work of four people, says her supervisor.

It is away from the sewing machine that she is betrayed by her illness. Her hands fidget. Her eyes focus and unfocus. She talks in a distant, somewhat slurred tone, like someone trying to recover from a dizzy spell. Those who know her say she has no sense of time or space.

Now 33, she had finished high school, was working in an electronics-assembly plant, and had begun taking nursing courses when she first lost control.

"I was working, but I was hearing a lot of voices," she says in that unsteady voice, trying to remember. "I was having a bad time of it." Supervisors, she says, were telling her to drink a lot of coffee. And to eat donuts. And to drink more coffee. "My neck must have been broken," she says of that time, "because my chin always rested on my chest."

Fifteen years later, Sandra still doesn't know whether anything that she recalls truly happened to her or not; the most real things in her life, after all, are the imaginary voices that are always filling her head.

The voices, she says, have changed over the years. These days, they're the voices of alligators and turtles. They're constant, she says, and friendly.

Used to them by now, she says the disturbing thing in her life occurs when she looks at other people. She sees their faces and hair. She sees their hands move and their expressions change. Then she tries to imagine her face and hair, her hands and expression. She can't.

"I don't know what I look like," she says.

MILEY JENRETT

Miley Jenrett's problems began in 1969. He was drunk. He took a gun and shot it in the air. The bullets went up, and then they came down, and then he went to jail for attempting to kill and attempting to wound.

Since then, Jenrett says, the problems have been steady. He set fires; he got frostbite and lost all his toes; he tried to beat up four police officers; he got caught with some marijuana; he's had a hard time staying away from liquor.

Now 44, Jenrett says he's hoping that Boley will straighten him out. He's faithfully taking his medications: Dilantin to control his epilepsy, Haldol to control his schizophrenia. He got his hair cut short, giving him a friendlier appearance. And even though he has no toes, he wears the Suncoast's favorite men's shoe style: white loafers.

"Nicest program you can ever hope to be in," he says of Boley. "They're helping me a whole lot."

His biggest problem, he says, comes at night. Unlike so many others, he says, he doesn't hear voices. But at night, he has had the same bad dream since he was 9 years old. "It's big and tall. Like a dinosaur. It breathes fire, and it's got beams out the eyes. I see people running from it. It's no lie."

PETER O'HARE

In 1971, Peter O'Hare was the best cross-country runner at Clearwater High. In 1972, he traveled through Europe. In 1973, he dropped out of 12th grade and began a tailspin that landed him in the state mental hospital in Arcadia 14 times and Horizon Hospital 30 times.

"I was on a big self-pity trip," he says. "I was severely disturbed. I had a bad attitude about people in general. I was mean."

He took psychedelic drugs. He sniffed gasoline. He drank Listerine and after-shave. "Anything to relieve the pain," he says. "God, I was suffering."

The pain was from schizophrenia. The suffering included voices that always said vicious things about him. Now, he says, "I'm doing better than I've ever done before."

He hasn't heard voices in several years. He plays the piano. He is reading magazines and taking his medicine faithfully. "I have a very bright future," he says. "I'd like a car, a boat, a wife. I want to get married. I want to go to college."

Thinking back to his stays in the state mental hospital, he says, "It's enough to depress anybody."

Thinking that there was a time when he might have had to stay in such a place for the rest of his life, he says, "If I'm doing right, I think I deserve to be out here. I think anybody does."

ELIZABETH

Like Charles Keys, Elizabeth, a manic-depressive in her 50s, is a success story.

Sitting in a restaurant one day last week, she couldn't help but notice some of the other people there. The men were in suits, and the women were in dresses. The talk was of business deals and grand, personal ambitions. There was a time when Elizabeth would have wanted the same things as they: a new car, a bigger house, a lot more money.

Now, she says, she wants nothing more than peace of mind.

Her problem was this. One day she was living in upstate New York, taking care of her daughter and grandchildren. The next day she was inexplicably in a St. Petersburg bus station, walking unsteadily toward a clerk to ask for help.

Only later did she learn that two-and-a-half months had gone by between those two days, a period of time she somehow survived but has yet to be able to reconstruct.

From the bus station she went to Horizon Hospital, and from Horizon she went to Boley. Given a bed in one of the homes, she remembers looking around at the people she was now being included among.

They looked odd, terrible, menacing.

Over time, though, she began talking to them. They ended up helping her a great deal. And now that she's out on her own—living in a duplex and working in a downtown St. Petersburg financial institution—her thoughts often go back to them.

She sees them sitting there in their small rooms and apartments, all fine people, all struggling mightily to get better.

"It's funny," she says, "When I was in there, I looked down on the people there. Now that I'm out, I'm sympathetic to them. I understand them.

"I thank God that I was able to make it."

Observations and questions

1) Finkel's lead attempts to capture how a schizophrenic thinks. Consider the problems of presenting alien thought and emotion. The reader must be able to understand the sentences, perceive them as strange, and yet empathize, all at once.

2) Finkel has to weave five schizophrenics and their stories with the bureaucratic complexities of a social program. Think about this balancing act in terms of emotional restraint, the need for clear explication, and reader interest.

3) Reporters traditionally dislike adverbs. What do you think of the adverb in this attribution: "The reason," she says *unabashedly*, "is the program she is in charge of."

4) Finkel says he organized the portraits of the patients from "worst off" to "somewhat hopeful." In terms of describing a successful program, do you think that structure succeeds?

5) Each of the portraits ends with a simple quotation. Think about the effect on the reader of the very simple language in each of these passages.

6) Notice how the last interview, although pictured outdoors, leads us back to the inside of the institution and the other patients. How does Finkel color the remaining patients with Elizabeth's success?

'Fat Albert' carves out an 891-pound niche

NOVEMBER 10, 1985

COCOA—Behold the fat man. Go ahead. Everybody does. He doesn't mind, honestly. That's how he makes his living. Walk right up to him. Stand there and look. Stand there and stare. Gape at the layers of fat, the astonishing girth, the incredible bulk. Imagine him in a bathtub. Or better, on a bike. Or better yet, on one of those flimsy antique chairs. *Boom*! If you're lucky, maybe he'll lift his shirt. If you're real lucky, maybe he'll rub his belly. Don't be shy. Ask him a question.

"What's your name?"

"T.J. Albert Jackson. Better known as Fat Albert."

"How old are you?"

"Forty-three."

"How much do you weigh?"

"Eight hundred and ninety-one pounds."

"Gawd! How many meals you eat a day?"

"Three."

"What—three *cows*?"

Go ahead. Laugh. He won't mind. He'll even laugh with you, slapping his hand on his knee and chuckling so hard that his belly's shaking. You'll have to excuse him, though, if his eyes seem to cloud over, but truthfully, he's heard your joke before. About a thousand times before.

He knows the rule: you pay your dollar, you get a show. So go ahead. Ask one more question, the one that's on your mind.

"What's wrong with you?"

"Hormones," he says. "Pituitary gland. I was born with a birth defect."

Ah, the carnival life. T.J. Albert Jackson knows it well. Billed as "The World's Biggest Man," he's been doing this for 17 years now, ever

since a promoter offered to make him the
featured attraction in a show called "The Horrors of Drug Abuse." All he'd have to do, the promoter promised, was sit there with a snake
around his neck, acting as if he was unable to
speak, while the promoter intoned dramatically
to the hushed and sickened audience, "Due to his
delicate condition, we prefer that you not con-
verse with him."

He turned that one down. But he did agree
to a second suggestion that he simply sit there,
looking big. And here he is, 17 years later.

"Hey, hey, hey," he rumbles, in imitation of
the Fat Albert character created by Bill Cosby.
"Hey, hey, hey."

This week, he's in Cocoa at the Brevard
County Fair. Last week, it was Louisiana. He left
there in the rain and drove straight through with
his wife Carrie ("You're married!?!" people
marvel) in his '71 Cadillac, the one with 73,000
miles on it and the heavy-duty shocks and the
special front seat. Next week he hopes to be home
on his 2 1/2-acre spread in east Tampa, where
he lives in a mobile home. "Double-wide," he says
before you can ask.

It'll feel good to get home, he says. The season
has been a long one, business has been down, a
summer-long drive across Canada was brutal.
Cocoa, though, should be an easy time. He's got
a good spot near the heart of the midway, down
the row from the Fat Boy's Bar-B-Q, next to
Flossie's Famous Funnel Cakes.

He arrived early in the day. With his wife at
his side, he drove across the grass and mud, stop-
ping directly in front of a narrow set of metal
stairs leading to his booth. He got out of the car
and stood up, no easy task. He made the tor-
turous climb up the stairs, hoisting his stomach
high enough to ride along the top of the hand
rails. He sat, *whooomph.* And he was in business.

Outside, the curious began to gather. Carrie,
seven months pregnant ("She's having a baby?
His baby!?!") flipped a couple of switches. On

came some lights illuminating a sign that says, "World's Biggest Man." On came a recorded announcement that would play over and over through an outside loudspeaker, repeating itself every 45 seconds, 90 times an hour, all night long:

"Your attention! For the very first time at your fair, the world's biggest man! Recorded in Guinness' World Book of Records, Fat Albert weighs 891 pounds, is 6-foot 5-inches tall and has a 116-inch waistline. Unbelievable size! Unbelievable man! At his present rate of growth, doctors predict that he will soon weigh over one thousand pounds. He's here, he's real, and he's alive. For an unbelievable sight of a lifetime, you must see Fat Albert...."

Sitting in his seat, spread over a flattened couch cushion, Fat Albert does in fact seem enormous. He holds up a shoe, the Pro-sports model by a company called King-Size. "Size 20 EEE," he says. He points to his shirt. "Size 96." He points to his pants. "I made them myself."

As if by rote, the fat facts come rolling forth.

Birth weight: 22 pounds.

Birth method: C-section.

Weight at age 5: 236 pounds.

At age 10: 337 pounds.

At 20: 800 pounds.

Now: 891 and climbing. That's more than twice as much as Sears' best refrigerator-freezer—a 26-cubic-footer with automatic ice and water dispensers on side-by-side doors. That's almost as much as a Steinway grand piano.

He weighs himself on scrap yard scales and at roadside weigh stations. He travels mostly by car, but sometimes by plane—when two first-class seats are available. He can walk up to 30 yards without resting. He eats three meals a day.

Favorite breakfast: two eggs, coffee, toast with strawberry jam. Lunch: two ham sandwiches, one slice of ham each. Dinner: Whatever. Maybe an Italian-sausage sandwich from a carnival booth. Maybe a salad.

"In a 24-hour period, I average maybe 2½ to 3 pounds of food," he says. "When I was young, I used to eat a lot—eight-egg omelets, with onions. But that was it. No breads or anything. See, it's not the food; it's hormones. They found when they took the food away, the growing didn't stop."

Most searing childhood memory: "I went to a carnival once, saw the big man and said, 'How can you do that?' I said, 'No way I'd ever let people gawk at me.' But things have a way of turning around. Now, here I am."

He was born in Mississippi. He says they wouldn't let him in school as a 5-year-old because he was too big. When he was 6, he moved to Philadelphia. When he was 14, he went with his father to England. Two years later, he was back in the United States, a 16-year-old weighing 600 pounds with no job prospects in sight.

He tried to wash cars. He tried to sell vacuum cleaners. He ran a little restaurant out of his house. He married, had four children, and got divorced. He became Fat Albert and began touring the country. He remembers the first day. "It made me feel like a king. Here I am, sitting in a chair, people are *paying* to see me. They're asking me the same questions they asked on the street, but now they're *paying*. I thought, 'My God, if only I had thought of this five or 10 years ago.' "

One day in 1979, he was in Baton Rouge when a 17-year-old girl came in, looked at him and said, "Are you Fat Albert?" It was Carrie.

He said, "Well, I'm not Pinocchio."

She said, "You don't have to get smart with me."

"It's just one of those 'true love' stories," he says now, thinking back to that moment. "She wasn't afraid of me."

They talked almost until the carnival closed. They exchanged phone numbers. She called him about 2 a.m., and they talked until dawn. That afternoon, she showed up with pork chops, rice, and gravy. She showed up the next day, and the next, and two weeks later, when the carnival left town, she was there for the ride, squeezed in beside him.

That was six years ago. Since then, she's learned a few things about people.

"They say, 'That's your *husband*?' I say, 'Yeah.' They say, 'Nah, that can't be your husband. He's just paying you to say that. That ain't true.' I say, 'It *is*.' They say, 'How do you handle this? Doesn't he squish you? What's the matter with you! You can't do no better than that?' I say, 'I don't care what people think of me. It's what I think of myself.'"

"My gentle giant," she calls him. Or "Fats."

"I like it when she calls me Fats," he says. "I like the way she says it."

They go everywhere together. While he sits, she sweeps up or takes tickets. On the road, he waits in the car while she makes sure their hotel room has a sturdy bed. Every night, she is there beside him, and when a customer gets overly abusive, she is there to defend him.

"When they call him a big, fat slob," she says proudly, "I say, 'You get away from here. He's not a slob.'"

Sometimes, she starts out after them. Fat Albert sees trouble coming and calls out to her to come back. "Carrie," he says, "it's okay."

She comes back.

He sits in silence. She leans on the railing and watches the people go past. On a busy night, it's a river out there. They come by holding food and stuffed animals. Some of them are drunk, some of them are on drugs. They stop and read the sign and are serenaded with the taped announcement: *Over eight hundred and ninety-one pounds of living flesh. You must see him to believe him....* They try to peek inside. "Hey, Fatso," they yell. Or, "You big wobbly body." Or, "Fatty, fatty, two-by-four, couldn't fit in the kitchen door."

They pay their dollar and come in. They look at him. They shake their heads. They poke him. They gape in silence.

"Don't just stand there," he says. "Do something."

They do. They ask questions.

"You eat all the time?"

"Only when I'm hungry," he says.

"How do you ever get up?"

"I stand up."

"You're fat like a whale."

"You're skinny like a stick."

"How'd you get so fat?"

"Hormones."

"Why don't you go on a diet?"

"Everybody comes in here and says, 'Why don't you go on a diet?' They say, 'I got a brother-in-law who lost 150 pounds. I got a sister who weighed 300 pounds and now she's down to 179.' Do you realize how big I am? This is a *disorder*."

"You don't mind being this big?"

"I have no choice. If I had a choice, I wouldn't be this big."

"Isn't Florida too hot for you?"

"No, it's good for me to sweat. I only sweat from my brow. I don't sweat from my ankles or anything."

"You do this for a living?"

"Yes."

"You own a tux?"

"Yes."

"Do you eat a lot?"

"No."

"You got a girlfriend?"

"No, I got a wife. She's right there."

"You get any?"

"Yes."

"I'm sorry. I don't believe you weigh 800 pounds. I've seen people who weigh 400 pounds, and you don't look a pound more than them."

"Thank you."

"It's pillows, right?"

"It's pillows? Is this pillows?"

He lifts up his shirt and shows there are no
pillows. His chest hangs to his stomach. His
stomach swells out like a great globe and hangs
to his knees. "It's all me," he says.

The shirt comes down. The people leave. They
walk down the steps, look back and say, "He's
disgusting."

"I know what they say," Fat Albert says. "It's
all right. You can call me a fat hog or a pig or
a slob all day long. That won't hurt my feelings.
I would be a pig if I let them bother me. I'm not
a pig. I don't have to defend myself."

It has been this way for 17 years, he says, and
it's not going to change.

In Louisiana, they call him "the human
blimp."

In the Caribbean, "They're willing to give me
$500 to stand up and take my pants off."

And on opening night in Cocoa, this: "Apparently, you're totally satisfied. You're not just
satisfied, you're happy." The tone of the question
is vehement, accusatory.

"Oh, *I am* happy," comes Fat Albert's sincere
answer. "I'm overjoyed because God put me on
this earth."

On it goes, all night long. It gets dark. The
crowd thins. Flossie's Funnel Cakes prepares to
close early. Then it rains, and the bugs come out,
including dozens of mosquitoes that invade Fat
Albert's booth.

What a meal they must see, huh?

But before the first one can begin feasting,
The World's Biggest Man springs into action. He
reaches to his left and rummages among the different bottles he keeps there. No, not the
Listerine. No, not the Ban, or the eyedrops or the
Vaseline. No, not the rubbing alcohol. Ah, there
it is. The Raid Yard Guard.

He picks up the can and sprays. He sprays
and sprays. He sprays until all the mosquitoes
drop.

He has sprayed too much, though. The air is
so thick with Yard Guard that it becomes im-

possible to breathe. Carrie, close to choking, heads outside toward the lights of the midway and inhales.

Fat Albert, of course, stays put.

Observations and questions

1) Finkel's long lead ("Behold...before.") speaks directly to readers in the second person. Readers see themselves performing actions in front of the fat man. Study this technique in terms of capturing and manipulating readers.

2) We attribute the questions quoted in the lead to the spectators rather than to the reporter, yet they are reporter questions: name, age, weight, diet. Notice how the dialect exclamation "Gawd!" changes the tone of the exchange.

3) Study the voices in this piece: generalized spectators, Fat Albert, his wife, a recorded announcement, and the reporter himself. Notice how Finkel plays the voices against each other.

4) Finkel plays on our curiosity about the sex life of an 891-pound man by weaving information about it throughout the story. Consider the alternative effect of concentrating this theme in one section.

5) What characterization of the spectators emerges from this story? Notice how they always function as a crowd rather than as individuals. Analyze how this characterization grows mostly out of quotations rather than description.

6) Do you feel guilty at the end of this piece? Why? What has Finkel done to make you feel guilty?

Joy Griffith's killing: act of love or murder?

NOVEMBER 17, 1985

MIAMI—He was a distraught man that day, a man who sang lullabies and wept. With one hand, he held a gun. With the other, he stroked the smooth face of his daughter, a 3-year-old existing in limbo between life and death.

An hour before, he had given her what he thought was a fatal overdose of Valium. But here she was still breathing, her tiny chest rising and falling rhythmically, if ever so slightly.

She was in a crib at Miami Children's Hospital, lying on her back. She had been there for eight months, since the day she nearly suffocated. He leaned over the crib railing and looked at her eyes. They were open. They stared ahead, mirrored no emotions, saw nothing. It was the same for her other senses. The damage to her brain was total and irreversible, and because of it, she couldn't hear his weeping, and she couldn't feel his last touch goodbye before he aimed the gun at her heart.

He shot her twice. He dropped the gun. He prayed that her suffering was over. He fell into a nurse's arms, cried and said he wanted to die. He said, "Maybe I should get the electric chair to make things even. I killed my daughter. I shot her twice. But I'm glad she has gone to heaven."

* * *

On Tuesday morning in a Miami courtroom, almost five months after the death of his daughter Joy, Charles Griffith is scheduled to go on trial for murder. The defense, says Griffith's attorney, Mark Krasnow, will be mercy. "It was an act of love," Krasnow says, "not an act of malice."

The case is troubling to everyone involved. Even the prosecutor, Abe Laeser, says he feels sympathy for Griffith. Nonetheless, the state has charged Griffith with first-degree murder because, Laeser says, "It's offensive to assume you can actively execute someone because you think it's a merciful act."

To Floridians, that line of thinking will probably sound familiar; in a highly publicized trial earlier this year, 76-year-old Roswell Gilbert was convicted of murdering his wife, Emily, who was dying of Alzheimer's disease. He, too, contended it was mercy rather than murder.

There are obvious similarities between the two cases. Both victims lived in South Florida, both were ill, both were loved, both were shot. But it is the differences that make Griffith's case especially pathetic.

While Roswell Gilbert was a successful engineer who at least had a long and fulfilling life to look back on, Griffith was adrift in depression and loneliness. And while Emily Gilbert was a dying old woman, Joy Griffith never had the chance to bloom.

She was, by all accounts, the center of her father's life. "Believe me, he worshiped her," says his father, Leroy Griffith. He took photographs constantly. He taped some of them to a wall in the place he worked, the projection booth of an X-rated theater owned by his father.

After her illness and death, the photos came down, but not before he wrote on the back of one of them in red pen, the one that showed her lying comatose and open-eyed in the hospital crib, "Our Father who art in heaven—why would You do this?"

The question referred to her accident. From the moment he shot her, he has taken responsibility for pulling the trigger. But the accident he never could understand.

It was a freakish thing. Joy was at her grandparents' house along with her mother, Becky. She went into the living room to watch TV. She began climbing onto her grandfather's recliner, poking her head through the space between the chair and the footrest. Somehow, as she tried to wiggle through, the footrest folded in a bit, closing on her neck. She began choking. She tried to get free, but the more she struggled, the tighter the chair folded up. She went a minute without breathing. Two minutes....

Becky, in the kitchen, heard the TV go on and began fixing Joy's lunch. Five minutes went by, perhaps eight. She walked out to the living room.

There was Joy, wedged in the chair, motionless, bluish in color, hanging unconscious.

"Had she not been found for another two minutes, she probably would have been dead at the scene," says Dr. Charles Wetli, assistant Dade County medical examiner. As it was, the lack of oxygen ruined her beyond repair. Much of her brain, and many of her nerves, were dead. It would take paramedics 40 minutes just to get her heart beating regularly.

"She was in what you call a chronic, persistent, vegetative state—virtually no hope of recovery," says Dr. Robert Cullen, the neurologist who treated her at Miami Children's Hospital. "The best they could hope for was that she would remain blind, spastic, perhaps off the respirator.... Basically, this girl had only one route, and that was to eventually die."

* * *

At the time of the accident, Griffith and his wife were still getting along, still talking. Estrangement, then accusations, and finally divorce would come later. But up until that moment—considering how idiosyncratic their life together was anyway—everything was fine.

They met in Miami in the late 1970s. To be sure, they had their differences. She was the daughter of Cuban immigrants; he was born in a traveling circus. She grew up in Miami; he was raised by his mother in North Carolina. She lived in a modest home; he dropped out of high school in 11th grade, left his mother behind, and moved into the estate his father had bought from running a string of porno theaters.

They also had their peculiar traits. He drank a six-pack of beer every day; she dabbled occasionally in a secretive, magic-filled religion called Santeria. They met when they both applied for the same job: training 33 poodles for a circus act.

Seven months later, they were married. And three years after that, on April 4, 1982, Joy was born.

They didn't have much money. They lived rent-free in one of Leroy Griffith's apartments. The apartment itself wasn't bad—at least it had air conditioning—but the neighborhood was. It was toward the southern end of Miami Beach, next to one of the Griffith theaters. The streets were filled with drunks, transients, and destitute refugees from the Mariel boatlift.

A few times, Griffith got into trouble. There were some arrests for burglaries and drugs, minor stuff. He got probation and drifted along. He went to computer school. He tried a few other dead ends. Always, he ended up back at the Gayety, one of his father's theaters.

Once, it had been a burlesque house. Now it was nonstop films. He got paid $100 or so a week for running the projector, and whenever things got really tight, his father would give him money, often folding a $100 bill into one of Joy's hands and having her present it to him.

The family survived. Joy turned 1, learned to walk, turned 2, started talking. Every morning, they would hang out in the apartment or at the beach. Then Griffith would kiss his wife and baby goodbye and head off to the theater. He would enter through a side door marked "Peep Show." He would climb the flight of steps leading past his father's office, go into the projection booth, thread up the first film, and settle in for a long day.

Sometimes he would read, sometimes he'd talk to his aunt who ran the box office, sometimes he'd look at the photographs of Joy taped to the wall: Joy sitting on a bench, Joy with a dog, Joy with some kittens. She always smiled. Her hair was getting long.

* * *

The day of her accident—Oct. 24, 1984—he was at the theater. Becky called, hysterical, and said Joy wasn't breathing, that the paramedics were there. But he didn't know how bad it was until he got to the hospital. Her heart was beating, but a respirator was breathing for her. Her color had come back, but she was lifeless.

He wouldn't leave. Both he and Becky stayed day and night, alternating shifts. For the first six months, Joy was never alone.

He would dab lemon juice on her lips. He would run a cloth under cool water, lay it on her leg, and say, "Joy, this is cold." He would put filters over a flashlight, aim it toward her eyes, and say, "Joy, this is red."

He would say, "This is Daddy. If you can hear me, move your toes.

"If you love me, blink your eyes."

He swore her toes moved and her eyes blinked. But the doctors told him that was impossible, that any movements were nothing more than reflexive.

She would sleep with her eyes open. She couldn't swallow. She was fed through a tube into her stomach. For the first few months, a bolt was inserted into her head to monitor any swelling in her brain: She was kept from further deterioration only through incredible medical wizardry:

Nystatin in her mouth to fight off infection. Lacri-Lube in her eyes when they got too dry. Tylenol as a suppository to control her temperature.

And an entire medicine cabinet fed into her through the gastronomy tube:

Pedialyte for nourishment, Colace for constipation, Phenobarbital to control seizures, Bactrim to control infection, Valium to relax her muscles and more.

How long can she live like this? Griffith once asked. They told him possibly only a few years, possibly until she was 50.

Nurses were in with her constantly. There was always a tube to check, a drug to introduce. When they rolled her over or were readying an injection, Griffith would yell at them, "Tell her what you're doing!" More than a few times, he could be heard shouting, "If you won't say anything, get out of here."

Stories began circulating about him. One nurse said he showed up reeking of liquor, another said he offered her marijuana, another said he threatened to hit her.

He and Becky began fighting, first about how much the nurses should be doing to Joy, then about everything. Becky filed for divorce and got a doctor's order limiting what kind of contact Griffith could have with Joy. She came to the hospital during the day. He came at night.

The only thing it seemed they could agree on was that they would never sign an agreement called a no-code, which would allow doctors to let Joy live or die on her own—no respirator, no heart massage, no help.

Then that changed. On her third birthday, Griffith came in dressed like a clown. He painted his hair orange and his face white and put on a red rubber nose. He thought she'd notice. He lifted her out of the crib, held her and sang to her, but she was stiff in his arms. He asked her to blink, but she didn't. He started to cry, put her back in the crib and left the room.

After that, she seemed to get worse. She got pneumonia and couldn't get rid of it. She began having seizures. She no longer moved her toes.

Griffith told doctors he would agree to a no-code.

But Becky wouldn't.

So on June 28, Griffith came to the hospital with a gun. It was tucked in a pocket along with some Valium.

A neighbor of his, Jeffrey Metcalf, told lawyers that Griffith had talked for a month about ways to "discontinue his child's pain."

"He thought about suffocation, but that was why she was in the hospital, so he didn't want to do it that way," Metcalf said.

* * *

He got to the hospital around 8 p.m. Becky was there. Joy was in her arms. He took her and cradled her. Becky left, and he started to cry. A nurse, Geraldine Goskey, got him some tissues. He thanked her and kept crying.

Around 9 p.m., he laid Joy back in her crib. He combed her hair. He caressed her.

He kissed her on the forehead.

He kissed her face.

Just before 10 p.m., when Goskey walked by the crib to check on Joy, Griffith put his hand on her, drew her close, and said, "Ma'am. I've got a gun."

He showed her the gun, a 32-caliber revolver. He told her he had crushed up 100 milligrams of Valium and fed it to Joy through her gastronomy tube. Scared, Goskey began to cry. Another nurse saw her and told the supervisor, Mary Leali. Leali walked over to the crib. She didn't know what was going on.

"Is she sleeping?" she asked.

"Not yet," she says Griffith answered.

"He was weepy-eyed," she said later. "He said, 'I don't want her to live like that any more. I don't want her to suffer any more.' And then he started in on God. 'If there's a God, why is He doing this? If there's a God, I want her to go where He is.'"

They stood there, against the side of the crib, watching Joy. After a while, Goskey moved off to feed another baby in the room.

Eleven o'clock came and went.

Leali said to him, "The nurses are going to wonder what I'm doing standing at this bedside for this length of time. Now why don't you take that gun, put it in your pocket, walk out that door, and no one will know anything."

She says he stood there awhile. "Then he ordered me to go call the police.

"So I did an about-face, prayed, and walked out the door."

Goskey was still in there. She was listening, but not looking, when he brought the gun close to Joy's heart and fired.

"I hear a shot," she said. "I turn around. I smell smoke. He has the gun in his right hand. He's standing over his child, right at the crib, near her chest area. He moves up again, closer, bends down a little bit.... Bang! I saw it, and I heard it."

He straightened up. Goskey stood absolutely still. He turned toward her. She looked at his face. "It looked very sad, very depressed." She watched as he knelt, put the gun on the floor, and pushed it away from him. She heard people running down the hall. He did, too.

He yelled, "Don't touch my baby! Don't come near my baby! Don't let them hurt my baby!"

They ran into the room, toward the crib. "Leave my baby alone," he screamed. "She's not going to suffer anymore. You're not going to cut her anymore."

They surrounded the crib, realized nothing could be done. They covered the body with a white blanket while a nurse held onto Griffith, who sagged in her arms.

"I shot my little girl," he said. "I killed my baby. I'm not an animal. Don't treat me like an animal."

* * *

His lawyer, Mark Krasnow, says he will attempt three paths of defense.

The first will be temporary insanity, an insanity that took root the day of the accident.

"Doing what he did certainly indicates that he has a mental problem," Krasnow said in court documents, "and if he did not have a mental problem before he did it, he sure had one after he did it, after he saw his baby die due to his own act."

The second will be that Griffith couldn't have killed his daughter because she was already brain dead, the standard of death in Florida.

"It's an interesting argument," says Laeser, the prosecutor, but "it has nothing to do with the case. She was never brain dead, and I've got the EEGs to prove it."

The third is the main one, the troubling one, the one based on emotions rather than legalities—the notion of mercy.

Even Laeser is bothered by this one. He has children. He had a father-in-law who lapsed into a fatal coma. "I'm sympathetic to him. I realize it was obviously very difficult for him during those several months," he says.

But he adds, "I don't have a legal question on it. I think the evidence is absolutely consistent with first-degree murder."

So starting Tuesday, unless a last-minute plea bargain can be worked out, the question of mercy will be put before a jury of 12, some of whom will be parents, some of whom may have confronted their own tragedies, some of whom will no doubt look over at Griffith and wonder how in the world he was able to pull the trigger. Twice.

For Griffith, it will be the first time he has been out of jail in quite a while. After he killed Joy, he was arrested, declared a suicide risk, stripped naked, and put in an isolation cell. Sedated, he slept on the concrete floor, woke up shivering, slept some more. Two days later, he was allowed to put on a suit and visit the funeral home for a viewing. Then it was back to the jail, where he has been since.

He has remained there in seclusion. He is in a cell decorated with 12 photographs of Joy, plus a drawing of her done by another inmate in exchange for three packs of cigarettes.

In a brief interview last week, he said, "I don't care what happens. They can't do anything to hurt me any more than I already hurt. The important thing is she's in heaven, she can move and talk and laugh."

He said a psychiatrist suggested he take down the photographs of Joy, but he hasn't.

He said he watches TV during the day and dreams at night that he is in the hospital, running down a corridor, Joy in his arms, doctors in pursuit.

"She's always in mind," he said.

He said that after Joy's burial, he called the cemetery and bought the grave site next to hers.

Says his father, who is helping him pay for it, "He must be thinking, 'If there's a heaven, and she's there, where am I going to go?'"

Observations and questions

1) Finkel's lead catches the frustrations of a father who has just failed to kill his daughter with an overdose of Valium, who will then shoot her twice in the chest. Read the first four paragraphs and watch how your sympathy switches from the father, to the daughter, and back to the father, who has just committed a murder before your very eyes.

2) Finkel contrasts Griffith's story with that of Roswell Gilbert, another Florida mercy killer. Where do the reporter's sympathies lie in this context-setting section?

3) This story proceeds along chronological lines, but the chronologies get interwoven and interrupted. Try to imagine this story written in straight narrative order, beginning with Griffith's youth and ending with the trial about to begin.

4) Finkel refers to the machinery keeping Joy alive and to her medical treatment. Notice how he spreads out the medical data and translates most of it. The few remaining terms seem transparent.

5) Study the scene where the nurses have to stand by while Griffith waits for his daughter to die. Notice the economy of language, the restraint of the description, the weaving of action and remembrance, and the trimmed quotations.

6) Why does Griffith's father get the last word? Look over Griffith's quotations earlier in the piece and see if you would want to move any of them to the end as a kicker.

A conversation with
David Finkel

DON FRY: Where did you work before you came to St. Petersburg?

DAVID FINKEL: I worked for *New Look* magazine in Gainesville, for the *Tallahassee Democrat,* for a magazine called *Urology Times....*

Urology Times?

Yes. I was a contributing editor. And then I went back to the *Democrat,* and then in 1981 to *Floridian,* the Sunday magazine for the *St. Petersburg Times.* The first year I wrote about 18 or 19 stories, and at the end of the year they congratulated me on being the most prolific writer in the history of the magazine.

Then what?

Then they folded the magazine in 1982, and I moved down to the City and State section, where I am now.

Was it hard to shift from the magazine to news?

When I came downstairs, I had to write one story a week, which I know sounds awfully luxurious. But coming from a magazine where I wrote one story a month or so, it was quite a bit of pressure. I would write the same kind of story, with the completeness of a magazine story, only once a week instead of once every three weeks. Once a week was my idea, and they agreed to it. If there's something in the state I'm interested in, I'll go write a long story about it.

When you come up with ideas, do you have conferences with the editors to refine them?

I'll come up with an idea, and I'll watch my editor's face to see if there's a smile there or a pained expression. If he doesn't like it, he'll say so eventually. Once they approve the idea, I'm pretty much on my own. If I'm stuck, I'll talk to the editor about it. I'll tell him every day how it's going, and when I'm going to have it finished.

I like your stories because you find such good interview subjects. How do you dig them out?

Sometimes editors suggest them, or I read the papers and the wires, or people call me. I read something, and it stirs something in me that says this is a good story.

Do you do most of your interviewing face-to-face?

Yes. I hate phones. I can't do it by phone.

You get a lot of information from the subjects besides what they're saying: letters, documents, and stuff like that. How do you talk them out of that material?

The way you would imagine. If you talk to someone long enough, you find common points. These things come out, and you ask for them. If I ask too early, they won't come through. But if we talk long enough and they feel they can trust me, then they'll hand over things.

How do you get them to trust you?

You know, it's getting harder and harder because so many people distrust reporters; they especially distrust television cameramen. I try to distance myself from TV journalism. I empathize because I've been offended by TV reporters. And I'll tell them about that and say, "You know, I'm really not out to do a job on you. I just want to listen carefully to what you have to say. That's why I'm here. That's why we're not on the phone." And eventually it seems to work out.

Your interviews tend to be quite long, don't they?

It depends on the subject. Sometimes I've written stories about people, but by the time I get to them, I only need to spend 30 minutes with them, no more. From other people I've talked to, I know all about them. You need to spend time with them to confirm what everyone else has said. But you're not going to get good quotes from them, because they're too polished.

They only give you "quote quotes."

And no matter how long you spend with them, there's going to be no break in that. So it's just a matter of getting some obligatory quotes to show that I talked with them. And then I just use everybody else to build a portrait of that particular person. Other times, when someone is good and honest with me, I'll spend as long as I can. If I have time, I'll spend days.

What's the longest you ever spent?

Probably John Lerro. I spent two full days with him without a break. And it was all necessary. We never went over the same thing twice. As soon as I got there, I could sense what had happened to that man. No matter whether he was at fault or not, there was so much tragedy in what had happened to him since the day he hit that bridge. But I didn't want him to say that to me. I wanted to be able to show it in the things he did, by the way he carried himself, by his posture, by the conditions of his life. He was leery of the press; he had had a lot of bad press. So I hung out for a couple of days until he felt comfortable enough with me to be himself. And tragically he was.

In your quotations, people don't seem to be posing. They seem very natural, not making speeches. How do you achieve that?

Well, for one thing, I don't use a tape recorder unless I have to. There's no unobtrusive way to bring a tape recorder into an interview. I don't know shorthand, so there are limits there. The quotes can't be that long because I just can't keep up with people.

What do you write down from a quotation? Let's say I speak three sentences to you. How much are you going to write down?

If I'm at a point in the interview where the mood is right and the person's going to say something quite telling, I'll begin at the first sentence. And if the second sentence sounds better and I'm not caught up yet, I'll stop the first sentence and start the second one, and then go from there. I can usually get three sentences down.

Do you write every word out, even "well," "you know," and "um?"

Well, I mean, sure. If a person speaks that way, I want to take it down.

But you don't leave those fillers in the quotations in the story.

Maybe I don't choose those quotes.

Tell me about working with a good quotation. Do you trim the quotes much?

No, no, the point of the story is to reflect somebody. They say it, and you write it. If you don't like the way they say it, maybe you can work it back in the interview later, get back to the point, build up to the emotion, and try to get the person to say it again.

Do you clean up bad grammar?

I can't think of an instance where I have, but it sounds too pure to say I haven't. If it's going to detract from the point of the quote, I guess I do. I can't think of an instance where I've doctored a quote to make someone sound more intelligent. Obviously no one doctors them to make a person sound less intelligent.

Do you think a person who makes a grammatical error sounds less intelligent?

Yes, but I notice it. Maybe a reader wouldn't.

I didn't notice any grammatical errors in the quotations in your pieces.

Good.

Either you're interviewing the correct people, or you're cleaning them up. (Laughter) Let's talk about Fat Albert a little bit. You present this story in the second person: "Behold the fat man. Go ahead."

It's an implied "you," isn't it?

Yes. You're seeing him almost entirely from the outside.

Well, there are a lot of quotes in this story, questions from people looking at the guy, and his answers.

You usually move in close to your subject and get rather intimate quotations. But this

story is different. Are you trying to show us what it's like to face this barrage of questions?

Well, he's been doing this for years and years. He knows how to answer questions the way a politician can answer questions. The point is not so much who he is, but the fact that people pay money to look at him, and that defines his life. I thought the best way to tell this story was to talk about him in the way that others see him.

This is not a very intimate portrait. It seems distanced from its subject.

But I see it as an intimate portrait. At the end, you know how people treat him, and you have a sense of what that does to him. It's not stated, but implied.

That's the way most of your stories are. Some things are stated, and many things are implied. You let us see things.

Do you think the approach is standoffish?

No, I think it's neatly done. Remember that the second-person point of view is very hard. It's not hard to start that way, but it's hard to maintain it.

But it was so easy. I was just one in a crowd that night. I almost didn't have to ask any questions, because the spectators were so direct and so rude. You pay your dollar, and you can ask the questions. All I had to do was stand there for hours and hours, and watch the people coming in and asking the questions.

I was glad there were people in there, because I wanted to look at him before I began asking questions. So I just stood there listening. I realized that those people were going to ask things that I would hesitate to ask.

One night when the carnival closed, I wanted to hang out with him, but he said no. So I came back the next afternoon and talked to him for a few minutes before the doors opened. Then people asked the same questions over again. My God, the things people asked!

Were you embarrassed by their questions?

Absolutely. *They* were the show to me, not him.

When they asked his wife about their sex life, I found that very offensive. Did that bother you?

Well, I was relieved that I wouldn't have to ask her, because the questions had to be asked. I was sort of looking down in embarrassment, taking notes at the same time.

This second-person technique implicates the reader. The reader, in effect, becomes a member of that audience.

Right. I was writing the story for all the people who were standing there looking at this guy, for all the ones who hadn't seen him, but who would probably ask the same kind of questions.

There was a sense of embarrassment within me. There was a little bit of anger. There wasn't much curiosity. I didn't find anything comical about it. He was a freak, and the people looking at him were freaks, too.

When you're doing the reporting, do you spin out the story in your head? Are you imagining the shape of it?

Yes, but that doesn't mean I stick to it. If you go through my notes, you'll see things like "(transition alert)," or something like that. I mark endings. I mark things that could be a lead while I'm taking notes.

Do you usually write quickly?

No, no. I'm a terrible writer. I have awful habits. (Laughter)

Oh, tell me some of your terrible habits.

I put off writing as long as I can. If I didn't have a deadline, I'd probably never write a story. That's why I wouldn't want to do projects: if I had six months, I'd probably begin writing at five months and 29 days.

What do you do with all your time?

Well, if I've got a week on a story, I'll spend three days reporting it. And then the next morning, I do everything possible not to confront my notes. I dread the moment when I have to begin to write. It's no fun at all.

So what do you do between the reporting and the first writing?

Oh, I wander around the newsroom and talk to anybody who doesn't look busy. I pace a lot, get coffee. I put it off as long as I can.

Roy Clark and I don't call that "procrastination." We call that "rehearsal."

Well, that's a nice name for what I call procrastination, necessary procrastination.

So you get to the point where you've just got to write. Then what happens?

I just sit at the terminal. I spend a long time going over my notes to be as familiar with them as I can. I do an outline. I write down on a piece of paper the name of the person the interview is with. Then I write down on a separate piece of paper the key points of the story in a column on the other side of the page. In the notebook, I underline quotes. If it's a real good quote, I stick a star next to it. Then I go over it again. Then I get some more coffee, and I pace.

I've seen you pacing in the *Times* newsroom.

Let me tell you a good story. Once when I worked at another paper, an editor pulled me aside and told me I couldn't pace anymore...

That'd be the end of news writing! (Laughter)

...because there had been complaints about it from the people writing two or three stories a day. To them it looked like I was goofing off. So he said, "If you want to pace, that's your business. Just don't do it in the newsroom. Just go down the street to the mall and pace." You're thinking while you're pacing, and eventually you come up to a point where you just want to sit down and write. So that's the story. At the *Times*, they let me pace all I want. They're very nice about pacing.

So after you pace, then what?

And finally, when it's time to write, I realize that all this preparing to write has left me in the mood not to write at all. So I pick up something, and read that to get back in the writing mood, maybe a copy of *Tropic* magazine.

Once you start writing, what comes first?

There are people who say they can start in the middle of a story if they can't come up with a lead, but I can't do that. I can't write the next sentence until I've written the one before it. How can you know what the next sentence is going to say until you see how you've ended the previous one?

Usually I write a lead and say to myself, "Well, that's a better ending than a lead." So I'll put that one away and try to come up with a different lead.

How much actual writing time did the Fat Albert piece, or any of these pieces, take?

The Lerro piece took about three days total to write.

How much of that time was revision?

I don't write and then go through and change everything. I edit as I go along. So it's all revision. I get into these silly arguments with myself: "Is it time for a simple sentence or a compound one? How's the rhythm going? If I have the reader at this point, does he have the same reading rhythm in his head that I have in mine?"

Hey, I like that term. What do you mean by "reading rhythm?"

You want the person to read it as you intended it. Syllables rise and fall. You want them to end up with the emphasis on the words that you intended.

I notice that all of your stories are divided into parts. Do you write your own subheads? Roy and I think writers should write their own subheads to keep control of the parts.

No, I can't write a subhead. But I designate the spot; I'll write in "SUBHEAD." My stories are long compared to most stories in the newspaper, so there are a lot of places for a reader to bow out. If you put breaks in the story, it gives the readers time to regroup, or another place to come into the story if they want to start.

My colleague, Mario Garcia, has discovered that many people don't start at the beginning of stories at all.

Right, which puts a lot of pressure on the way you start the next section. It had better be a helluva sentence.

So when you finish the first draft, you've finished the piece. Do you read it aloud?

Aloud? No. I can hear it in my mind better than I can say it. I almost always go through the whole thing again, not for major changes at that point, but mostly simplifying.

Let's talk about the Haber story. How did you get involved in it?

The children of the man who was killed found out that Mrs. Haber was maneuvering to be released from prison on good behavior. They were so offended by the murder, and 10 years later they were so offended that she might get out, that one of them called the paper. My editor asked me what I thought, and I said I liked it.

There are a lot of people talking in this piece, but the family gets the last word.

I think they should. It's their story.

But in the ending, they are all telling why she should not get out. Did you have an agenda here?

Well, not before I started this story. Journalists are not supposed to decide anything. But I went through her prison file. I talked to her. I talked to her lawyer. I talked to the kids.

How'd you decide who would get the ending?

It was more a story about the kids than it was about her. Even if the court system operates effectively, it doesn't clear up all the hurt. They were the ones still hurting.

Almost at the end of the story, you're explaining the legal processes ("So she was recommended for a commutation..."). Joel Brinkley calls such factual sections "boring but important," or "BBI" for short. Tell me how you handle BBI, not just here, but in general.

"BBI, boring but important." That's a good phrase. It has to be in the story because the first obligation is to report.

But you seem to cluster BBI. Do you run a risk by clustering it, the risk that the reader will get bored and quit?

I guess you do. But if I don't put the facts in, I can lose readers, too. If I tell the story quickly enough from the top, maybe the reader will stick with me through the boring stuff. After all, it's in there because it needs to be in there.

The trick is where you put it, and how you frame it, isn't it?

Yes. In most of my stories, I'll end up liking best what you call "BBI." I don't know where it should be in a story, but I know it needs to be in there. When I get to it in the writing, I know that this is the place for it. There *are* stories where I sprinkle it throughout. But you use it where you need to use it.

Do you have the ending in mind when you begin to write?

Almost always. But that's not to say I have preconceptions going into a story. When I've done

all the interviews, I know what I want to say.
I know where the story ought to go, and what
the tone ought to be.

A lot of your pieces end with quotations.

I use quotes at the end more often than I'd like
to. A quote's an easy way out, which is not to say
it's ineffective. The Lerro story, for instance, ends
with a quote, but it's a terrific quote. That was
a nice way to get out of that story.

**Tell me what you want to accomplish in your
writing.**

First, I want the reader to finish the story. The
last thing I would want him to say is, "That's
a helluva *writer*." Instead, I want the reader to
say, "That was a great *story*."
   Sometimes on the way to work, I listen to
country music stations. Country songs tell nice
simple stories, which is what I'm trying to do
with my stories. Not to be confusing, not to be
elaborate, just to tell a nice simple story. The
pieces I like best are the ones with the most simple sentences in them. It's just the easiest way
for a reader to get through.

**Let's talk about how you achieve all that
simplicity.**

In the final editing, I usually go through the story
and tear down the sentences quite a bit. The
point is just to tell a nice little story. If it's an
emotional story, I want to leave the reader feeling kind of tingly.

**I admire the simplicity of those sentences
and the simplicity of the storytelling. You get
to the narrative in a hurry.**

Believe me, I could do it a lot quicker, and it could
be a lot simpler.

Do you work in a high-pressure newsroom?

The pressure comes from grimaces I imagine my editor giving me, which is to say, the pressure pretty much comes from within me. By now, they know how I work best, and they pretty much let me do it. It's a nice climate for me.

What kind of positive feedback do you get?

Not enough, right? Nobody gets enough. The best reaction I've ever had was on a story I wrote last year, one of my favorite stories. It was about a widow of a Marine who was killed by a sniper in Beirut. She and her husband had lived this idyllic 1950s life. Their dreams, what they wanted out of life, were so simple. I felt very strongly about this story, and I've never had an easier time writing. It was there. It was done in a day.

And I really wanted my editor to like it. And he got up, and he came over to me, and he put his hand on my back. He didn't say anything. He just stared off into this vague distance. He was obviously very choked up. And he said something like, "Just terrific." And then he just walked away. It was great.

What did you like so much about that story?

It was such an honest story. Everything worked so well. I liked the way I presented it, nice and simple. After I wrote that story, I felt comfortable with my career. The pressure was off to finally write a story that I liked, because I wrote one that I liked.

You seem to feel close to your subjects.

Well, Madeleine Blais once said that she can't begin writing a story until she has a definite feeling about the characters. And that's a true statement. I had a lot of feelings about Charles Grif-

fith and about John Lerro and about the widow
I was talking about before. I'm striving for the
simplest way to tell a story, which is through one
person's eyes.

It's easier to empathize with one person.

Yes, but I wonder if that cheapens the story
because you're not being representative.

"Cheapens" isn't the word I would pick.

"Limits," maybe. But the stories I like best are
the ones that focus on a particular person, and
tell a problem through that person's eyes.

Do you like being a reporter?

Sure. I get entry into situations I could never get
in otherwise. I'm learning things from my stories.
I'm talking to guys who killed their little girls,
the same age as mine. There's a lesson in that
for me to consider when I think of my own life,
and it's a tragic lesson. I'm seeing people at their
best and their worst. And I'm learning how a life
ought to be lived. In a way, it's selfish, but I'm
using my newspaper to teach me things that I
want to find out about.

I wish more reporters wrote the way you do.

My job is so luxurious compared to other reporting jobs. I have more time than most reporters,
and I don't have to get bogged down in what you
call "BBI." So I don't think my stories can teach
broad lessons in journalism. I think somebody
can look at them and learn a bit about phrasing.
But my stories are the exception in newspapers,
not because they're good or bad, but because I
have the luxury of taking my time and approaching subjects one-on-one. And it's not covering a meeting....

If I sent you to cover the city council, you'd come back and write a story...

I'd come back and get fired because I'd write this wistful story! (Laughter)

You'd come back. And you'd write a story that would be simple. And the quotations would be simple. And the sentences would be simple. And the motives would be clear.

And by the time I handed it in, it would be a week late! (Laughter)

Well, that kind of simplicity and brevity takes time.

Right. That's true. Except how can you argue brevity when I'm writing 250-picas and they're writing 50 picas?

Because most writers outside journalism would treat your 250-pica stories at book chapter length, that's why. Think of the Haber story. Is that a book chapter? Yes, it is. Charles Griffith's story? That's a pull-out section at least. Do you see what I mean?

Well, sure. I could have gone on....

But you don't. You pare it down. Your whole act is paring it down. Most writers try to mash it in, not pare it down. They're not doing what you do so well, which is to cut it out.

If I had more time and more money and a different format, I could go on a lot longer. But that's not what I want to do at this point with my writing. I just want to write nice stories for the newspaper.

Good for you.

Bradley Graham
Deadline Writing

BRADLEY GRAHAM, 33, grew up in Chicago and Pittsburgh. He attended Yale University, where he became editor of the *Yale Daily News* and interned at the *St. Petersburg Times* and *The Washington Post*. He covered city hall for the *Trenton Times* and later took an M.B.A. at Stanford University. He joined *The Washington Post* in 1978 as a business writer, became Bonn bureau chief in 1980, and headed the Warsaw bureau in 1983. In 1985, six weeks after moving to the Buenos Aires bureau, he covered the disaster at Armero.

Colombian volcano erupts, killing thousands

NOVEMBER 15, 1985

MARIQUITA, Colombia, Nov. 14—A volcano in central Colombia erupted last night, triggering floods in valleys below that buried large sections of at least two towns under tons of mud and rubble. Government and Red Cross officials said the death toll could reach 20,000.

President Belisario Betancur declared a national emergency as Army, Civil Defense, and Red Cross teams rushed to the disaster zone located around the 17,400-foot Nevado del Ruiz Volcano, about 85 miles northwest of Bogota.

"The tragedy is immeasurable," said the president, who visited the devastated region this morning. "It is a new tragedy that has hit Colombia," he said, alluding to the siege of the Palace of Justice in Bogota last week in which 97 persons were killed. "But I'm sure that with the solidarity of the world and in the country, we will overcome," he added.

Part of the volcano's top exploded late yesterday, breaking off chunks of snow near the summit. The ice melted rapidly into cascading waters that gathered dirt and debris and turned the rivers at the mountain's base into killer currents.

The inundation took inhabitants of this farming region by surprise during the night, despite recent warnings that the mountain might erupt. It had been dormant for 400 years but had become restless in recent months.

Colombian geologists said the volcano, the second highest peak in Colombia's central range of the Andes, might continue erupting, further threatening populations below it.

The government issued urgent appeals for medical supplies, potable water, and transport equipment to help in a rescue effort hampered by the destruction of bridges and roads. Colombian radio and television advised people in the disaster zone not to drink from local water supplies, which were feared contaminated by sulfur.

(In Washington, the U.S. Agency for International Development said 12 helicopters were dispatched to the scene from a base in Panama, at the request of Colombia. A statement said AID relief expert Paul Bell and Darrell Herd of the U.S. Geological Survey in Reston, Va., who has studied the volcano, were en route to offer assistance.)

The most seriously affected town was Armero, with a population of 25,000, about 18 miles east of the volcano. It was said by some residents to have been 90 percent submerged.

Several neighborhoods in the city of Chinchina, population 75,000, on the west side of the volcano, also were reported to be buried. Minor damage occurred in the town of Honda, here in Mariquita.

Survivors reported that thousands had drowned in sweeping torrents of hot mud and rock that overcame them as they tried to flee. A flight over Armero this afternoon showed much of the town covered by wide swaths of mud that appeared in many places to rise as high as the second floors of buildings.

Several hundred people could be seen standing in one of the few streets cleared of mud, apparently awaiting rescue.

One of the two policemen in Armero to survive said he was saved by being in the center of town when the flood came. "Many more than half of the people in the town were taken by the river," said Jose Victor Otalvaro. "Where the town is, you can't recognize anything." Armero had 22 police.

Osvaldo Echeverry Almanza, the chief of personnel at Armero's hospital, said he had been awakened last night by a noisy downpour of ashen rain. He said town residents began panicking after 10, racing into the streets.

From the hospital, where he went after waking, he said he witnessed an avalanche of mud come roaring around one side and then the other of the hospital, swallowing trees, cars, houses, and people in its path.

"You could see people tumbling in the mud," Echeverry told reporters, who found him at a hospital in this town, six miles north of Armero. He said many were "screaming and going crazy," and the air had a light sulfur smell.

The mud, he said, rose 3 to 6 feet high, and even higher at times. The town church—a 5- or 6-story building—was almost completely buried, he said.

Echeverry made it to safety, he explained, by building a bridge to high ground with bits of wood, picking his way past pieces of pots, television sets, homes, and bodies.

Speaking calmly but bitterly, the hospital administrator criticized government authorities for hesitating before declaring an emergency. Despite reports of volcanic activity by 8 p.m. yesterday, he said, national radio stations were still advising people in the area to remain calm instead of evacuating.

"The danger was imminent," he said. "I know there is an emergency plan. I have studied it. Why didn't they tell us to activate it sooner?"

(The U.N. Disaster Relief Organization said after midday that "4,000 bodies have already been recovered," United Press International reported.)

A senior civil defense official said the flooding of Armero had come after a natural dam of rocks and stone above the town broke under the force of onrushing waters.

The destructive mud flows had been predicted in a report presented only yesterday by Colombian geologists. The report was ordered several months ago after Nevado del Ruiz started showing early signs of reawakening. It was the scene of an earthquake in 1845 that set off floods and killed about 1,000, according to historian Joaquin Acosta.

The last time lava flowed was in 1595. Although clouds of ash and pieces of volcanic rock spewed miles into the air in last night's explosion, there has been no confirmed sighting of lava streams this time.

The geological study had estimated the probability of an eruption of ashen rain or gas emissions to be 67 percent and had foreseen the flooding of several rivers and mud slides as a result, causing damage to homes and fields.

But less accurately—as last night's events proved—the report also predicted that the flow of mud would be slow and easily permit the evacuation of surrounding populations. Citing Armero specifically, the study—as summarized in today's editions of the Bogota daily *El Tiempo*—said the town could be cleared within two hours without danger.

The volcano is situated in a central air-traffic corridor, and its explosion last night was witnessed by several pilots en route at the time.

The pilot of a Colombian Avianca cargo plane, flying from Miami to Bogota, reported seeing a red flash at about 10 p.m. that sent clouds of ash mushrooming upward and filled his cabin with dense white smoke.

With his vision clouded, the pilot said he was forced to make an emergency landing in the southwest city of Cali, guiding himself in by sticking his head out a cockpit window.

Observations and questions

1) Analyze Graham's lead in terms of mixing the general and the specific. Remember that he wrote it in an obscure area less than 24 hours after the event occurred.

2) The town of Armero first appears in the eighth paragraph. Graham says he wanted to "give the scope of the disaster in the sense of the country moving into action before getting into some of the specifics." Would you be tempted to move Armero higher, even at the expense of pushing the contextual material lower?

3) Graham lets the reporting show, telling us about arriving reporters, answers to reporters, etc. Should the press appear in stories not about the press?

4) Many of Graham's sentences consist of lists, sometimes more than one in the same sentence. Think about listing as an organizational device.

5) The fourth paragraph ("Part of the volcano's top...") graphically describes an explosion that no one saw. Graham explains that he wrote it from an animation he saw on TV. Think about the possibilities for distortion in using artistic material from one medium in another.

6) The story ends with a blinded pilot trying to land his plane. Discuss the effectiveness of this long view in terms of human interest and symbolism.

Survivors recall night of horror

NOVEMBER 15, 1985

MARIQUITA, Colombia, Nov. 14—It came over them in the black of night, with the suddenness and force of a giant wave, swallowing everything in its wake.

Survivors of Armero, the Colombian cotton-growing town drowned in a river of mud and stones after the Nevado del Ruiz Volcano erupted, told today of a night of horror in which family members were torn from each other as they struggled for air and secure ground.

Caked with mud, burned by the scalding temperature of the river of dirt and debris that overwhelmed their town, cut and battered from being dragged hundreds of yards across the valley floor, some of the victims of Armero were brought here to this neighboring village by Red Cross, Civil Guard, and Army units.

They were unloaded from helicopters and transported in jeeps, trucks, and other makeshift ambulances to a small, overcrowded country hospital. There they lay on crowded beds or cots and waited, many with tubes in their arms feeding medicine, to be evacuated to hospitals in Bogota.

Some wept. Others, dressed only in the underwear or bedclothes they had on when the disaster struck, shivered in shock in the warm air here.

The stories they recounted had haunting similarities—about awakening in their homes before midnight to cries of alarm and a heavy rain of ash, about grabbing children and the elderly, then fleeing to the streets, about finding nowhere to run as the Lagunilla River, normally just a tributary of the valley's main Magdalena River, turned into a raging mass of liquid earth.

Doris Rico Aldania, 21, said the river of mud and rocks came crashing through the doors and windows of her home, pursuing her and her family as they climbed to the second story to pray for their lives.

Sandra Patricia Perez, 13, her face badly scratched and her head wrapped in a white cloth, said she nearly choked beneath the mud but somehow remained conscious as she tumbled away from Armero in the flood.

Hortensia Oliveros, 19 years old and eight months pregnant, saw the rushing water sweep their 11-month-old child out of her husband's arms. In the panic, she heard her husband shout to her to grab a branch, but that was the last she heard of him. She ended up near a road outside of Armero, screaming for someone to help her.

A 25-year-old truck driver, Pedro Mancera, and his wife grasped the hands of their two children before darting from their home. A first rush of water tore the children away from their parents, and a second blow separated Mancera from his wife. He said he was carried to a farm field, his left arm broken and his body a mass of aches.

Luis Vicente Suarez, 24, a fruit vendor, remembered that someone in Armero instructed him to take cover in the stadium. There, he saw perhaps 3,000 people pressing against the entrance when the torrent of hot mud came over them.

He, too, was immersed in the flood, he said, which scalded his body. Holding to a tree branch, he drifted six miles to the town of Guayaval, where at 5:30 this morning he was rescued. "I was just about to give up," he said. His wife, eight months pregnant, has not been found.

In this town, about six miles north of Armero, floodwaters knocked out a bridge spanning the Guali River and demolished 10 to 20 waterside homes, said residents. Some people decided to evacuate, but hundreds of curious onlookers lined the narrow avenue from the one-runway airport, which now is a center of relief operations, and the hospital.

Rifle-toting Colombian Army soldiers stood around the perimeter of the airport as a C-130 cargo plane and other military aircraft landed with boxes of emergency supplies. Several light aircraft carrying reporters and photographers also received official clearance to land here and, later, circle the Armero disaster zone.

Observations and questions

1) The lead contains two unspecific pronouns: "it" and "they." Try to rewrite this lead with specific nouns replacing "it" and "they." What do you gain and lose?

2) The middle of this piece contains a list of survivors and their stories. Discuss this structure in terms of economy of presentation and speed of writing.

3) The characters in this section describe themselves in motion. Study Graham's choices of verbs to capture the repeated personal disasters. Note his choice not to focus on emotions.

4) Graham wrote this piece, the color sidebar, before he wrote the previous straight news story. He says he felt more emotion about it, and expected it to be easier to write than the news story. Think about this tactic of purging emotion before writing the straighter account.

5) The piece ends with the first event Graham witnessed, his own arrival at the airport. Like the first story, it ends with an airplane landing after passing over the chaotic scene. Ironically, our point of view draws back as our reporter arrives.

Ill-equipped rescuers dig out volcano victims

NOVEMBER 16, 1985

ARMERO, Colombia, Nov. 15—From beneath the rubble of what was Armero, now a mass of broken concrete slabs and twisted corrugated metal, of scattered belongings and crushed bodies buried under brown, watery slush, came the cries today of survivors, alive two days after a volcanic eruption caused a flood of mud that swallowed this town.

But few were here to save them. Officials in Bogota, who had declared a national emergency after the eruption Wednesday of Nevado del Ruiz Volcano, reported that aid had begun to arrive from the United States, Europe, and international agencies. But only a tiny amount of material and a small number of volunteers have arrived so far at this main scene of disaster.

Relief workers, laboring in hot, humid weather amid the rising stench of spoiled food and decomposing bodies, said there was a desperate shortage of supplies and personnel. As they worked, more tremors and rumbles were felt from the volcano.

The government of Caldas State warned people living near rivers flowing down from the volcano to "take security measures" because of the "potential danger of a new avalanche."

A Health Ministry spokeswoman in Bogota said preliminary reports said 21,559 persons were dead or missing and 1,436 were listed as injured. Margarita Vargas said more than 19,000 were left homeless.

Walter Cotte of the Red Cross said many of the dead were buried in mass graves without being photographed or fingerprinted. One relief official said it would probably be necessary to declare Armero "holy ground," leaving many of the dead buried where they died. Hastily constructed tent hospitals were set up in the nearby towns of Mariquita, Lerida, and Guayabal, civil defense officials said, but there were few helicopters to carry the victims there, and none of the roads into Armero were passable. "We don't have the help we need," said Raul Alferez, who is in charge of the Red Cross medical unit here. "We need people, we need equipment, but we have next to nothing."

The magnitude of what has to be done is overwhelming. What was once a picturesque country city of 25,000 inhabitants is now a mangled mass of junk and corpses. Traces of ruined lives lay strewn across an area about 70 acres wide, where a raging river of mud and stone swept over this town. Today, Armero resembled a giant junkyard bathed in brown ooze.

Only a few of the buildings that once made up Armero's center are still standing.

Over where the coffee warehouse once stood, bags of beans floated on the muddy mess.

There is no organization, no plan, to search for the living. It is a hit-or-miss operation. Survivors have been located most often when their screams or cries were heard by passers-by.

Once survivors are found, the process of freeing them is a lengthy, arduous effort.

One team of workers spent much of this morning trying to pry a 34-year-old man from his collapsed house while, a few yards away, another team chest-deep in water sought desperately to lift to safety a 13-year-old girl whose feet were pinned by fallen concrete.

The man, Efrain Gomez Primo, a peanut farmer and candy vendor, was stuck under his collapsed house. He talked about his ordeal as rescue workers hacked away with machetes at the boards that imprisoned him.

He said the walls of his house fell in Wednesday night as he was trying to flee the raging current. After the volcanic storm had subsided, he said he started screaming for help. His brother found him at 6:30 yesterday morning and told him not to worry, that the Red Cross, Civil Defense, and Army were on their way. The brother never returned.

A Civil Defense worker who arrived soon afterward lacked the necessary tools and left. It was not until late this morning that a rescue squad arrived.

By then, a middle-aged woman, who had been caught in the wreckage with him and was in great pain through last night, had died. Her corpse lay facing up on a sheet of tin.

"I'm half dead," he said, as the effort to free him began. No one had given him anything to eat or drink for more than 36 hours. Gasping for air, he exclaimed, "I can barely breathe."

When he was finally pried loose and carried to the evacuation zone, medics had no splint for Gomez's broken right leg. They tied a strip of cardboard around it.

Just a few yards from Gomez was the girl, Omayra Sanchez. She had been found just after dawn yesterday by an Air Force officer working in the rescue campaign. The first problem was how to pry loose the stiff arms of the girl's dead aunt, who had grasped the child the night of the tragedy.

Sanchez said the waters of the ravaging Lagunilla River had prevented her aunt from opening the door of their house. All during that stormy night, before she died, the aunt kept apologizing for not having managed to rush the family to freedom, the niece recalled.

The girl's eyes were bright red and swollen. When rescue workers called for an anesthetic, there was none.

She asked for cookies, but there were none of those either. Somehow the girl managed to stay calm and lucid, closing her eyes in pain at times, breaking into tears at other moments.

She would wrap her hands around the neck of a rescue worker standing in the water in front of her and try, with all her might, to tear herself free of whatever was keeping her feet pinned down. But she could not budge.

Workers dug around her, lifting out huge blocks of broken concrete. Rescuers feared that rising water would drown the girl if they couldn't get her out soon. Her head was just above the water line.

Watching the desperate attempts to save the girl, Alferez, the Red Cross chief, shook his head in despair.

"This makes one feel useless," he said. "What can we do?"

Jaime Hernandez, a 22-year-old farmer and Armero resident who survived the avalanche, stood surveying the destruction, chewing on a coconut he had cut open with a machete.

Food is a serious problem, said Hernandez, explaining how he had scrounged for the coconut. As visitors arrived during the day, children ran up to them, hands extended, begging for something to eat or drink.

In the low hills above the city, several hundred persons have camped in makeshift huts with tin roofs. They are the lucky ones, those who managed somehow to escape the waves of hot mud and debris that swept through Armero.

But they were not being evacuated. Relief officials said priority for seats in the nine or 10 helicopters ferrying people to and from the disaster site was given to the injured.

On the northwest side of Armero, several bulldozers were pushing back the mud, trying to open a road into the town. But it could be days before emergency land vehicles can reach here.

The Red Cross has set up a tent and evacuation area in a clearing several hundred yards from where the mud stopped. Only five medics and 15 volunteers made up the Red Cross team today, according to Alferez. Also helping in the rescue effort here were about 10 blue-suited Air Force members and about the same number of orange-suited Civil Defense workers. Yesterday, emergency teams pulled survivors off the roofs and trees where they had climbed to escape the avalanche. Today, the rescuers searched for those buried alive in the mud.

Alferez estimated that 1,000 persons could be trapped alive in the city's ruins. An Argentine medic participating in the relief effort, 23-year-old Alejandro Jimenez, guessed that there could be 2,000.

As of early this afternoon, Red Cross director Alferez, who was not keeping exact records, said about 65 injured survivors had been found and flown out today.

Describing how ill-equipped rescue workers here are, Alferez rattled off a list of urgently needed supplies: power generators, water pumping machines, medicine, bandages, stretchers, food, and drink.

He said the supplies being sent by foreign countries were going to an Air Force base.

"I was there this morning and there was a lot," said the 20-year-old Red Cross volunteer who hopes to study medicine in the United States. Asked why he thought the material had not reached this primary disaster area yet, Alferez replied, "Poor communications."

In another part of what had been Armero, one man was scouring the wreckage for whatever could be salvaged—a television set, some plastic plates, a spool of wire. Wiping the mud off the spool, he tested the strength of the wire and appeared satisfied. Where neat rows of buildings once stood, there is now just a sea of mud. A few isolated rooms jutted above the mud.

In one such room—a three-sided concrete box with the front missing—several men were sifting through the remains. It used to be an appliance store. A fan, a blender, and some spare cords were found.

Scavengers are everywhere. Rodrigo Salcedo, 27, from the neighboring town of Honda, spotted an artificial Christmas tree and perched it on his head.

"Those of us who survived have a right to live," he said when asked about his new possession.

Two boys from the town of Guayabal, several miles up the valley from Armero, had stuffed their pockets. One collected dozens of ballpoint pens, a precious commodity in this poor region. The other collector pulled a bottle of perfume and another of deodorant from his jacket pocket, showing off his finds.

The people of Armero are bitter about the disaster. In interview after interview, residents who survived said the loss of life could have been prevented. They said the government knew the volcano might erupt, and when it did, officials failed to react fast enough to evacuate the town.

When the ashen rain started falling heavily around 6 p.m. Wednesday, many in Armero turned on their radios. They heard Jairo Monroy, the local radio announcer, saying reassuringly that there was no cause for alarm.

So the people of Armero went to sleep.

It was only four hours later that the alarm was sounded. By then, the volcano had exploded, sending broken hunks of melted glacier ice racing down its slopes into the valley below.

But even then the signals that authorities gave were confusing.

Alirio Oliveros, a farmer, said that to warn citizens and wake up the town, police shot their guns into the air at about 10 p.m. Wednesday. Oliveros mistook the shooting for an attempt by the M19 guerrilla group to take over the town. He said that instead of running into the street and to high ground, he and his family "hid even more" in their house, which subsequently was washed away.

Observations and questions

1) Analyze Graham's lead ("From beneath... town.") in terms of the information it contains. Note how the sentence flows with no sense of strain despite the number of details. Graham anchors it with a central verb and subject: "...came the cries."

2) This story brims with sources. Study Graham's decisions on which sources to identify specifically, and which not.

3) Graham says that he can write quickly because he takes notes in subject "blocks," which he transfers almost whole from his notebook in the writing process. Analyze the structure of this piece to see if you can identify the blocks.

4) Graham uses small quotations as little kickers for subsections. Think about how these quotations serve both as closers and transitions.

5) Two victims appear at length in the middle, Mr. Premo and Ms. Sanchez. How do their plights illustrate Graham's theme of ill-equipped rescuers? Note the restraint in these presentations.

6) Graham saves his best quote, "Those of us who survived have a right to live," almost until the end. Try moving this vignette of the scavenger around in the story for different effects.

7) Graham says his ending plants the seeds for a developing theme, the issue of blame. Think of alternatives to his anecdotal mode here.

Hopes ebb for victims of volcano

NOVEMBER 17, 1985

ARMERO, Colombia, Nov. 16—Efforts to save hundreds of people trapped in the wreckage of Wednesday's flash floods were stepped up today, but Red Cross officials in the disaster zone in central Colombia said victims not lifted to safety by tonight stood little chance of survival.

The number of survivors being dug out of Armero's rubble had dwindled to a few by this morning. Only two had been found between dawn and 11 a.m. today. Relief workers, who yesterday estimated that 1,000 to 2,000 people might be alive in the submerged town, today said they believe that 200 at most were still alive.

In Bogota, the government said about 22,300 people had died in the floods and mud slides that followed Wednesday's eruption of the Nevado del Ruiz Volcano.

Unconfirmed reports of new activity at the top of the volcano triggered a panic in several towns around the mountain. A pilot flying by the volcano claimed to have seen a dense cloud of sulfur, and radio stations broadcast reports that there might have been one or two new explosions. But other reports early this evening indicated that the situation was not threatening. In this town, where most of the destruction from Wednesday's volcanic eruption and mud slides occurred, doctors continued to complain of insufficient medical supplies, manpower, and salvaging equipment, while the search for people still alive beneath the morass of collapsed buildings and twisted vegetation had little direction.

At Palanquero Air Force base 36 miles to the north, headquarters for the military relief effort, Gen. Alberto Melendez, the base commander, acknowledged that Colombian authorities were staggered by the enormity of the tragedy. He said the task of digging out Armero, a town of 25,000 almost totally destroyed when the volcano erupted Wednesday, causing hunks of glacial ice to melt and flood rivers below, was more than official agencies could manage quickly.

"There are just too many people to search for, to fight for," the general said in English to a group of foreign reporters. "I don't know if anyone in the world could figure out what to do. If he could, then he is quite close to God."

As he spoke, crates of clothing and medicine were being loaded onto two U.S. military CH-47 cargo helicopters, part of a fleet of 12 American choppers flown to Colombia from Panama yesterday and today by the U.S. Army's 210th Aviation Battalion of the 193rd Infantry Brigade. The helicopters were put into service transporting the wounded and ferrying supplies to several field hospitals set up yesterday in neighboring towns in the Magdalena River valley.

The U.S. Air National Guard also flew a C-130 cargo plane to Colombia yesterday filled with 500 tents, each large enough to sleep six to eight people. But, according to Navy Cmdr. Frank Evans, spokesman for the 105-man U.S. contingent sent to Colombia, a decision on what further American assistance to provide was awaiting a report by a U.S. aid official who toured the devastated region this morning.

Tons of emergency material have been shifted south from Palanquero to the civil airport at Mariquita, now a military-controlled staging point for relief operations.

Melendez said the number of sorties flown by military aircraft out of Palanquero carrying emergency supplies tripled today over the number flown Thursday. But hardly any of the supplies are being forwarded to Armero. Part of the reason appears to be bureaucratic.

Additionally, authorities supervising the salvage effort have decided to limit rescue and medical operations in Armero because of the absence of electricity, potable water, telephones, and other basic services.

Fernando Bendeck, national vice president of the Colombian Red Cross, said today he had dispatched only 15 volunteers to Armero.

"We can't leave more people there because there are so many difficulties with water and food," he explained at his operations base at the Mariquita airport.

He said the Red Cross had mobilized 2,000 volunteers nationwide to help in the disaster but had stationed them in hospitals and relief centers away from Armero.

Bendeck expressed his own disappointment at the sluggishness of rescue operations, saying workers lacked equipment to do the job. He had little hope of finding any more survivors in Armero after today.

"After three days, conditions are critical," he said. "Today is the crucial day."

Clusters of rescue workers continued today to pick their way across the mud-covered remains of Armero, listening for cries of help. Several helicopters hovered overhead, also hunting for signs of life.

The search had no formal organization or design. And it had major setbacks.

One came at 9:45 this morning when a 13-year-old girl, whom rescuers had spent much of the past two days trying to free from the crushed remnants of her house, died. The attempted rescue of Omayra Sanchez had been widely reported, with photographs of the round-faced, dark-haired girl appearing in newspapers around the world.

Her body lay limp this morning in a pool of brown water out of which she had struggled to climb, held back by broken concrete slabs pinning her feet. She died of a heart attack induced by exposure, according to Alejandro Jimenez, a Red Cross medic.

"We were up all night trying to save her," he said.

Someone had draped a blue-and-white checkered cloth over the girl, a graceful symbol of mourning among ugly splintered timbers, chunks of concrete, and corrugated sheets of tin.

Eduardo Talero, another Red Cross medic, said the small-scale rescue operation here was in desperate need of such basic medical supplies as antibiotics, typhoid vaccine, and bandages.

"It will become necessary soon to start burning bodies, because otherwise there will be an epidemic of typhoid," he said. "Most importantly now, though, we need to have more first-aid equipment."

An attitude of resignation has come over some Armero residents who said they have given up searching for lost relatives and friends.

"The place is already buried, it is already a grave," said Antonio Rubio Guzman, a construction engineer who lost 25 relatives in the catastrophe.

A mass grave has been designated in Guayabal, the closest town to the north of Armero, where about 200 bodies reportedly have been deposited. Pope John Paul II, who, according to the papal nuncio to Colombia, wept when he saw pictures of the disaster here, has declared the area sacred ground so bodies can be left where they are.

In the towns around Armero, residents remained fearful of further volcanic explosions and mud slides. Rumors of imminent disaster swept through Mariquita, Honda, and Lerida yesterday, triggering a stampede of people looking for higher ground.

In the streets of Mariquita today, hundreds of people milled around nervously.

Colombian geologists have said that ice flows triggered by the restless volcano may be blocking some rivers at the mountain's base, which now have shrunk to narrow streams. Government authorities have warned residents in the area to be alert for new flooding.

This evening, Communications Minister Noemi Sanin made a radio broadcast urging residents of the area around the volcano to begin an evacuation immediately. An hour later, however, she made a second broadcast saying there was no imminent danger of a new avalanche.

"The state of alert remains, but fortunately it seems that this eruption will not have the grave consequences of the one three days ago," she said.

In the early evening the government said it was sending a team of international experts closer to the mountain to survey what had happened. One expert raised the possibility that there had simply been an intense electrical storm around the volcano's summit, rather than a new eruption.

The emergency field hospital in Mariquita was sent by Mexico along with 45 soldiers to run it. Their commander, Gen. Jose Luis Gutierrez Cedeno, rescued people from the rubble of Mexico City following September's earthquake there.

The general said conditions here are much worse.

"In Mexico, there were still buildings standing after the earthquake with facilities and supplies," he remarked. "Here, we are in the countryside. Everything is more difficult."

Observations and questions

1) Graham tells us that he controlled his "own sense of outrage at how poorly the rescue effort was going" by reporting the story "as straightforwardly as possible." Note the wording of his lead in terms of this tension.

2) Graham says he had difficulty finding standards for judging the rescue effort. How can the reporter in the field see things from the local point of view, avoiding inappropriate comparisons?

3) This piece plays events in Armero against a background of world coverage, especially on TV, and ends with a comparison to the Mexico City disaster. Graham explains this technique in terms of giving "a point of reference to the reader...as part of a continuing story." Does the reporter need to remind readers of what they already know?

4) More than halfway through, Graham tells us that Omayra Sanchez has died. Discuss how and why he subordinates this striking event, seen by millions on TV, to his theme.

5) Throughout these four stories, Graham avoids gore, sensational detail, political criticism, and excessive emotion. Think about how journalistic forms and standards aid the isolated writer reporting catastrophes under difficult conditions.

A conversation with
Bradley Graham

DON FRY: Where were you when the Armero story broke?

BRADLEY GRAHAM: I had been on the job as the South American correspondent about six weeks. I spent a week in Bogota before the Armero tragedy, reporting on the aftermath of the attack on the Palace of Justice. I was about to leave Bogota to cover elections in Brazil when the Nevado del Ruiz Volcano erupted and sent a wall of mud sweeping over Armero.

How far is Armero from Bogota?

Well, by car on narrow, winding, mountainous roads, it's about three to four hours. By plane, it's about 35 minutes to the closest airport in a small town called Mariquita, 12 miles north of Armero. Together with Joe Treaster of *The New York Times* and Julia Preston, who was then with *The Boston Globe*, and several other reporters, I chartered a plane and flew to Mariquita. Every morning we'd get up very early, rush out to the airport, and try to find a charter. We were competing with the networks, other news media, and the government, which had appropriated many of the small aircraft of the country for the rescue effort.

The morning of November 14 we flew out to Mariquita and watched as the first survivors of the tragedy were brought in either by helicopter, by military and Civil Defense teams, or stumbled in under their own power. And it had been just a night of horror.

Did you file from Bogota?

We'd have to scramble back to Bogota for a long-distance line. Sometimes we would have to hitch rides back on whatever aircraft was going back. Once we hitched a ride on an old DC-3, another time on a police plane. It was quite chaotic.

We flew over Armero the first day. You couldn't get to Armero by road because all of the roads into and out of the towns had been washed away. The only way in was a long trek on foot or by helicopter. But most of the space on the helicopter was reserved for the victims.

What kind of equipment did you take in with you?

Well, I traveled all the time with my Radio Shack 200; it works on batteries. I carried a map of Colombia, a raincoat, and a hat, but I didn't carry food. The idea was to be as mobile and have as little equipment as possible, because we were having to jump in and out of helicopters and run around the disaster area.

Did you take notes on the lap computer or in a notebook?

In a notebook. But the machine was quite important in terms of meeting the deadline. I could start writing on the airplane and in a taxi from the airport back to the hotel.

How long did it take you to write the first piece?

Well, I did two pieces the first day. I got back about 4 o'clock, and the deadline was 7 o'clock. So I did the color piece first, and then the main piece, and I just made it.

Do you normally revise a lot?

Well, it depends on the piece. On a deadline piece, there's not much time to revise. But normally I agonize over my stories.

When you're in the field, how do you organize the material in your notebook?

Well, I underline all the names as I go along so I can refer to them easily when I go back. I try to indent notes and quotes so they can be easily found. If I'm certain I want to use some reference or quote as I'm writing it down, I put a star next to it. Sometimes on my way to talk to the next person, I'll go over the notes again and make a mark.

When you're reviewing your notes later, do you use codes and mark the good stuff?

No, I was constantly trying to structure the story in my mind as I took notes, particularly on the lead. I've always had the hardest time with the first few paragraphs. And then I'd structure the rest of the story in block terms, sometimes even outlining on a piece of paper.

So you test leads in your head and think in blocks.

Well, on a breaking story, you have to. Organization is a lot of it. There's a constant play between the main points you want to make, the developments you want to highlight, the constant play between that effort and finding the right people to talk to.

Do you write a lead first?

I usually do. If I'm having too much trouble with the lead on deadline, I skip it and go on with the rest of the story.

Let's talk about the first story, beginning "A volcano in central Colombia erupted last night, triggering floods in valleys below that buried large sections of at least two towns under tons of mud and rubble. Government

**and Red Cross officials said the death toll
could reach 20,000." Nice hard-news lead.**

Well, I felt we had to say what happened as
straightforwardly as possible. At that point, there
were still a lot of details we didn't know about
what did happen inside the volcano, what time
it erupted, and so on. The number of dead was
still a very rough estimate.

**I like this fourth paragraph, describing the
eruption: "Part of the volcano's top exploded late yesterday, breaking off chunks of
snow near the summit. The ice melted rapidly into cascading waters that gathered dirt
and debris and turned the rivers at the
mountain's base into killer currents." How
long did those two sentences take to write?**

Not long, because I could see it in my mind. A
Colombian scientist explained what probably
happened in a graphic animation on TV while
I was writing the story. That visual impressed
me, and so this part came quite easily.

**The simplicity of the wording impresses me.
Do you work hard at such simple diction?**

Well, it helps on deadline to keep the thoughts
as short and simple as possible. If I have more
time, my diction will get a little more complicated, my sentences longer. So the deadline
pressure helps keep my writing clear.

**Armero doesn't appear until the eighth
paragraph. Why did you save it so long?**

Well, Armero is not exactly a household name.
I thought it was important to give the scope of
the disaster, the sense of the country moving into action, before getting into the specifics.

**Tell me about this anecdote at the end, the
pilot blinded by smoke.**

Well, I thought it was memorable and graphic. It leaves one with a sense of drama and obscured vision, and that's what the whole week was going to be about. I heard that story on the radio.

You seem to use all the media for supplementary sources.

The two main newspapers in Bogota, *El Tiempo* and *El Espectador*, did excellent reporting on this crisis. I drew information from both newspapers throughout the week. In some countries, you find yourself relying on local press coverage. And when it's good, it makes a difference. The more confusing the situation, the more sources you have to use to try to piece the puzzle together.

Let's talk about the second piece. Why did you write two stories?

Well, because the desk said, "Give us two stories." A little after 4:00 that first day, I called Washington and said, "I got close to the disaster scene. I got a lot of color. It's a mess here." Our day editor immediately could see room for at least two stories, one with a lot of quotes and eyewitness accounts from the victims, and the other one the main story announcing what had happened and the rescue effort and so on. So he said, "Put it in two pieces, and give us the color one first." So I opened my notebooks to these eyewitness accounts and just filed that. That piece took only about 45 minutes to write.

I notice that many of your sentences have lists in the middle of them. Listen to this sentence in the third paragraph: "Caked with mud, burned by the scalding temperature of the river of dirt and debris that overwhelmed their town, cut and battered from being dragged hundreds of yards across the valley floor, some of the victims of Armero were brought here to this neighboring

**village by Red Cross, Civil Guard, and Army
units." Actually, that sentence has two lists.**

Well, part of the challenge is trying to get so
much information into a limited amount of space,
and sometimes the best way to squeeze in all this
information is just to list it.

**The whole piece is a list. Six paragraphs
down you introduce your list of witnesses:
"The stories they recounted had haunting
similarities." You capture five people
describing themselves in motion, not how
they felt.**

The quotes we got result in part from the questions we were asking. We were not asking how
they felt because we could see how they felt. They
were in shock. We were more interested in just
what happened: "What happened? Where were
you? Then what happened?" So the accounts in
my notebook were action accounts.

**I admire the simplicity of these accounts. Did
that take much doing? Or did that just come
out that way?**

It took some concentration at the top of the story
to try to weave together the separate accounts
into a sense of the horror of the night, giving bits
and pieces of what had happened to different people. It wasn't necessary to hype this story.
Because if you just reported things as they were
and as people explained it to you, it just leapt
off the page. The drama and the terror of what
happened spoke for itself. It didn't need any
embellishment.

**You end this piece with an airport scene:
"Several light aircraft carrying reporters
and photographers also received official
clearance to land here, and, later, circle the
Armero disaster zone." Why did you decide
to end with that sequence?**

Well, partly because I had to get to the main piece of the day. This was the easiest to write of the day's two pieces because I felt more emotion about it. And I wanted to add a paragraph about the scene at the airport, which is what we first saw when we landed.

You're letting the reporting show.

Right, I felt I owed it to the reader. When someone's watching television, it's quite clear where the camera is positioned, and where the correspondent is positioned. When someone's reading a newspaper article, it's not clear. I felt an obligation to show where I was.

Let's look at the next story, headlined "Ill-equipped rescuers dig out volcano victims." Here's the lead: "From beneath the rubble of what was Armero, now a mass of broken concrete slabs and twisted corrugated metal, of scattered belongings and crushed bodies buried under brown, watery slush, came the cries today of survivors, alive two days after a volcanic eruption caused a flood of mud that swallowed this town. But few were here to save them." Good lead.

Well, I wrote it sitting on top of the rubble. I had been sitting right next to one of the rescue efforts I described, the attempt to save Omayra Sanchez. I'd been watching them struggle to pull this girl out of this pool of muddy water where her feet had been trapped by fallen bits of concrete. And it just seemed so hopeless and so frustrating.

And then I turned to the back of my notebook to try to scribble out a lead. And all around me was this rubble and these broken slabs and twisted metal, and so I just set out to describe that. And I also had the strong sense of the survivors out there. One heard people say that they heard voices. I was also struck by how few rescuers were there. And so the lead was written right on the scene.

Tell me about the frustration.

Well, there's a question that reporters may be confronted with in tragedies of this sort, that is, the tension between being at a scene in a professional capacity, where you're there to record what's happening and get back to file, versus the human obligation one has, the moral obligation to put down your notebook and get involved yourself in saving a life.

How do you deal with that?

Well, it's tough to know where to draw the line. My feeling is, if there is some immediate action you could take to help, then you should do it. On the other hand, as a representative, particularly the *only* representative, of an organization that has to report to hundreds of thousands of readers and to governments, you have to get back in time to fulfill that obligation.

Let me ask you a personal question, something I wondered about in all this coverage, and particularly last year in the Ethiopian famine. You're reporting in a place where people are starving, but you have to eat. Do you know what I'm talking about?

Yes. It's the same problem where people are dying, whether you get involved in the rescue effort versus whether you're just there as witness. There is no exact place to draw that line, except that in the end, you have to file.

There's a detail in one of these stories about how children would run up to you in the street and beg for food.

If I'd had any food, I would have given it to them.
But I didn't carry food.

**Let's talk about Omayra Sanchez, the little
girl trapped in a pool. I'm struck by this
description: "The girl's eyes were bright red
and swollen. When rescue workers called for
an anesthetic, there was none. She asked for
cookies, but there were none of those either.
Somehow the girl managed to stay calm and
lucid, closing her eyes in pain at times,
breaking into tears at other moments."
That's so simply written.**

Well, in a situation like this, I just write down
what's happening in my notebook in short
sentences. And when I go back, I just list out in
my notebook the observations that I have. And
in a situation as dramatic as this, it's enough to
keep the reporting simple and write it exactly
as I saw it and recorded it.

**Tell me about the scavenger who showed up
wearing a Christmas tree on his head.**

We were all sitting there watching the rescue effort around Omayra Sanchez, and this man with
a Christmas tree came wandering by and stopped
to watch. And we asked him what he was doing
with the Christmas tree. It seemed so out of place,
comical almost, black humor.

**This is the best quotation in all these pieces:
"Those of us who survived have a right to
live."**

Well, that's exactly what he said. I think he was
speaking for most of those who had come to pick
their way through the ruins. People do tend to
say things that just sum up the moment exactly. And the things that people were saying to us
were just incredible. It made writing the story
that much easier because they were great quotes.

Why did you end this story about rescue efforts with a police anecdote from the night before?

Well, I felt it was important towards the end of the story to talk a little more about the controversy that I could see was growing, over who was to blame for this tragedy. In covering a story like this, you have to be conscious not only just of what is happening that day, but also of the developing issues and themes, so you can weave them through your coverage. I could see early that blame was going to become an issue that would survive the actual tragedy itself.

So you're already planting the seeds for the next story. Tell me about collaborative efforts with other reporters.

A lot of this reporting was a result of pooled effort. It was impossible to be everywhere at once. There were three of us, and sometimes as many as six or seven of us would exchange quotes and information.

For instance, while I spent most of my time watching Omayra Sanchez, two of my colleagues were nearby watching another victim. The Christmas tree quote was taken down by these two colleagues. And on the way back to Bogota, we would try to pool what information we had.

You wrote the lead sitting on the rubble. Where and when did you write the rest of the story?

I wrote the rest on the plane ride back. At the airport I found a long-distance line and filed the top half of the story. And I wrote another part of the story on the taxi ride from the airport to the hotel, and I finished the story at the hotel and sent the rest from there.

Amazing. What's the total writing time?

Under two hours.

You're writing these stories so fast, under such terrible conditions, and yet they're wonderfully cohesive. I get no sense of dribs and drabs, or of just blocks of things coming at me.

It normally doesn't come so easily. I've been known to take four or five days to do a story the length of this piece, and it doesn't come out this coherent. It makes a big difference to feel a story and to have the information all right there in blocks in your notebook.

The last story, headlined "Hopes ebb for victims of volcano," has this lead: "Efforts to save hundreds of people trapped in the wreckage of Wednesday's flash floods were stepped up today, but Red Cross officials in the disaster zone in central Colombia said victims not lifted to safety by tonight stood little chance of survival." What a desolate lead.

Well, I was feeling this story very passionately. For one thing, I was getting very tired and feeling the desperation grow. I was constantly wrestling with myself to report the story as straightforwardly as possible, wrestling with that professional obligation versus my own sense of outrage at how poorly the rescue effort was going.

How do you deal with anger and despair at a scene like this?

Well, the best way I found was to factor out the emotion and simply pinpoint those elements of what I was seeing that were making me feel this way. I was criticized afterwards by the government of Colombia and by some U.S. officials for being too critical of the rescue effort. As I look at these stories again, I don't see much editorial comment.

Neither do I. How do you judge something as unusual and chaotic as a rescue effort?

Well, I had to wrestle with a judgmental issue: what standard to apply to judge how the rescue effort was going. A U.S. rescue team and the U.S. government would have handled something like this differently. It's important for any reporter to know what kind of standard to expect while witnessing an event. Readers need to know that what they are reading about should be judged by a standard different perhaps from what they're used to. I knew not to expect American efficiency. But what I saw was so short of what I regarded as minimal organization and supply that I couldn't help but feel compassionate and frustrated.

And the more foreign a country becomes to one's own experience, the more difficult it is to bridge this gap. And sometimes the more emotional an event, the more difficult it is to remember the importance of keeping one's perspective on the country involved.

So you keep the readers' needs in mind. Who are your readers?

Well, the foreign desk says we should write for the Bethesda housewife. The problem is that sometimes the Bethesda housewife might be married to the secretary of state. Particularly on a human-interest story like this, I have a composite picture of someone who has never been to Colombia and never seen a major tragedy, but needs a lot of detail to get a full sense of the overwhelming impact of the disaster.

Let's look at the death of Omayra Sanchez: "The search had no formal organization or design. And it had major setbacks.

"One came at 9:45 this morning when a 13-year-old girl, whom rescuers had spent much of the past two days trying to free from

the crushed remnants of her house, died. The attempted rescue of Omayra Sanchez had been widely reported, with photographs of the round-faced, dark-haired girl appearing in newspapers around the world.

"Her body lay limp this morning in a pool of brown water out of which she had struggled to climb, held back by broken concrete slabs pinning her feet. She died of a heart attack induced by exposure, according to Alejandro Jimenez, a Red Cross medic.

" 'We were up all night trying to save her,' he said.

"Someone had draped a blue-and-white checkered cloth over the girl, a graceful symbol of mourning among ugly splintered timbers, chunks of concrete, and corrugated sheets of tin."

Talk about that scene, please.

That day, because of helicopter problems, we only had about five minutes on the ground, so we went in shifts. We touched down for those few minutes just after the girl had died. And the Red Cross team was especially depressed about their failure to save her, and they described what had happened. And one of us ran over to the area where she had been, and came back with this description. I didn't go. I stayed to talk to the medics.

Why do you pull back to "the newspapers around the world?" Everything has been so close-up until now.

Well, I wanted to remind the reader of this person they had seen in *The Washington Post* or on television the day before, to give a point of reference to the reader. This was a part of a continuing story, and I felt it important to remind the reader of that context.

She was incredible. We were shocked that she had died. It was just totally unexpected. They were working so hard on her the day before that we all assumed she would be saved.

Why did you choose to end with a general talking about the Mexico City earthquake?

Well, I thought it was important to give a sense of balance, a sense of the obstacles that the officials involved in the rescue effort were facing. I had described some of their failures and shortcomings in such detail. I also felt it was important to note that they were working under very difficult circumstances, not only being in a Third World country with things like basic cutting tools or water pumps hard to come by, but also being out in nowhere. And this quote came from someone who had been involved in another recent rescue effort, the Mexico City earthquake. And so he had a comparative view of why this disaster was more difficult to deal with.

Well, this is the long view in history, even though the history is quite recent. Was there anything you saw in Armero that was so awful you had to leave it out?

I left out some political impressions I couldn't prove. But there was no gruesome detail I left out, unless I blocked it out of my mind. On the contrary, the challenge was to try to describe the bodies and the destruction in detail.

Well, I think you succeeded admirably well. Were these stories edited much?

Surprisingly, no. Usually one finds out they've changed something only when the paper shows up weeks later in the mail. But I adopt the advice a veteran reporter once gave. When asked how he'd managed to survive so long as a foreign correspondent, he replied that the secret was that he never reads his stories once they appear in print. (Laughter)

How do you function without a newsroom, with no editors to talk to?

Well, in foreign bureaus, you have sort of an umbilical cord. During a breaking story on a crisis, there is contact at least daily and usually several times daily, as opposed to quieter times when weeks pass without phone contact. There's a lot of reliance on the correspondent in the field to let the paper know what is important and what isn't.

In a sense, your newsroom consists of your colleagues in the pools, in the field, an extended newsroom, if you will.

Well, that's true. There's much more contact with other foreign correspondents and local reporters than with editors and reporters back home.

As I listen to you talk about the pooling efforts, it sounds like a good basketball team, whose success depends on people not being selfish, and passing a lot.

Well, in overseas disaster coverage, it is essential in order to keep on top of the various fronts. And everybody gains in this pooling effort.

You certainly lead a hard life in the field.

Well, it's a different life. After tours in Bonn and Warsaw and now Buenos Aires, it's beginning to feel normal. I'm beginning to worry about that. (Laughter)

Well, I think you're very cool under fire and a wonderful writer. *Adios*.

Adios.

Roger Simon
Commentary

ROGER SIMON, 38, was born and raised in Chicago. He majored in English at the University of Illinois at Urbana, graduating in 1970. He started his journalism career writing for the City News Bureau in Chicago before moving to the Waukegan (Illinois) *News-Sun* as a general assignment reporter and columnist. He moved to the Chicago *Sun-Times* in 1972 and to the Baltimore *Sun* in 1984. Simon has won numerous writing prizes, and he is the only non-black columnist to win the National Association of Black Journalists writing award. In 1985, he published *Simon Sez,* a collection of his columns.

The children in MOVE house 'were just kids'

MAY 15, 1985

PHILADELPHIA—Anthony Williams knew the people who lived eight houses down the block. He knew the people they called MOVE.

He is 13 and he played with the kids who lived in that house and he sometimes saw their parents up on the roof, carrying rifles and staring out into the West Philadelphia night.

"They were just kids," Anthony said of the MOVE children, "They didn't talk much about what went on inside the house. We would just play.

"But then, the adults put raw meat in the driveway and we couldn't play there any more. We'd hold our nose whenever we went past the house. It smelled bad."

Anthony was sitting in the basement of the St. Carthage Church with the other burnt-out families. The Red Cross had set up a disaster relief center there.

He was wearing a gray, quilted jacket, a striped, boatneck T-shirt, jogging pants, and Puma running shoes. He has one other change of clothes. And that is all he has.

This is not a slum here. It is a neighborhood of neat row houses with struggling, postage-stamp lawns and people who sit out on their front porches and take note of what is going on.

Because it is not a slum, the people here did not like the MOVE house and what they called the filth that existed inside and out.

Today, that house is charred rubble and so is Anthony Williams's house. The police dropped a bomb, a percussion grenade—call it what you will—on the roof of the MOVE house and 60 surrounding homes went up in flames.

Only the walls between the row houses still stood, everything else was blackened ruin and the blocks looked like the gap-tooth grin of a jack-o'-lantern.

While Anthony's father, Milton, and his mother, Sherry, were trying to find out who was going to rebuild their home and replace all their worldly goods, Anthony sat on a metal folding chair and tried to piece together the last 48 hours of his life.

"I got up Sunday to go to the corner store, to Dee's, to buy some potato chips," he said. "But when I got outside, I saw two men on our porch."

The men were plainclothes cops and they told Anthony's parents that they would have to evacuate their home by 10 p.m. that day. But they told them not to worry, because they could come back in 24 hours and everything would be fine.

The police had come to the neighborhood to serve warrants on and evict the MOVE people and they came prepared for trouble. In 1978, the police had besieged a MOVE house for nearly two months, trying to starve the residents out, when finally they stormed the place. A policeman was shot and nine MOVE members were convicted of murder.

But this time there would be no lengthy siege. The police and the mayor had decided if there was trouble they would move decisively.

"We spent Sunday packing," Anthony said. "My mother and father told me and my brother, his name is Christopher, he's 6, not to worry. That we'd only be gone overnight.

"I knew the adults in the MOVE house were dangerous. The kids were OK. They were just kids. But the adults. Well, they were scary."

Anthony didn't take much with him. He packed a change of clothes and his radio and that was it.

"You didn't take your homework with you?" I asked him.

He grinned. "I don't care that my homework got burned up," he said.

Anthony's mother was nervous, but tried to look calm in front of the children. She took only an overnight bag. She told the kids not to worry.

Sunday was Mother's Day, of course, and her mother, Leona Murph, came over for dinner.

"I knew of the MOVE people," Mrs. Murph said. "And I remembered what happened before. It was a very stressful day. I was concerned from the very moment we left the house."

The Williamses packed their few possessions into their car, locked up the house, and drove over to the Murphs' home, 18 blocks away.

Anthony's father went back to his house Monday afternoon, but couldn't get very near. By then, the shooting had already broken out and the situation had moved from tense to serious to grave.

As he turned away from the scene, it occurred to him that all the family documents and records, all the irreplaceable items that a family collects, were still inside his home.

Not long after that, about 5:30 p.m., the police dropped the bomb on the MOVE house.

"We saw the helicopter come over and drop it and then we saw the smoke," Anthony said. "Then we ran back inside to watch it on TV."

TV got good pictures. The cameras in the helicopters picked up the flames quite nicely. The kids were excited as they sat in front of the television and watched. But the adults knew what those flames were doing.

It is funny what goes through your mind at times like those. It struck Mr. Williams as he sat there and watched his house burn on TV how fortunate it was that his and his children's Mother's Day gift to his wife—gold earrings costing $62—were still safely at the jewelry store, all picked out, but not yet delivered.

Yesterday morning, Anthony and his mother went back to their house. Or what was left of it.

Though the gaggle of press and tourists were kept at bay, residents were let in for a peek.

Christopher, the 6-year-old, had not been told about the fire. He had left his Mr. T doll, his most valued toy, at home when he went to his grandmother's and had not yet missed it. Nobody wanted to remind him of it.

Anthony looked at the rubble that had once been his house. "The whole place was just sort of...gone," he said. "There were the walls, but nothing else.

"I liked that house. I had my own room. I've been living there since I was 6. I know everybody on the block. I don't want to move.

"It was more than a house. It was a home."

He straightened up in the chair a little bit, as if pulling himself together.

"I was scared when I saw it," he said. "I was upset. I cried. My mother cried. There wasn't anything else to do."

I asked him who he blamed for what had happened.

"I don't blame the mayor," he said. "I like the mayor. The MOVE people should have left the house. I think the mayor did his best."

Even though your house and everything in it was burned up? "The mayor promised us he would rebuild our home," Anthony said. "I heard him. The same home on the same place. He promised and I am going to hold him to it. I am."

And so it will all turn out OK? Your brother will get a new doll and you'll get new clothes and everyone will get a new house and it will all be OK?

Anthony looked down at the floor. "No," he said. "There's something else. Something I didn't tell you." He took a deep breath.

"Mittens," he said. "My cat. When they said we had to leave, I didn't take her because my grandmother has a cat and they don't get along.

"And so I left her. I left Mittens. I left food for her and water. But I left her. She was 6."

He had been acting very brave and very adult answering my questions. But now he was just a kid again and his lower lip trembled.

"They said we were coming back," he said. "And so I left Mittens. But they said we would be back in 24 hours.

"They said it would be all right. They did. They said. They promised."

Observations and questions

1) Simon wrote this column in 45 minutes on a portable computer while standing up on a hot day in a busy street. Do you see any signs of haste?

2) Simon's column would gain unity and punch by focusing on Anthony as a single source, but he would have to forgo the enriching viewpoints of the family members. Think about this tradeoff in general newswriting. Study how Simon weaves the other characters around Anthony.

3) Simon uses words like "gap-tooth," "gaggle," and "peek" in an essentially serious piece. Think about such light language and its effects. Does it ease the sense of tragedy and loss? Does it pull the punch on devastation? Does it restore a sense of normality in scenes of chaos?

4) Simon struggled over the inclusion of Anthony's statement, "It was more than a house. It was a home." While most journalists will not improve a quotation, what do you do when a subject delivers a statement that will strike your peers as too perfect? Would you have risked the inevitable questions or would you have left it out?

5) Simon ends on a rather sentimental note, with the child starting to break up over his dead kitten. He consciously risks being accused of writing "a sob story" or "delving too far into the kid's emotions." Would you be tempted to end this column seven paragraphs up, with the sentence "I am?"

6) Simon regards his ending as hopeful. Do you?

The lesson of the salt tray

JULY 28, 1985

It was a small thing in a way. And it was certainly not the worst thing I saw in South Africa.

People had shown me scars of shootings and beatings. They had told me tales of prison and torture.

I had seen how some lived without electricity or running water. And I had learned that to be black in South Africa was to die before your time.

As of 1981, the mortality rates for black infants between 1 and 4 years old was 10 times as high as that for white infants. Life expectancy for blacks was 58 years; for whites it was 72 years.

A couple of years ago, the South African government took out slick ads in American publications explaining how everyone was treated fairly there regardless of race.

South Africa spends millions on such publicity campaigns and they have an effect. Often, I get letters and phone calls from Americans who buy the South African government's official line: that blacks are treated very, very well in that country.

And when I was there, I met some of those blacks who were, indeed, treated well.

True, they were denied the same human rights that their poorer black brothers were denied, but they did enjoy a large measure of material comfort.

They had worked and struggled, and they had achieved something.

One day, I was introduced to such a man. He was not an apologist for the apartheid system. He was no Uncle Tom. He was a black man who, from a material standpoint, had "made it."

We arranged to meet in the city of Durban where I was then staying and where he was visiting on business.

I asked him to lunch at my hotel, one of the few hotels in the entire country that allowed black men and white men to eat together in its restaurant.

The restaurant, like Durban, was beautiful, reflecting the old days of British rule. Indian laborers had been brought to Durban by the British, and the city is still the center of South Africa's Indian population.

Indians, officially classified by the government as Asians, have more rights than blacks, but nowhere near the rights of whites.

If all this sounds confusing, that is because the South African race classification system is a kind of refined madness. When I was there, Indians were classified as Asians, Chinese were classified as a subgroup of coloreds (mixed-race), and the Japanese were classified as honorary whites.

The restaurant of the hotel was decorated in a grand style with the Indian waiters dressed in gleaming white jackets and red turbans.

I got to the table first and as my guest entered and I rose to greet him, I could see the faces of the waiters harden.

That is because in South Africa, Indians are not used to waiting upon blacks.

But they could hardly refuse. They could hardly refuse because this black was the guest of a white.

Confusing? Ridiculous? Not in South Africa. In South Africa, this is a way of life.

My guest sat at the table and we began to talk about his life. How he had risen, by dint of hard work, from the lowest of the low to his current level of success.

He could dress well and live well and provide well for his children. And, really, what more was there to life?

We ordered and after a few moments the soup arrived. The restaurant was so fancy that the salt on the table was not in shakers, but heaped on tiny crystal trays.

My guest took a pinch and then handed the tray to me.

But before I could take it, a waiter rushed up, took the tray from his hand, and disdainfully dumped the contents on the floor.

Then the waiter handed me a tray from another table.

My guest froze. For a second, I did not know what had happened.

After a long moment, my guest spoke quietly without lifting his eyes from the table. "Now you see," he said. "Now you see what it means to be a 'successful' black man in South Africa." And I have always remembered that little, seemingly insignificant incident. I have always remembered how easily the image of success can be shattered, how quickly the comfortable veneer stripped away.

I have always remembered that no matter how far a black man rose in that country, he was still considered unfit to touch the same salt as a white man.

A week ago, the government of South Africa began taking even more Draconian measures against its black population. Nearly a thousand people have been arrested and nearly a score killed.

As a sign of protest, the government of France decided to freeze new investments in South Africa and withdraw its ambassador.

The government of the United States is not even considering such things. It would be counterproductive, we say. It could only make things worse.

And whenever I hear that, I always wonder the same thing.

Worse than what?

Observations and questions

1) Simon wrote this column when papers were focusing on the issue of disinvestment, a subject he does not mention until the very end. Try rewriting the beginning to get the idea of disinvestment high up.

2) The lead uses the unspecified pronoun "it" twice. We assume that "it" refers to the incident told in the middle of the column. What does Simon gain from dangling the reader that long?

3) Simon delays telling the incident itself. Discuss the role of suspense in this circuitous telling.

4) Simon wrote this column in 1985 about an incident in 1978. He blurs the time scheme in the clause "and when I was there...." Why doesn't he simply tell us the date?

5) Simon interrupts his narration with this exclamation: "Confusing? Ridiculous? Not in South Africa. In South Africa, this is a way of life." Consider how this uncool outburst punctures his very restrained surface.

6) Simon uses only one quotation in this column, the black man's two sentences. Consider how the isolation of this one quotation strengthens its effect.

7) Who is the "we" in the penultimate paragraph? Compare Simon's implicating "we" with Jonathan Freedman's.

Nagasaki frenzy overlooks why atom bombs fell

AUGUST 7, 1985

Remember Pearl Harbor?

I'm not sure we do. Not based on the things I've read and heard over the last few days.

It is the 40th anniversary of the week we dropped the atomic bombs on Hiroshima and Nagasaki, and there has been a great questioning in America, a great soul-searching.

We feel guilty about doing what we did. Or at least some people do.

Good. Fine. A little guilt is sometimes healthy.

But from what I've been hearing on the news, you'd think we snuck over to Japan during peacetime, dropped an atomic bomb, and giggled all the way home.

It didn't happen that way. We did what we did during a war, a war we did not start. War is, almost by definition, madness, and now all the argument is about just how mad you are allowed to be during war.

I know what some will say. That this is the anniversary of Hiroshima and Nagasaki, not Pearl Harbor, and that is why there has been so little linkage, so little thought.

But that is the trouble with these anniversary frenzies. They view history as isolated incidents rather than as a continuous flow of events.

But you can't look upon the dropping of the atomic bomb in isolation. It is not fair.

Let us ask ourselves what we were doing in World War II and whom we were fighting.

We were not fighting for territorial expansion. We were not interfering in the history of another nation for our own ends.

We were fighting the spread of fascism. We were fighting two powers, Japan and Germany, that sought to enslave the world.

World War II, as Studs Terkel said in his book on the subject, was our "good war," our last "good war," perhaps.

And do not think for a second that had Japan or Germany developed the bomb first, they would have hesitated to drop it on New York or Los Angeles. And I doubt either the Nazis or the military in Japan would have worried about it 40 years later.

One newsman, NBC's Tom Brokaw, tried to touch upon this subject this week with Japanese Prime Minister Yasuhiro Nakasone.

He asked Nakasone if he thought, maybe, the atom bomb had saved Japan from itself, if ending the war saved Japan from the military-industrial clique that had plunged that country and the world into war.

Nakasone didn't think so.

The atomic bombings were "inhuman acts," he said. They were war crimes, he said.

I waited for him to go on. I waited for him to mention Pearl Harbor. Or the Bataan Death March. Or the atrocities carried out by Japanese soldiers against civilians throughout the Pacific.

But Nakasone did not mention those things. In his estimation, America had been inhuman. We were war criminals. Those other events did not enter into it.

But I think they should. And I think all those reporters who went to Hiroshima this week should have made one little stopover first. It is on the way.

And once you are there, it is only a short boat trip. The view is splendid, a natural harbor ringed with volcanic mountains.

At your destination, you alight onto a platform and, inevitably, you look down.

The water is crystalline and beneath the waves you can see the red rust and the green algae on the USS *Arizona*.

It is always quiet. Even the children fall silent without being told to.

One gun turret still sticks above the waves, and you can see the hull through the clear water, lying broken and twisted on the harbor floor.

Small, fluorescent fish dart in and out where more than 1,100 crewmen, from admiral to apprentice seaman, still lie trapped.

After a few moments, you hear the low burble above the wind. It is a recording of the name of every man who died on board this ship.

A 1,000 pound armor-piercing bomb crashed through the deck behind the forward gun turret, pierced the decks below and ignited the powder magazine.

The 30,000-ton battleship was lifted from the water by the force of the explosion. No one below decks lived. The Japanese attack on Pearl Harbor was three minutes old.

On the day I visited the *Arizona*, many of the tourists there were from Japan. They were, like the Americans, solemn. They were, like the Americans, paying their respects.

And, this week, we have reason to be solemn about and pay our respects to the dead of Hiroshima and Nagasaki.

We have reason to think about those terrible weapons we dropped. We should know about the horrors of atomic bombs and the madness of war.

And we should make sure we never repeat what we did.

But there is another lesson to Hiroshima and Nagasaki. One that is being forgotten.

Nations that start wars eventually have to pay for them.

And the price is often high.

Observations and questions

1) Where does Simon's lead end? Does this column have a lead? Must a column always have a lead?

2) Simon creates a dialogue with imaginary questions asked by imaginary readers, structuring his piece with these questions. Divide the column into parts according to these questions, and notice how the answers overlap.

3) Halfway through, Simon takes us on a tour to the USS *Arizona*, but he saves the name of the ship for four paragraphs. Study the colorful details as he leads us into this scene, almost like a travel brochure. Think about the contrast of this pretty vista with the horrors in the next few paragraphs.

4) The column ends in a flurry of large themes, advice to nations in general. Would you be tempted to write one more paragraph applying these lessons to American foreign policy, just so the reader will not miss your point? Why do you think Simon stopped where he did?

5) Simon received over 1,000 letters in response to this column; he believes it validated what many people felt. How can a columnist perceive what needs validation at any given time? Can columns be seen as articulate statements of what many think? Alexander Pope said, "What oft was thought, but ne'er so well expressed?"

6) Simon expresses well in very simple language. Study how his little words reinforce his large themes.

Citizen's oath gives U.S. story happy ending

OCTOBER 11, 1985

WASHINGTON—Walter Polovchak stood there in the white hot glare of the TV lights, dwarfed by the splendor of the room.

It was one of those huge Senate hearing rooms with glowing wood paneling and green marble, and it had bronze lamps made to look like torches.

Walter put his left hand on the Bible and raised his right hand and swore his allegiance to this country.

Then a black-robed judge said: "Mr. Polovchak, it gives me pleasure to declare you a citizen of the United States of America."

There were tears in Walter's eyes and in the eyes of his sister and in the eyes of his lawyers. I had a little trouble seeing, too.

A reporter nudged me. "You know this kid?" he asked.

It's a long story, I told him.

I first met Walter Polovchak when he was 12. He was a small, handsome, frightened kid, who wanted only one thing: to be free.

Today, he is 18. And a citizen. And his story is the story of America.

His parents left the Soviet Ukraine and came to America with their children in 1980. A few months later, his father decided he wanted to return.

But Walter did not want to go back.

So he asked for political and religious asylum, and the United States granted it.

The Soviet Union howled. The American Civil Liberties Union screamed. And for the next five years, both worked tirelessly to ship him back to the U.S.S.R.

Last week, an op-ed page piece in one of America's leading newspapers accused me of making Walter's case a personal crusade.

Never have I pleaded guilty to an accusation with more pleasure.

Though the legal fighting was complicated, to me it was always a simple story, a simple question: Was America still a place of refuge? Was America still a place where the oppressed could come and be free?

Many people said no. A *New York Times* editorial said those who supported Walter were demonstrating "shallow chauvinism."

As one who has spent a good part of his career criticizing the things wrong with this country, it never seemed to me that praising the liberties offered here was either shallow or chauvinistic.

A few years ago, I was on a plane with Walter. I didn't want to turn the time into an interview. So we just talked.

And I told him that his accent reminded me of my grandfather's, who also left the Ukraine when he was a young man and came to America.

Walter looked at me. "And they did not make him go back?" he asked.

Oh, no, I said. He stayed and became a citizen.

"And your parents, they are here? Here in America?" he asked.

Yes, I said. Sure.

He looked out the window for a moment, out to where America was spread beneath him.

"They are very lucky," he said quietly. "You are all very lucky."

He didn't know the half of it. We are all so lucky in this country we have forgotten how lucky we are.

For five years, the court battle raged.

Walter's lawyers, Julian Kulas of Chicago and Henry Mark Holzer of New York, fought with a tenacity that surprised their opponents.

Now, it is over. Walter turned 18 last week. And since he is officially an adult, there is no question of his being sent back.

He is living in Chicago, finishing high school and planning for college. But he flew to Washington this week for a big citizenship ceremony. Before it began, he showed me a cable his father had recently sent him from the Ukraine:

"Dear Son, Walter,

"Greeting you on your birthday is your father, mother, brother, and sister. We wish you the best in your life."

To me, this does not sound like the words of an angry man. I think they are the words of a man more happy for his son than he is allowed to say.

I asked Walter if he loved his parents.

"I could never say I do not love them," he said. "I am a son and they are my parents and definitely I love them.

"I wanted only to live in the country I loved. To live in the U.S.A. If they come to U.S.A., we will be together again."

I asked him if he had ever thought he would lose, if he had ever thought he would be handcuffed and taken on a plane to the Soviet Union.

"The fear was deep inside me," he said. "That was the hardest. In the beginning, I spoke no English. I had no friends. There was only the fear. The fear I would have to go back."

So why didn't you just go back? It would have been easier.

"I would have lost America," he said. "And I could not do that."

Before he took his oath of citizenship, Walter made a short speech before the TV cameras. He ended it by saying, "I know many, many people take freedom for granted. But I never will."

Then from the middle of the crowd of spectators, a man began to sing "God Bless America." And the crowd took it up and everyone sang it.

It was one of the corniest things I had ever witnessed. And one of the most beautiful.

When it was all over, they presented America's newest citizen with a big birthday cake. And he did something he hasn't done much in the last five years: he smiled.

I said his story was the story of America and it is.

But this week I found out something I was never sure of: the story has a happy ending.

Welcome home, Walter.

Observations and questions

1) Simon wrote a long series of columns over a period of six years about Walter Polovchak. In such a continuing series, how can columnists avoid taking knowledge on the part of the reader for granted? Can they even assume that readers read the latest column?

2) Simon calls this piece "a column conveying emotion more than argument." Study how much argument he uses to buttress his emotions.

3) Close to the end ("I asked him..."), Simon shows himself asking a question, whereas reporters try to keep themselves out of their stories. Does this prohibition apply to columnists? Should we even apply it strictly to news stories?

4) Walter, the Russian immigrant, speaks perfect English in this column. Would you be tempted to let a little dialect slip through in his speech, just for color or verisimilitude?

5) Simon tells us that he is "just corny about certain subjects," about "aspects of the American dream." Six paragraphs from the end, he admits the corn, even flaunts it. Think about the risks and benefits of such openness.

6) The column ends rather obliquely. What does Simon mean by this statement: "But this week I found out something I was never sure of: the story has a happy ending."?

Split d'accord: when city folks go oh-so woodsy

OCTOBER 21, 1985

My neighbors are talking about wood.

No. It is worse than that.

They are not only talking about wood. They are buying it and cutting it up and stacking it.

Usually they talk normally. But when they get around wood, they begin speaking in strange accents.

"Yup, split me 'bout a cord, cord 'n' a half," said a neighbor. "Good 'n' seasoned. Make a mighty fine fire, come first frost."

"You grew up in Queens," I told him. "And you went to UCLA. Where did that accent come from? Did you buy it with the wood?"

He said something about me not getting in the spirit of things. Then he spat on his hands, rubbed them together, and grabbed his ax.

I still speak to this neighbor. I just don't shake hands with him anymore.

For years I lived only in apartment buildings and condos. None had a fireplace. The residents never talked about wood.

We talked about sensible things—silverfish, roaches, noisy neighbors—and how to kill all three.

Then, a few months ago, I rented a house. The first thing I noticed was a large hole in the living room that led up through the roof.

I was about to call the housing authorities when one of the movers told me it was a fireplace and a chimney.

"They are considered desirable," he said.

I can't think why. For the past few weeks, strange, battered pickup trucks with high, slatted sides have been driving through the neighborhood.

In the front seat there are usually two burly guys, with squashed baseball caps and flannel shirts, with the sleeves rolled up to reveal tattoos that say, "America—Love It or I'll Kill You."

In the back of the truck there are great stacks of wood, and sometimes there will be a kid sitting on top playing a banjo.

I figured either these guys were selling wood, or they were here to shoot *Deliverance II*.

The truck will slowly cruise the street as one guy hops out and goes from door to door.

In apartment buildings nobody goes from door to door. Somebody comes to your door in an apartment building and you yell, "Get away from that door! I got a gun!"

So I have been hiding from the wood men. But my neighbors welcome them. And some buy huge stumps that they then bust up in their driveways with sledgehammers and wedges and axes.

Normal human beings who just last week were wondering whether a Pomerol or a Margaux went best with squab are now grunting and sweating and whacking at wood.

And when they are done, they stack the wood out where everyone can see it. One guy has built a little crib for his wood. Another has removed his Weber and has filled his deck with wood.

Decades ago, our forefathers used wood for heat and survival. Now it is a status symbol, like having a BMW in the driveway.

Last week I was caught outside when the wood truck came up the street. I ran into the house, but the wood men had seen me.

One rang the doorbell.

"I've got a gun!" I screamed.

"Ah lahk guns," he said. "You show me yourn, and Ah'll show you mahn."

I opened the door a crack.

"Wood," the guy said.

I sighed. I gave up. I told him I would buy wood.

"Come on then," he said, leading me to the truck.

I hate pretending to know about things I don't know anything about.

That's why I hate buying cars. The salesman always insists I look under the hood, and I look under there and say something like, "Well now, *that's* an engine."

So I looked at the guy's wood.

"It's very...woody," I told him.

"Oak and maple," he said. "Seasoned right good."

I kept looking at the wood. It could have been bamboo and seasoned with salt and pepper, for all I knew.

"Great!" I said. "I'll take 5 pounds."

He took off his cap and scratched his head. And explained that wood was not sold by the pound but by the rack or the cord.

I kept nodding as if I knew what the hell he was talking about. He sold me a cord for $105.

I figured it out. At those prices the Arabs missed their bet. They should have gone into wood, not oil.

But he said the price included stacking, which he proceeded to do. I watched him from the porch and tried to make conversation.

"I like my beer in longnecks, don't you?" I said.

He kept stacking.

"Ever kill a man in Texas?" I asked.

He kept stacking.

"Well, which is best with squab?" I asked. "A Pomerol or a Margaux?"

He took off his cap and wiped his forehead.

"Wahl, it really don't make me no never mind," he said, "but Ah'd go with a Cote du Rhone or mebbe even a Nuit St.-Georges—less'n you think that'd be a mite sassy."

When he was done he thanked me and said he would be back at midwinter to see if I needed another cord.

Now, every night, I sit in front of my fireplace and watch my wood.

And I can hardly wait for midwinter.

Because when he comes back, I'm going to ask him how to light the stuff.

Observations and questions

1) Simon plays Woody Allen in this piece. With whom does the reader identify, the Yuppie nerd or the woodsman? Or both?

2) This piece turns on a series of "zingers." Notice how Simon has spaced them to allow set-up time for each.

3) The speaker tells us that "normal human beings" discuss "whether a Pomerol or a Margaux went best with squab." When did you last discuss Pomerol or Margaux or squab? Who then are the "normal human beings" here?

4) The narrator advises us that "somebody comes to your door in an apartment building and you yell, 'Get away from that door! I got a gun!'" You can take the boy out of Chicago, but you can't take Chicago out of the boy.

5) The woodsman says, "Ah lahk guns....You show me yourn, and Ah'll show you mahn," borrowing the line from "Doctor," the children's game where boys and girls offer to exchange looks at their private parts. Simon plays games with macho pretenses in this simple exchange.

6) Why do we expect close adherence to truth in newswriting, but allow overt fiction in columns? How can the reader tell that this column is not to be taken at face value?

7) Which *does* go better with squab, a Pomerol or a Margaux?

A conversation with
Roger Simon

DON FRY: Since you won the ASNE award in 1984, you've moved from Chicago to Baltimore. What's it like having to learn a new town?

ROGER SIMON: It turned out to be challenging, but somewhat easier than I thought. All towns are different, but in a lot of basic ways, people are the same. It wasn't like going to the dark side of the moon. It's just a matter of learning new streets and getting to go out and talk to people. You do a lot of listening in the beginning rather than a lot of talking, which is probably good for a columnist anyway. (Laughter)

Let's talk about Walter Polovchak, the teenager who refused to go back to Russia with his parents. That's an old Chicago concern of yours, isn't it?

That was probably one of the longest-running stories I have ever done, in terms of the most columns.

What were you trying to do in this column?

This was a very emotional piece. Although there are a few paragraphs in there trying to sum up the issue, this piece describes an emotional moment.

You said that "his story is the story of America."

Well, here was a person who had fled conditions and oppression elsewhere, sometimes just less economic opportunity, to come to the land of

unlimited freedoms and unlimited opportunities.
And if that's not the story of America, what is?

This piece is about both of us. I'm talking
about a journey that we both took together,
Walter and I. It was one of those rare pieces when
I enter the column in very explicit ways,
although I like to think that columnists are in
every column. Sometimes it's explicit, sometimes
it's implicit.

**All through the column you're leading him
along. You explicitly show yourself as the
questioner.**

Right. Reporters and columnists go to great and
unnecessary lengths to disguise the fact that they
ask questions. We're all taught quite properly
that we're not part of the story. And for news
stories I think that's a fine rule. However, some
columnists forget that they can break that rule,
and that there are no rules. Communication
seems to me to be the only basic rule. And rather
than going through intricate sentence structures
to disguise the fact that you are a human being
asking another human being a question, why
don't you just repeat the question?

**The answer makes more sense if you can see
the question.**

Exactly. And it's fairer, because you can see exactly what the person was asked and exactly how
he replied, rather than having this person just
expound as if you walked into a room and he
started babbling.

**I notice that Walter speaks perfect English.
Do you clean things up a little, take out
dialect, grammar problems, and so forth?**

I try to do that as little as possible. You can read
through all my pieces on Walter and see his
English improve over the years, and it has im-

proved. Walter has attended an American high school and done numerous interviews by now. The clause "The fear was deep inside me," is somewhat stilted and very much the way Walter talks.

That ceremony was a big moment for both of you.

It was. I remember one of the most valuable lessons I ever learned was on a sign posted on the bulletin board of my first journalism class. It was a headline that said, "Don't get excited by excitement." If you're a reporter covering an exciting event, and you get overwhelmed with emotion, either happy or sad, you probably won't be able to do your job. As a columnist, you have to temper that normally good advice every now and then. In the case of the Polovchak piece, I was happy I did temper it, happy that I let a little emotion show.

I think you let a lot of emotion show. In fact, I think you really let your hair down. Listen to this: "Then from the middle of the crowd of spectators, a man began to sing 'God Bless America.' And the crowd took it up and everyone sang it. It was one of the corniest things I had ever witnessed. And one of the most beautiful." You're really naked there.

One of the hardest things for a columnist to face in his early years is the fact that a lot of the people you see have just read some of the most private, intimate thoughts which you have voluntarily decided to share. And sometimes you draw back, and some columnists get very isolated for that reason and cut down on human contact. But I don't want to be isolated from people. I try not to be afraid of showing emotion if the emotion is sincerely felt. If it's sincerely felt, it's the truth, and we're in the truth business. I am, as anyone knows who's read my column for a period of time, just corny about certain subjects, especially about aspects of the American dream. I am a child of immigrants who made the same journey that Walter made, and not to let that show is not to let people know where the emotions come from.

How did you get the idea for the Nagasaki piece?

This was one of those rare pieces resulting from an outside suggestion, where a reader calls and says, "Why don't you write about X?" The ratio of calls that turn into columns is maybe 20-to-1 or even 100-to-1. Newspaper columns validate opinions that people already hold. Many times you'll get letters where people say, "I've felt that all my life. And I'm glad you said it." This was a case where I got two or three phone calls in one morning, following a lot of TV specials on Hiroshima and Nagasaki.

A woman called and said, "I'm not anti-Japanese. I consider myself a liberal. But I just think we've gone too far. Certainly we had a reason. Doesn't that count for anything?" I had seen the interview with Premier Nakasone on TV, and it just crystallized into a piece based on one very simple theme: this war was conducted for a reason, and we have to examine the historical context of what we did.

I like the way you set up your argument. You say, "Let us ask ourselves what we were doing in World War II and whom we were fighting." And that question generates the next whole part leading into Nakasone.

Right. I like the technique of asking the reader to ask himself a question. Because that's how I come to opinions.

You think that way?

Yes, and it often shows up in the column. Also, I try to raise the questions that the other side might raise, and not just straw men.

Richard Aregood, who won the prize for editorials last year, says he feels an obligation to represent different viewpoints in the society. So he has to ask himself the questions others would ask.

Yes, I think that's true. Fairness also requires that if you know a good argument against your position, you should raise it and address it.

But, Roger, remember the disease of editorial writers: "on the one hand, on the other hand." Nobody would accuse you of being wishy-washy, but how do you avoid that?

I only wrote editorials for a few weeks once to fill in at the *Sun-Times*. I wrote one reversing a long-held editorial opinion of 40 years, so I was relieved of that odious position. I call it the "paralysis of gray."

The paralysis of gray?

The paralysis of shades of gray. You realize that there are arguments for and against everything. You can get into the mind set of seeing so much on both sides that you're reduced to paralysis. I heard of a professional football coach who worried about what he called "the paralysis of analysis." He doesn't want his quarterback out there peering over the center and analyzing so much he can't throw the ball. Not everything is shades of gray. There are shades of truth and shades of falsity. But some things are right, and some things are wrong.

Is there a difference in fairness for columns and fairness for news stories?

I think both have to be fair. It's fair to hold everything in the paper to the same standards of truth, while keeping in mind that an editor should run a column whose opinion he does not necessarily agree with. Not all editors are capable of that, by the way. Not all editors like columnists, and not all columnists like editors. I've been fortunate to find editors who say, "Well, I don't agree with it, but you're writing the column."

If you raise the counter-issues, you should be able to argue effectively against them. You don't have to be paralyzed by doing "on the one hand and on the other hand." You should still be able to get to your central point. If you can't, you probably should not write the piece.

I'm struck by the way you lead up to the USS *Arizona*. You move from Nakasone with the suggestion that "all those reporters who went to Hiroshima this week should have made one little stopover first." And you give three paragraphs of description before you name the *Arizona* and three more before you mention the 1,100 dead. That's a long dangle for the reader.

Yes, and it's a purposeful dangle. (Laughter) I wanted them to feel the place and the moment before the punchline obscured it. It's going to ring a lot of bells with readers anyway. Pearl Harbor was that moment by which they measured events in their lives, just as for a different generation, it was the death of Kennedy.

Everybody has a personal view of the *Arizona*. We've seen pictures. If you just mention it, it's going to call up our own view. But you very carefully select the details that we're going to remember.

In a less obvious way, I am weaving in my emotional reaction to the *Arizona*, what stuck in my mind: the darting fishes, the clear water, the fact, to me the overwhelming fact, that the men are still trapped below there.

Let's look at your ending: "But there is another lesson to Hiroshima and Nagasaki. One that is being forgotten. Nations that start wars eventually have to pay a price for them. And the price is often high." Is that the theme of the piece?

That's one of the themes of the piece. You would have to be a rock head not to realize this applies to more than just Japan. And I don't have to say, "This goes for a lot of other countries, too, including ourselves, if you just look back at our own history." You have to give the readers some credit. Anyone who buys a newspaper is an intelligent person by definition.

What sort of response did you get, angry letters?

It was the largest mail response column I had gotten in five years. There were less than five hostile letters out of more than a thousand.

More than a thousand letters?

Yes, more than a thousand letters. And it pushed a button that was really out there, and I knew it was going to push that button. This was an example of the issue being out there, and a columnist expressing something that was widely felt. People wanted that validation. They wanted to see it expressed. That's when they believe the columnist is acting for them as their representative.

Let's move to the firewood piece. When you're writing satire and humor, what's the role of fiction? How much can you exaggerate? How much can you make up?

Oh, I think you can do imaginary dialogue, if it's clearly a satirical piece and the images are broad enough. I don't think Art Buchwald has to worry that people are going to confuse his characters with reality.

Is any of this imaginary?

Oh, sure. I did talk to a wood salesman, but there was no wood salesman beating on the door, saying, "You get your gun, I'll get mine."

Did your wood salesman have an opinion on wine?

No, but when I'm bringing up a cultural stereotype, I like to reverse it. Up to this point, you think this guy is a hillbilly because I paint him that way.

Particularly quoting him in dialect.

Right. But while we've all been reading through these paragraphs and thinking this guy is dumb, in fact he's a wine connoisseur. And that's not just meant to be humorous. It also shows that stereotypes and dialect don't always tell you what you think they tell you about a person.

You say your column gives you the freedom to put yourself into the story. Can you talk about how you create yourself as a character, particularly in this piece?

Yes. When I create myself as a character, invariably I am the butt of the humor. I am not just the victim, but usually the straight man. And the other guy gets the good lines and gets to make fun of me. It's more fun to exploit your own foibles that people either identify with, or say, "He's a bigger jerk than I am."

You play Woody Allen. It's essentially like his early movies, a series of zingers centering around himself as a character.

Columns work on many levels, especially humor columns. Before I wrote the piece, I looked up in wine columns what would be accurate wines. I didn't have to. I could have made up wine names. And most people who don't know anything about the wines would have gotten the joke anyway. But I think it's an added benefit for people who really understand something about wine to get the joke on yet another level. And so even the humor does not free you from the obligation to do real reporting and research sometimes.

Let's talk about the MOVE piece. As a Baltimore columnist, why were you reporting in Philadelphia?

I was in the newsroom, and the managing editor said to our national reporter sitting next to me, "John, I think you ought to go there." And he turned to me and said, "If you want to go, I think it'd be a good story." And I said, "Yeah, sure. Great." So we drove up together.

How did you organize your reporting?

The first decision is, are you going to be an independent gatherer of information? Answer: yes, if you can do it, do it. Two, do you walk the streets and soak up mood and color like a sponge, and then squeeze yourself out onto the keyboard later? Well, yes. But why not go out and do the interviews yourself? Some papers are worried about what is called "big-footing." If you send a columnist out, is he just going to step on the reporters?

Do you ever get your information from the reporter instead of first hand?

Sure, sometimes, but not in this case. If both people know they've got their stories and suppress their egos, you can work cooperatively. And many times you get a reporter saying, "Hey, this would be a great interview for you across the room."

How did you find this family?

There was a church that was being used as a center to provide cots, and clothing was being gathered for the people who had been burned out. I found Anthony's grandmother first, and then she led me to Anthony. Anthony sort of faded in and faded out, just wandering around that church basement.

You don't stick with Anthony all the way through. You bring in other characters because Anthony can't tell you the whole story.

Precisely. You could do the piece just from Anthony's point of view, but Anthony, as you said, does not know the whole narrative. He was not there for all of it. He does not have the viewpoint of his grandmother.

You did a lot of reporting for this column.

I would have done as much reporting as I could, although sometimes pieces become cumbersome because of that. You gather all the information, and you decide what not to use later.

Talk for a minute about reporting for a column.

There are only two elements to a column: having something to say and saying it well. The best kind of column tries to put them together. And sometimes having something to say means that you've done a lot of reporting, but not always.

I didn't do any independent research on the Pearl Harbor column, and that's fine. But I don't like that as a steady diet. I would prefer to do reporting. All my background is reporting. It's where I came from.

It also keeps your mind working. How did you organize all your materials?

I have left the church basement for the last time. And I know I'm ready to go write the piece. So I get into my car, which gave me a reasonable amount of quiet. But the front seat was too hot and uncomfortable, so I did it standing up outside. And I'm just looking at my notebook, flipping the pages. I know already that Anthony is going to be my centerpiece.

Do you mark the pages as you go through them?

Yes, when I have the leisure and the luxury, I do it with a red felt-tip pen. In this case, when I don't carry red felt-tip pens with me, I mark the right-hand edge of the paper with double slashes, sometimes a star, two stars. Underlining is usually too clumsy. I mark quotes I don't want to miss, because that's the easiest thing to do.

Okay, you've marked up everything. Then what?

Marked up everything and a quick read through the notes, we're talking about probably less than five minutes. How I begin the piece is very, very important to me, because everything flows from beginning to end. All columns have to start somewhere, and where they start is not always obvious. Sometimes you put shackles on yourself and write in only one style, only one approach. But to me, the joy of writing a column is to be able to use any number of styles, any number of approaches, and to challenge yourself on how you're going to do it.

How did you get from marked-up notebook to the first words?

I decide what my lead is going to be, plunge in and try to do a good middle. Now sometimes I will not be able to get a beginning that I like, and I will dispense with it. Usually in pieces done on deadline, you don't have the luxury of not having a beginning. With computers it's easier to put a new top on a story. But sometimes I will dispense with the beginning and start with what I know is going to be the fourth or fifth or sixth paragraph, and get to the end, and then go back and say, "What's the beginning to this piece?" Sometimes I have switched endings for beginnings.

Some of your endings and beginnings could be switched.

Yes, some of them have been switched. (Laughter)

How long did it take to write the piece?

The whole piece was done in maybe 45 minutes tops, through the miracle of electronics on a Radio Shack Model 100 lap computer on the roof of my car while I was standing there typing it. By being able to write quickly when you need to, you can work the story longer. There's no advantage in writing faster just for the sake of writing fast. If you have three hours and you can do better in three hours, take three hours. But by writing fast you can stay with the story longer.

So you're standing up beside the car, typing on a lap computer on the roof.

It's a hot day out there. And I'm typing away. Every now and then people come up to me, kids in the neighborhood, and say, "What are you doing, man?" A cop asks, "What is that? Is that one of those computers?" "Yeah, it's one of those...." I answer their questions, but no one hassles me, which is fortunate. You can easily conceive of circumstances where you might be locking yourself in the car and doing the piece.

Amazing.

Let me digress a minute, if you will. Anthony delivers a line that's almost too good.

I know which one: "It was more than a house. It was a home." I wrote beside that line: "A kid said this?"

Exactly. That's what my editor said, and my wife, "Did a kid say this?" Columnists hear enough speech so they know how people will react. And I knew that some people would read that and say, "Is the columnist improving the quote, faking the quote in a very obvious way?" And so I had the choice of leaving it out, and I was about to. And then I thought to myself, "I'm changing reality here. I'm afraid that a kid said something too bright, and people will think that I faked it. I was there. The kid said it. I'm going to print it." This was obviously a snap judgment, made standing up outside, typing on the top of my car.

But that's what he said: "It was more than a house. It was a home."

Exactly. Maybe someone had repeated it to him earlier. Maybe he had heard it on TV. Maybe he's just a bright kid, which we shouldn't rule out. And what also hit me was the fact that he's a young, black kid. Young black kids do say bright things. Why should I be afraid of letting him say it?

Anthony says some terrific things. You must have asked good questions.

All of us were weary, me, them, everyone. And you think about what has become the buzzword now, "the pornography of grief," and how far you can press people to describe the terrible moments of their lives. I tried to stay on what I thought was the fair and tasteful side of it, while still trying to tell what happened.

Let me test your ending against that statement. This is Anthony talking about his dead cat: " 'And so I left her. I left Mittens. I left food for her and water. But I left her. She was 6.' He had been acting very brave and very adult, answering my questions. But now he was just a kid again and his lower lip trembled. 'They said we were coming back,' he said. 'And so I left Mittens. But they said we would be back in 24 hours. They said it would be all right. They did. They said. They promised.' "
Tell me about that ending.

Again, you make the judgment. Some people are going to read that and say, "That's just a sob story." Some might say that's delving too far into the kid's emotions. Obviously, I don't think it's either, or I wouldn't have written it. He is talking about an emotional moment in his life. He has dealt with it, and he'll get over it.

I take it as a hopeful touch. I don't think you want to end this story in despair.

Right. Life did go on. Obviously I'm going to go back and do a follow-up on Anthony and his new home and perhaps his new kitten.

I'm ready to read that.

I'm ready to write it.

Jonathan Freedman
Editorial Writing

JONATHAN FREEDMAN, 36, was born in Rochester, Minnesota, and grew up in Denver. He was graduated from Columbia University in 1972 cum laude and Phi Beta Kappa. After traveling on the Cornell Woolrich Writing Award, he joined the Associated Press in Sao Paulo and Rio de Janeiro, Brazil. From 1976 to 1981, he free-lanced, writing fiction as well as columns for *The New York Times*, the *Chicago Tribune*, and the San Francisco *Examiner*. He published one volume of short fiction, entitled *The Man Who'd Bounce the World*, which he also illustrated. He joined the San Diego *Tribune* in 1981 as an editorial writer and became a Pulitzer Prize finalist in 1983 and 1984.

Abolish American apartheid

MAY 9, 1985

They live in polluted squatter camps. They toil in factories by day, but at night they are hunted like animals. They produce the crops, but they are not permitted to own the land. They serve in homes but sleep in shacks. They have no rights, no representation in government, no freedom of speech in a land which is a democracy. If they are passive and do their work, they are tolerated by the white elite. But if they protest, they are fired and returned to their homelands. Periodically the owners of the land become appalled by the squatters and bulldoze the camps. Their children, born far from their homelands, are strangers in the new land and strangers in their fathers' land. Generations live in a separate society, serving the main society, but denied its rights and privileges.

These victims of apartheid are not thousands of miles away in South Africa, but here in America—in San Diego. We call them illegal aliens, but their status and their living conditions are not that different from the blacks of Soweto.

Americans are justly incensed by the horrors of apartheid in South Africa. But students protesting against apartheid at the University of California at San Diego are blind to the system of illegal alien farm labor in San Diego County. Concerned Americans raising money to boycott South Africa are unaware that the waiters and busboys serving them at fund-raisers are illegal aliens. The joggers who eat fresh strawberries at the roadside avert their heads from the field workers stooping in the sun, who live in the squatter camps of California.

South African apartheid is evil, a system which dooms that land to despair and bloodshed.

But South Africa is at least honest about its separate and unequal society. America is not. An estimated 6 million to 12 million illegal aliens live in this country, picking our crops, working in our sweatshops, an invisible minority.

Yes, many are better off economically than their brothers in their distant villages. So also the blacks in Soweto are better off than those in the impoverished homelands. But the illegal aliens are not free. They live in constant fear of being caught in the wrong place and deported. They cannot, in many places, go to a bus station or eat in a restaurant without being detected and deported.

And yet they are working for the benefit of employers who know they are illegal, know they have no rights, and exploit them.

Many Americans want to disinvest from firms doing business with South Africa. But we do not disinvest from farms and factories and restaurants and hotels that hire illegal aliens in America. We maintain a system by which it is legal to hire illegal aliens but illegal for them to work here, a system equal in hypocrisy to the pass laws of South Africa.

Americans look the other way when dealing with their own system of apartheid. And Congress, by its repeated deadlock, has ratified the system of illegal immigration and illegal labor. Some sing of the virtues of illegal labor for the United States economy. They resemble the Afrikaaner apologists for apartheid who turn up at newspapers, arguing the justice of their system, or their predecessors in the American South, the gentlemanly apologists for that benign, Bible-recognized institution, slavery.

Apartheid is racist wherever it exists. It is inhuman in South Africa and inhuman in southern California. It destroys the moral fabric of our society and leaves a legacy of discrimination and suffering.

But we are blind to it. We point our finger at the South Africans and feel self-satisfied at our

enlightened society. While the waiters bring us
fresh strawberries picked by illegal aliens living
in ravines and hootches. Here. Today.

We have no direct power to halt apartheid in
South Africa. But we can and must stop illegal
immigration and exploitation here. We must
make it illegal for employers to hire illegal
aliens. We must offer amnesty to aliens, to bring
them out of hiding. We must abolish apartheid
in America.

Observations and questions

1) The first nine sentences use the pronouns "they" or "their" 15 times. Study this sequence in terms of rhythm produced by repetition. Does such repetition grab readers or bore them?

2) Freedman gets to the news peg in the third paragraph, students protesting apartheid. Would you prefer to dive into this editorial with a short lead using the peg? What would you gain and lose?

3) Notice the simplicity of Freedman's sentences, even the longer ones, and the alternation of long and short sentences.

4) In paragraph four, Freedman spins the paradox of South Africa as less hypocritical than America in its treatment of suppressed people. Does the harshness of this judgment undermine its potentially useful shock value?

5) In the latter part of the editorial, Freedman switches pronouns from "they" to "we." Think out all the applications of this "we" from the reader's point of view. Put ungrammatically, who is "we?"

Police Canyon of the Dead

JUNE 17, 1985

Colinia Libertad, one of Tijuana's poorest neighborhoods, is the gateway to America for thousands of illegal aliens. They ride buses for days from their impoverished villages in the interior of Mexico and from Central America, reaching Tijuana exhausted but hopeful. Here is the entrance to El Norte, where jobs await them in farms and hotels and sweatshops. Jobs that pay in a week what they can earn in months at home. Jobs that provide food for their families remaining behind in villages named for Christian saints and pre-Columbian gods, villages cursed by hunger and disease.

But before they can reach those jobs, the illegal aliens must cross the Canyon of the Dead, *El Canon de los Muertos*. It is a ravine running parallel to the international boundary, on U.S. territory, less than a mile east of the most heavily used border gate in the world. The aliens who enter America with visas enter a world of rights and freedoms.

But the way through the Canyon of the Dead is the path to an illegal world, of manhunts and attacks by bandits, of ghettos and exploitation. An apartheid world without rights or freedoms for illegal aliens working in the land of liberty.

The aliens are called *pollos*—chickens—but they show great courage in crossing the border. The physical danger is not from the Border Patrol, which generally avoids violent encounters, but from the bandits who attack and rob and rape and sometimes kill the *pollos* crossing the canyon named for the bodies found in its depths. The bandits, called *asalto-pollos*, come from both sides of the border. But most fade into Colonia Libertad when dawn comes and the

Border Patrol counts up its apprehensions and the successful *pollos* make their way north and the victims crawl out of the no-man's-land or remain face down in the dust.

During the day, hundreds of *pollos* gather openly at a place called the "soccer field," on U.S. territory, overlooking the canyon. The ground is covered with broken glass and there are remains of a bloody towel, an abandoned suitcase. Three taco vendors shaded by umbrellas serve food to *pollos* who may not eat again for days before reaching hiding places in America. Men laugh as a woman passes, joking, "Who'll get her tonight?" She flinches and walks on, clutching her small bag. A sunburned man says he's been caught six times in five days by the Border Patrol, but he's waiting to try again. A peasant husband and his wife, with braided hair, clutch two infant daughters wearing ruffled Sunday dresses and white shoes. They hope that the children will protect them from the *asalto-pollos*.

The sun lowers above the Pacific. A Border Patrol van glints on the bluff. A dozen *pollos* head together down the canyon. *Asalto-pollos* follow them, their shadows moving like daggers. Over the hill, people wait blithely in cars to cross the border legally, oblivious to the nightmare unfolding in the Canyon of the Dead.

The Americans who opposed the Simpson-Mazzoli immigration reform bill for civil-rights reasons should come to the soccer field and explain to the *pollos* waiting to cross the Canyon of the Dead that this is better than a guest-worker program that would give them visas to cross legally. The Mexicans who protest the mistreatment of illegal aliens in the United States should explain why the Mexican police do nothing to halt the *asalto-pollos*.

The *pollos* are forsaken by both countries, preyed on by Mexicans and Americans. Yet they plant the fields of California, serve food to our tourists, care for children in our homes. They also send remittances back to their families, giving their countries millions of dollars of revenues.

If the United States needs foreigners' labor, it must rewrite its immigration laws to treat them like human beings. If Mexico values its poorest emigrants, it should police its side of the border, as the San Diego police now patrols our side.

As long as this tragedy is allowed to continue night after night, year after year, to thousands of people whose crime is to cross the border illegally to feed their families, the symbol of American immigration is not the Statue of Liberty, but the Canyon of the Dead.

Observations and questions

1) Freedman opens his editorial with the phrase, "gateway to America." Notice how this cliche colors the horrors that come later, emphasized by the repetition of "America" and the final image of the Statue of Liberty.

2) The journeyers begin as "aliens," then become "*pollos*," and in the last two paragraphs become "human beings," and finally "people." Freedman's nouns show us the transformation of a class of people into animals; then he shows us how we should regard them.

3) Read the last sentence in paragraph four ("But most...dust."). Freedman explained this sentence to me in terms of a camera panning in a circle. Notice the effect of ending with the word "dust."

4) Study the language of paragraph six ("The sun....Dead."). Discuss how Freedman uses the connotations of simple words to conjure up a sinister scene and the irony of unconscious tourists.

5) Good editorials aim at the general reader, but their final call for action targets specific people who can effect change. Who is the target audience at the end of this editorial?

The silent scream of no-care babies

OCTOBER 21, 1985

The premature infant writhes in a maze of tubes, her mouth contorted in a scream. But there is an eerie silence in the intensive-care nursery. The baby, born with defective heart and kidneys, is on a respirator. A tube bypasses her larynx, muffling her cry.

This is the silent scream of a baby whose mother received no prenatal care. It is not heard in the nursery. It is not heard in the hospital administration. It is not heard in the county or state health departments.

It is not heard because we don't want to look into that crib and see that child born to suffering.

We don't want to see the mother sick with anemia because she didn't receive proper nutrition.

We don't want to see the $75,000 hospital bill for the baby who survives two months in intensive care. And we don't want to see the little coffin of the baby who didn't survive.

No, we want to see the healthy pink babies in the well-baby nursery. We want to look at the happy parents and hear the healthy cries of hunger—cries that can be answered with a feeding, not an intravenous tube.

We want to think that we are doing everything we can to give babies of all colors and backgrounds an equal start in life.

But we are not giving them an equal start. Some are doomed even before they are born, because their mothers do not get prenatal care.

We have an excellent public program to give proper care to mothers and babies. It is called the Comprehensive Perinatal Program of San Diego County. It costs $1,150—$250 from the patient and $900 from the state. The program provides total prenatal medical care, nutrition and counseling, delivery of the baby, postpartum care, and a well-baby checkup. The program is effective in reducing the chance of low birth weight, premature birth, and other health problems.

The number of women who can participate in the progam is limited by a lack of state funds and by a shortage of hospital beds at UCSD Medical Center, which is the only participating hospital. Last year, the program turned away 1,200 women. This year, it expects to turn away 1,600, because of an increasing number of women who arrive at the hospital in labor, without previous contact with the hospital, and occupy maternity beds that otherwise would be available for the perinatal program.

Many of the women who want prenatal care but are turned away go on to deliver healthy babies. But a high proportion of them have complications that could have been avoided. Complications are enormously expensive. And because many of these mothers don't have private health insurance, the bill will be paid by society.

The UCSD Department of Reproductive Medicine sponsored a comparative study of mothers and babies who received prenatal care in San Diego and those who received no prenatal care. It shows the average hospital cost was about $2,500 higher for those who received no prenatal care. That's more than twice what it would have cost to put the same women in the program. And that doesn't even begin to count the human suffering, or the toll of medical and social services which society will have to pay for the maintenance of sick babies who become handicapped adults.

The program has sought maternity beds in other hospitals. So far, no other hospital has stepped forward to take its share of patients. This is unfortunate. There is a surplus of maternity beds in this county. But many hospitals prefer not to have needy patients, with a higher incidence of complications. State funding for the care of such patients is less than the cost to the hospital. With the cost pinch, the hospitals say they can't afford the program.

The state must provide more funding for prenatal care in San Diego, which is carrying a heavy burden because of the large illegal alien population here. The Hospital Council and the Medical Society should join together to encourage doctors and hospitals to care for needy mothers through this program. And private charities and individuals could contribute funds. All mothers in San Diego who want prenatal care should be given access to it. It is not morally defensible or economically sane to deny prenatal care to women who request it—and to doom defenseless children.

The silent scream of no-care infants must be answered with funds for prenatal care and with desperately needed maternity beds for needy patients. San Diego must show that it cares for the no-cares.

Observations and questions

1) Freedman borrowed the phrase "silent scream" from the anti-abortion movie of the same title. Does this very loaded phrase risk distracting the reader into thinking about abortion in an editorial about prenatal care? Or does it raise the alternative of abortion without talking about abortion?

2) The first six paragraphs interplay vision and hearing, mostly by denying sound and sight ("it is not heard," "we don't want to see"). Study the pounding repetition of this section. Do you find it overdone? What would happen if we moved it to the end?

3) Notice the use of the pronoun "we" in paragraphs four through nine. I named this device "the implicating we," and Freedman calls it "the democratic we." Think about these two terms in the light of the editorialist's function to bring about action.

4) Identify all the numbers in this editorial. Think about how to rewrite it with a more economic and governmental focus, with less emotion at the top. Would the second version prove more effective with certain audiences?

5) In the final sentence of the penultimate paragraph, Freedman argues on two grounds: "morally defensible or economically sane." Freedman struggled over the two words "defensible" and "sane." What other terms could he have used? Keep the surrounding sentences in mind.

6) Freedman's kicker is a *tour de force* of wordplay. Does such play help cement his point, or is it merely decorative?

Bathhouse cubicles of death

DECEMBER 14, 1985

A fire broke out in a cubicle of a gay bathhouse downtown at 8:25 a.m. on Saturday, Nov. 30. When the Fire Department reached the scene, firemen found a man clothed in a towel hanging outside a window. Inside was a maze, painted black, lit with dim colored light bulbs. There were about 30 cubicles. In a room called "the brig" there was a leather hammock with chains, manacles, and wrist bindings. Walls were covered with pictures of nude models wearing hats of sailors and Marines.

The bathhouse clients were rescued. The fire was extinguished and the bathhouse has been closed, its masonry exterior hiding what went on inside.

But questions about the safety of bathhouses remain. Fire is only one danger. Bathhouses are also a breeding ground of the deadly AIDS virus. While most Americans agree that everything should be done to help treat AIDS victims and to take precautions to slow the spread of the fatal virus, there is sharp disagreement over what to do about bathhouses. Public health physicians point to the danger of bathhouses breeding AIDS, where anonymous multi-partner sex passes on the virus.

The San Francisco Health Department tried to close the bathhouses. But owners protested civil rights infringements and won. The bathhouses remain open, though they are monitored.

In Los Angeles, the leaders of the gay community advocated the closing of bathhouses. The Los Angeles County Board of Supervisors ordered bathhouse owners to prevent high-risk sex from going on, or be shut down.

New York state amended the sanitary code to require local health officials to close facilities where high-risk sex goes on. New York Mayor Koch said the restriction threatened civil rights and asked bathhouse owners to prohibit high-risk sex voluntarily. A gay bar was closed by the authorities, but as far as we can determine, no gay bathhouses have been closed permanently in San Francisco, Los Angeles, or New York City.

In San Diego, where AIDS fatalities are doubling each year, three gay bathhouses remain open. The oldest of the three is across from the county Administration Center. There is no sign, just an address on a nondescript building.

At the entrance window, a customer is asked to join the club by paying a $7 membership fee. He is required to sign a release saying he is a consenting adult and doesn't hold the club responsible for any mishaps. But there is no verbal or written warning about AIDS at the entrance. The man's valuables are put in a safe and he is given a key and a towel.

The 24-hour bathhouse is dark inside. To the right is a small alcove where notices are posted, including circulars from the San Diego Department of Health, warning of AIDS. A mimeographed letter from a private individual says, "Bathhouses don't spread AIDS—people do." But the notices are small and hard to read and tucked away in a corner.

The main lounge, done in plush carpet, has a fireplace with a Santa Claus poster and a television. Two men, wearing only towels, chat on a raised and carpeted platform. A corridor leads to the steam bath, sauna, and toilet, where a machine sells condoms. Condoms are believed to help prevent the spread of AIDS.

The same corridor leads to a large room with five bunk beds. On one, a nude man lies on his back, waiting.

Stairs lead up to a second floor, where a large room has been subdivided into 27 cubicles. They are two paces wide and three paces deep. Each has a cot, an ashtray, a mirror, and a hanger. The door of one is open and a naked man lounges on the cot, looking up when someone passes.

Music pulsates a heavy beat. But the red light is too dark to clearly make out faces. The room encourages anonymity and the cubicles provide beds for encounters.

In one newly rented cubicle, the bed is still mussed from the previous occupants. Cigarette butts fill the ashtray. The walls do not go up to the ceiling, so sounds carry.

A corner doorway opens to a pitch-black room filled with 10 stalls. They resemble privies, except there is no toilet hole. A swinging door opens to a narrow bench. Two people could fit in these compartments only by standing up.

At the opposite corner is a television viewing room, showing a pornographic film, with saloon doors. During a five-minute period at 11 a.m., three sets of bare feet approached the swinging half-doors and three heads, hard to distinguish in the darkness, peeked over the doors.

Outside, men circulate in towels, looking up when passing another man. Those who know the risks of AIDS but can't stop themselves enter cubicles loaded like the chambers of a revolver in a game of Russian roulette.

There are no warnings about AIDS on this floor. There are no condoms, no lights. The Health Department's advisory to check partners for signs of AIDS would be impossible to perform in the darkness. The darkness, the cubicles, the TV, and the stalls encourage anonymous, multi-partner sex among strangers.

Over the hill from the bathhouse stands UCSD hospital and the nearby San Diego AIDS Project, on Vauclain Point.

A couple of evenings each week, people who think they may have AIDS symptoms come to the UCSD Medical Center. There they wait to go into the cubicles where doctors examine them. Inside the cubicles, they wear hospital gowns. Everything is sterile. And the warnings posted on the walls are too late for some of the men.

It is too late for the men in a room on the 10th floor of the UCSD Medical Center. The door has a sign, "Enter isolation. Blood precautions."

Inside the room, two young, handsome men, gaunt and wasted from AIDS, talk with visitors. One man lies on the bed while his visitor keeps up rapid conversation. The man toys with a gift balloon and stares off into space.

At the San Diego AIDS Project there is a wall made of plexiglass. It has the names of 121 victims of AIDS written in black. And beside it are Christmas wreaths being sold by the Mothers of AIDS Patients.

The drive from bathhouse cubicle to hospital cubicle takes about five minutes. The virus caught in the bathhouse could take from six months to four years to incubate into AIDS.

We can't stop the people who have already been infected from getting AIDS. And we can't— and shouldn't—interfere with the civil rights of consenting adults to have sex in private.

But bathhouses are businesses posing as clubs, where darkened rooms become cubicles of death. If gays were being forced into cubicles and injected with a deadly serum to wipe them out, we would protest and halt it. But here the cubicles of death are tolerated, while the virus decimates the gay community and threatens people outside.

The gay community must act now to close the bathhouses voluntarily. If the bathhouses won't close, the health and fire departments should shut them down.

Observations and questions

1) Freedman entered the bathhouse without identifying himself as a journalist. He did not regard himself as disguised because he did not intend to interview anyone. Debate the issue of disguise in this reporting process. Must journalists always identify themselves at a scene?

2) Freedman unifies the two parts of this editorial by repeating the word "cubicle." Study the other similarities he describes between the bathhouse and the hospital.

3) Freedman's editor felt that this editorial needed to include the news peg (the fire) and the contextual paragraphs on other cities; Freedman thinks that those six paragraphs delay the entrance into the bathhouse too long. Team up with a partner and debate this issue, taking the parts of editor and writer.

4) Study this piece in terms of what it does *not* describe. Beyond the question of taste, consider the role of the reader's imagination in making a scene graphic. Pay particular attention to the 11th paragraph ("The same corridor..."), especially the last word, "waiting."

5) Freedman tells us that his editor wanted to cut the gift balloon in paragraph 21 for reasons of space. Some editorial decisions have nothing to do with journalistic or literary effects!

6) The author presents a series of tableaus, with virtually no moving characters except his own observing presence. Yet the language of the piece teems with imagery of motion.

7) Freedman aims his call for action at the gay community. We might think that he need not describe a bathhouse for that audience, who probably had seen one. Or we might say that the writer shows people the world around them as it really is—in this case, deadly.

8) Freedman reduced the risk in printing such an editorial by eliminating value judgments in depicting the bathhouse. Can we trust our readers to supply the necessary value judgments?

A conversation with
Jonathan Freedman

DON FRY: Well, sir, you've had an interesting career, even though you had no formal training as a journalist.

JONATHAN FREEDMAN: I call it more of a careen than a career. I always wanted to write. I read that Jack Kerouac went to Columbia University, so I went to Columbia and majored in English. I won the Cornell Woolrich Writing Fellowship, named after the detective writer. When I graduated in 1972, I took the $2,500 prize and traveled down the Pan American Highway. I ran out of cash in Rio. I met a girl, who said, "Do you speak English? I think I know where you can get a job." She took me over to the Associated Press where by luck there was a fine bureau chief who went to the Columbia Journalism School. He hired me, although I had never written a newspaper story. He promptly sent me down to Sao Paulo. And the bureau chief there said, "Whoa, you've never had any journalism experience." So he threw the *AP Stylebook* in my face, and said, "Read this. This will teach you how to be a journalist."

Whoa! The *AP Stylebook* is going to teach you how to be a journalist? (Laughter)

I didn't understand any of it. And he said, "Rewrite your lead." I didn't know what a lead was. But I had written a lot of fiction, so I knew how to write a story: start very quietly, and slowly build up details until the climax, which comes at the end. And the first story was thrown back on my desk. "What the hell are you doing here? It's all upside down and backwards!" So that was my training.

How did you get from Sao Paulo to San Diego?

I quit AP because Hugh Mulligan, one of their great writers, read one of my short stories and said, "Boy, you should try to write fiction." So I did try it. I free-lanced from '76 to '81, had a lot of adventures, did a lot of writing, and published a book. But I didn't make any money to speak of. Finally, I sent some clips to a blind-ad box in *Editor & Publisher*, and Ralph Bennett called me up and said, "I'm from the San Diego *Tribune*, and we'd like for you to come out for a tryout." Ralph later became my mentor, and has done more for me than anyone else.

Did you start there as a reporter?

No, I became an editorial writer, without ever having worked on a newspaper. I'd never written an editorial, and I must confess I'd never read many either. But I'm an opinionated type, and Ralph is a great teacher. So Ralph and I collaborated on a project on illegal aliens, and we were runners-up for the Pulitzer Prize my first year.

Your career's so odd that we couldn't even called it checkered. (Laughter) How many editorials do you write per week?

Too many. Three a day at the worst, two a day often, and at least one a day. We just don't have enough people to fill our page without doing that kind of work. But Ralph immediately started sending me out of the office to do reporting for the editorials. So that started the tradition of my leaving the office.

Do you pick your own subjects, or are they assigned?

We speak for the publisher, not for ourselves. That's part of editorial writing. But Ralph's system here encourages people to have strong beliefs. And if that's what the paper wants to say, those beliefs get in the paper. But you're not required to write things you don't believe.

Well, it certainly shows in your editorials. There's no uncertainty in any of them. Tell me the background on "Abolish American apartheid."

When Ralph suggested doing a series of editorials on illegal aliens, a lead popped into my mind, something like: "The border is where the great water projects, the great flow of water from Northern California and Colorado stops, and the great human flood of people crosses northward."

Terrific lead!

I thought that was quite profound, and Ralph said, "Look, you don't know anything about this. I want you to go and write about the border from confronting it." And he sent me out to the border fence and to ride with the Border Patrol, and eventually to a farm and the INS office downtown and to Washington, D.C.

"Abolish American apartheid" was provoked by reading in the paper that the students in our local university were protesting the treatment of black workers in South Africa. I got mad because these students, who are eating fresh strawberries and benefiting from illegal farm labor, don't realize that equal and horrible human rights injustices are going on right here in San Diego. So I just blurted this editorial out. I wrote it in maybe an hour, and then I rewrote it.

I find this a very controlled editorial. How do you control anger in your editorials, keep it from breaking through the surface?

I resent editorials where you rage against the readers and push them around. Sometimes I vent my anger against the subject matter rather than against the reader. I really am angry at the reader in a certain sense and angry at myself, angry at us, the American people, for not being able to see this situation in our own backyard.

The first sentences are dominated by the pronoun "they."

The editorial begins, "They live in polluted squatter camps." And we don't know who "they" are, or where we're talking about. And I say, "These victims of apartheid are not thousands of miles away in South Africa, but here in America, in San Diego." That "they" is a universal "they." It becomes very specific about a third of the way into the editorial.

The next sentence begins, "We call them illegal aliens...." That's the first time you use the pronoun "we."

It's "they" and "we." I don't use that "we" the way editorial pages use "we," *The Wall Street Journal*, for example, as "we the capitalists of America" or "we distinct from the readers." In this editorial I'm using that "we" as "we the people, we the United States, we the Americans."

Listen to the pronouns in the last paragraph: "*We* have no direct power to halt apartheid in South Africa. But *we* can and must stop illegal immigration and exploitation here. *We* must make it illegal for employers to hire illegal aliens. *We* must offer amnesty to aliens, to bring them out of hiding. *We* must abolish apartheid in America."

Well, here it's the "we" of "we the people." We the people have the power to change it, if we are willing to see ourselves with the clarity with which we see others.

Let's talk about repetition and rhythm. Do you think in those rhythms?

I think like a fiction writer, a person who started out trying to replicate speech, write dialogue, do description, invent personas who speak in their own way; I use all that in editorial writing. This is a simple voice, controlling anger, speaking all the more quietly the angrier the person gets, and letting the simplicity of the sentence structure and the repetition make a point that can be lost in a more complicated way of writing. What I'm trying to say here is so simple and so true that we don't see it. The prose is trying to make a simple analogy between South Africa and America, with clarity and emotional force coming from the repetition.

Do you read aloud? I thought maybe you did because of the rhythm.

No, although I've caught myself saying things aloud while I'm writing. A character in my mind speaks this. It's a person on a darkened stage speaking in a kind of a half light in a simple voice.

What's the relation of this voice to the real you? Do you impersonate these characters or spin them out of yourself?

Well, novelists say that they invent characters out of people they know and out of themselves. I can see from almost every different point of view. While I'm talking to him, I understand the farmer's dilemma. He's in competition with another farmer who's hiring illegal aliens, so he has to do it, too. At the same time, I always have this other voice in me arguing with him. In my editorials, I try to show the point of view of the person I disagree with, before slamming in with my own point of view, with my newspaper's point of view.

Newspapers speak in two voices anyway, the news voice and the editorial voice.

Yes. Editorial writing can be a form of realism. The American newspaper is based on the premise of objectivity, but the opinion page is that part of the paper which says we are not being objective, we are being opinionated. But opinion can give a kind of truth, a kind of realism, which can't come out of objective writing.

What do you mean by "realism"?

It's a realism which says, "This is opinion. This is not an objective point of view. This is a partisan point of view. But it's a caring point of view, similar to the kind of human reactions that each of us has when confronted with the situation." An objective journalist coming to the illegal alien situation often has a hard time conveying the hypocrisy and the suffering, because there is no point of view to deal with this matter.

So realism can be achieved in part by saying we are going to express our emotional reaction to what we are portraying, and the readers can agree or not. But we're going to tell them how it feels, smells, and tastes, and how it feels inside your rib cage.

Give me an example.

For me, the greatest writer and journalist is George Orwell. In *Homage to Catalonia*, he writes about having been a partisan in the Spanish Civil War. You know he's a partisan, and you know his own views are changing as he confronts things from the point of view of someone involved, just the opposite of an objective journalist. But he is such a good writer that he can tell you his prejudices and his point of view and still make you feel what it's like to be in Barcelona on the day of liberation. And you may or may not agree with George Orwell, but you come away from that book with a very strong feeling for what the Spanish Civil War felt like. And that is realism in a certain sense, the kind of realism that good editorial writing can produce.

Orwell said that good prose is like a window-pane. He gives you a window on what really happened, but he doesn't pretend that he's not filtering the light. Would you go so far as to say that the objectivity and the implied realism of straight news writing are really illusions?

It's a commonly held illusion, in a positive sense. The writer and the reader and the editor all agree that we're going to call this illusion "objectivity." News is our best attempt at saying what happened, and we will collectively hold this illusion as fact. But I don't think that's the only way to get at fact or to get at reality.

I like your idea of the reader as accomplice in this fiction.

The reader *is* an accomplice. And many, many readers now say to me that they don't trust journalists anymore. They don't trust what they read. And I always say, "Well, you shouldn't believe what you read in the newspaper. You shouldn't accept any fact from any source without being skeptical about it."

Right. When I read a poll that tells me that only 84 percent of the readers believe their newspapers, I think to myself, "We've got to do something about that 84 percent. They have to learn some skepticism." Tell me about the second piece, "Police Canyon of the Dead."

Well, I went down to Tijuana to meet the mayor and the police chief, with our veteran Tijuana correspondent. And later we drove to a slum area of Tijuana called *Colonia Libertad* (the Liberty Neighborhood), on the route the illegal aliens come down. People were gathering on the soccer field, and I asked a woman who was selling tamales under a beach umbrella what this area was called. And she called it *El Canon de los Muertos* (Canyon of the Dead).

You can write an editorial about issues, but if you go there to the border and see it in person, it affects you in a different way. In a certain sense it becomes less simple, and in another sense it becomes simpler, because you have a simple human reaction to things. I thought I would just like to present the Canyon of the Dead to the readers, and let them decide what they think about it. This is an attempt at realism. Most of this editorial paints the picture, and then I try to bring home the moral conflict near the end.

Reading the picture you've painted, I now realize that I don't really know what the ravine looks like, because you've described the scene in terms of the people in it. It's not topography, but essentially a human landscape.

I like that term. It *is* a human landscape. I try to make people aware that the illegal immigration problem involves people: not numbers, not immigrants, not aliens, but people.

At the beginning of the fourth paragraph, you say, "The aliens are called *pollos*— chickens." You use the word "aliens" down to that point, and then you use *pollos* almost to the end. Two paragraphs from the bottom, they become "human beings." In the last paragraph, they become "people." Those nouns parallel the structure of your argument.

That's very perceptive on your part, but unconscious on mine. The reader starts by seeing them as illegal aliens, and then as they are called by their own people, *pollos*. And then I try to humanize them so they emerge as universal people, any one of us. I'm trying to lead the reader on a journey, not just to a place, but to a conclusion that we should deal with these people as human beings rather than as illegal aliens or *pollos*.

Nice piece. Shall we talk about "Silent scream of no-care babies?"

Sure. One day, Ralph Bennett said, "Why don't you go look at the county health program," and I spent a couple days doing that. I found out that this perinatal program was doing a good job, but was hurting because it didn't have enough money. But I didn't write about it then because we were looking at the larger issue of indigent care.

Later I heard of the title of that movie about abortion, *The Silent Scream*. And I remembered those babies I saw in the nursery screaming their heads off, but you couldn't hear it because they had breathing tubes down their tracheas. So I wrote it then.

Listen to the second and third paragraphs of your lead: "This is the silent scream of a baby whose mother received no prenatal care. It is not heard in the nursery. It is not heard in the hospital administration. It is not heard in the county or state health departments. It is not heard, because we don't want to look into that crib and see that child born to suffering."

There's that "we" again. I didn't realize I used this device so often.

We ought to give that "we" a name, like "the implicating we."

Yes, it's not "the imperial we." It's "the democratic we."

You make an unusual linkage in the penultimate paragraph: "It is not morally defensible or economically sane to deny prenatal care to women who request it—and to doom defenseless children."

Well, economics and morality are not always on the same side, but in this issue they are. When you have the knowledge to help mothers give birth to healthy babies, it's morally wrong not to give it. When you deny a minimal payment for basic preventive care, you inherit a baby who is going to cost hundreds of thousands of dollars in the nursery and for the rest of its life. So economically it's not sane. Maybe "sane" is not the right word there.

I like that word. You don't want to repeat "defensible."

I think that's why I put "sane" there. I couldn't figure out what else to say except "defensible."

I particularly like the way "defenseless children" picks up "not morally defensible." It's repetition with a slight change, a little twist. Journalists, particularly editors, dislike repetition, regarding it as flat. But in argumentative writing like this, it can become very effective. It has rhythmic effects. It has ritual qualities. It shows you different sides of the same thing.

Right.

These editorials seem free of ideology.

Well, my editor is a very open person. He wants the editorial to have something to do with reality rather than just ideology. I think some good editorials can be written from ideology, but we're not ideologues around here. We're much more interested in trying to find out what reality is in terms of what we confront.

Some people might take your certainty of tone as ideological, but I see it as the product of getting down to grips with real things done by real people.

I hope I'm not preaching. I'm trying to burn a picture into the readers' minds and cause a reaction, to cause action.

I'd like to talk about the bathhouse story. Reporters covering AIDS stories are very concerned about issues of presentation in family newspapers, basic problems like explicit description, endorsing lifestyles, problematic language, etc. You handle all that rather well.

Well, we've done our share of editorials about AIDS. But there was one thing in our community that people didn't agree about, and that was whether we should keep the bathhouses open or closed. The Health Department was telling us the bathhouses are a good place to disseminate information about AIDS, and that AIDS was not being spread in them. So I talked Ralph into letting me look inside a bathhouse.

I asked Ralph, "What should I do if they ask me what I'm doing here?" And he said, "If they ask you, tell them you're a journalist. If they don't ask you, you don't have to say anything."

So you worried about the ethical problem of disguise in reporting?

I was mostly worried about AIDS. And I was worried about not harming anybody individually. I usually tell people, "I'm not a reporter. I'm writing opinion. And I'm not going to quote you.

Or if I quote you, I won't identify you." In this case, I did not intend to reveal any of the individuals I saw in there, and I was hoping I wouldn't meet anyone in there I knew. (Laughter)

Indeed. So you didn't have to debate the question of disguise.

Well, Ralph had given me the guidelines, and I trust him. If I had interviewed people, I would have told them. The only person I quote is from a mimeographed letter by a private individual. That was signed, but I didn't put the name in.

Remember that my original objective was to see the warnings in the bathhouse. How prominent were they, and what effect were they having? I just wanted to go there and see that.

So you went to the bathhouse.

Yes, I went. You had to become a member, so I said I wanted to be a member, and they asked me my name, and I paid them $7, and they looked at my driver's license, and they said, "You're a member now." And they gave me a towel and opened the door, and I went in.

I had never been in a gay bathhouse before, and I didn't really know where to go or anything. But they gave me a key to a little cubicle, so I walked slowly through the place, went up to my cubicle, and closed the door and took out my notebook and wrote down everything I saw.

I didn't know what to do then, and I didn't feel clean about taking my clothes off. So, like an idiot, I just go out and walk around the second floor with my suit on. (Laughter) And I'm getting eyes, and I think they thought, "Well, this guy is really kinky, you know. This guy wears a suit. Everyone else is in a towel." (Laughter) And I came back into my cubicle and wrote more about it. I did four little forays that way, into different parts of the bathhouse, trying like a camera to note down everything. And then I left, driving back to the office to write.

What were you thinking about?

I thought: "It's going to be hard on the gays to paint that picture of the bathhouse. It's going to sound scurrilous and seamy. We're dealing with a tragic situation, a painful situation, people dying. And it's going to look like we're exploiting it as a lurid place. Anyone who wrote about it would paint a lurid picture."

Indeed.

I decided a real storyteller would tell what happened in the beginning and what happened in the end. So I drove to the hospital where the people were being treated for AIDS and dying of AIDS, the University of California at San Diego Hospital. I asked a woman there who was very helpful to journalists if she would show me where the AIDS patients were, and she took me into the clinic. Then it hit me: there were cubicles, about the same size as the cubicle I had just come from in the bathhouse. And there were curtains and all kinds of warning signs.

And men lying around.

And they were the same guys, more or less the same age group, the same people. And the situation was sterile, cold, frightening, and dangerous. The bathhouse had been dark, with pounding music, sensuous in a strange way, and no warnings except the ones posted near the doorway. But the hospital was just heartbreaking.

So then I brought this stuff back, and I said to Ralph, "This is going to be really hard, but just trust me and let me see if I can write it." In the old days, this newspaper used to paint the testicles off dogs in photos, so Ralph was really taking a chance. So I wrote it, and the editors okayed it, and we ran it on the editorial page.

You wrote it pretty much as it appears?

Yes. Ralph added two things, the news peg of the fire and the context of other cities. I think the latter takes too long, because I'm trying to get the reader into the bathhouse quickly, and that part delays it.

Your description has very little motion; it's almost a dumb show. And there are no emotional reactions; it's all description.

There's no emotional reaction. That was intended. Instead of being vivid, I'm trying to tell what's in the camera's eye, and not tell what's not in the camera's eye.

The camera's eye shows no homosexual activity. Did you see any?

I heard it. I saw people being picked up, and I was approached. But I didn't see any sex acts.

Did you leave anything out that you saw there, anything that you really had to struggle over?

Well, you've got to remember I was there in the morning, 11 a.m. So I didn't have to leave out a lot because I didn't see a lot. I did not want to step over the bounds of taste. For example, I didn't describe the man lying on his back, that he was ogling me with his eyes, and how his thighs were open and his penis half erect. I left that out.

You simply wrote, "a nude man lies on his back, waiting."

The word "waiting" was the restrained way of saying all the rest.

What does that do to the reader? Is it more real, in a way?

It lets the reader imagine more than he would see if I had painted it. Sometimes when you don't describe every naked detail, the reality is stronger and clearer.

Hemingway said not to tell the reader too much, to leave room for the imagination. What kind of conversations happened on the desk when you came back?

We decided to remove all value judgments in the portrayal of the bathhouse. The only value judgment in the editorial is protection of the health of the gay community and of the entire community.

Did the editorial have any effect?

Since the editorial appeared, there has been a debate in the gay community about what to do. And I think this editorial may have had something to do with promoting that debate. But I don't want to be in the position of preaching, so much as provoking thought.

A good editorial can be a catalyst in the community. How much action can an editorial bring about? Is it enough just to start the debate? And are you responsible after that to keep it going?

In 20 or 30 years, there will have to be a Martin Luther King to free illegal aliens. People might look back and say, "Well, this guy was saying that this was a human rights problem, not just a question of being invaded by aliens, and not an economic problem."

That's playing to history. Do you find it frustrating that your editorials don't provoke action now?

Yes. But on the other hand, I'm just a writer. Maybe there's a good reason why actions aren't taken.

When you don't get results from your editorials, are you tempted to write louder?

Yes, that's a good point. "Abolish American apartheid," which I think is a pretty loud editorial in its own way, was written after a lot of frustration.

Do you read other people's editorials, other than your own paper's?

Yes, I read *The New York Times* sometimes, and the *Los Angeles Times*, and *The Wall Street Journal*. I like *The Wall Street Journal* editorials, although I don't agree with them. But they have a delightful wit and a tongue-in-cheek quality. They have a very definite audience and a very definite perspective. But they do the opposite of what I do. They don't get close to their subject matter and grapple with it on a human level. Their "column one" is great for exploding myths and getting close up. That's more like my editorials, where I try to get close to the material, and give the feeling, and be disarmingly honest sometimes, and try to show the complexity of the thing.

You have a very, very distinctive voice in your editorials. Does that voice stand out from the other editorials on your page?

People tell me that they can recognize my editorials. Each of us has our voice on this page. Ralph lets the differences stand, so it's a page that speaks with voices, but not with bylines. The joke here is that my editorials are so long that no one will ever read them. (Laughter) But I think that sometimes a very long editorial will get more readers and will get people to read all the way through, because there's enough room to involve the readers and not repulse them with shorthand.

Thank you, sir.

Larry King
St. Petersburg Times
Finalist, Deadline Writing

Larry King, 29, was born and raised in Indianapolis. He received a bachelor of journalism degree from the University of Missouri in 1979 and joined *The Charlotte News* as a night general assignment reporter, later moving on to police and city hall beats. In 1981 he moved to the *Greensboro Daily News (Greensboro News & Record)* on general assignment, again at night. He received several awards from the North Carolina State Press Association. Since 1983, he has worked as a general assignment reporter for the *St. Petersburg Times*, also serving as the Tampa bureau chief. He is now assigned to the projects team.

King writes deadline news with enterprise and depth, including stories about abortion clinic bombers, a citrus farmer struggling with freezes (reprinted here), a 13-year-old girl who wants to play tackle football on the boys' team, and the vision-filled world of a supermarket bomber. His pieces teem with apt quotations, insight, nice turns of phrase, and human interest.

Citrus farmer hopes groves can be saved

JANUARY 23, 1985

WINTER GARDEN—A feeble little fire burned Tuesday morning outside the equipment barn of Jerry Chicone's orange groves. A couple of logs, not much heat, smoke that wanted to play tag, but still an excuse to rub cold hands and speculate.

"Unemployment line, here we come!" hollered Jody Berry, one of the grove's two full-time tenders.

"How 'bout the soup line?" said Walter Moore, the other tender, laughing in spite of things.

Up drove the boss in a chocolate-colored jeep wagon, signaling the start of a day's work on these freeze-wounded groves in Orange County. Berry mounted a tractor and puttered off. Moore left on foot, toting a chain saw.

The boss is Jerry Chicone Jr., age 50, status uncertain. He likes these men who work for them, and doesn't want to lay them off. He likes growing oranges and doesn't want to abandon it or sell his family's land. He also likes to make money, but lately all he's done is pay it out.

"Listen, I love to grow citrus. It's a great way to spend your life," Chicone says. "But I'm not stupid. I'm not going to beat my head against a wall."

Nonetheless, there are a lot of northern citrus growers going around with bruised foreheads lately. A freeze nipped them in 1979. They pruned and replanted. Same thing with the freezes of 1980 and 1981.

But when the cold wave of Christmas 1983 turned out to be a lot meaner, strafing tens of thousands of acres north of Interstate 4, some growers invested only in for-sale signs.

Still, many others stuck with citrus, only to meet the granddaddy of them all. This week's record cold is expected to finish off many of the northern trees spared in 1983. Those that live may be barren of fruit for two or three years to come.

So people like Jerry Chicone have some tough thinking to do. Their wallets and their common sense are doing some talking. Their hearts and their stubborn streaks are whispering in the other ear.

Sell it, this is crazy. Get to work, it's in your blood. Move south, it's warmer there. Sit out for a year and see what develops.

Chicone is doing a little of each. He has 60 acres in the shadow of Clermont's famed Citrus Tower. This tract's trees were killed in the 1983 freeze and Chicone has put it up for sale (so far, no reasonable offers, he reports). He recently traveled south to scout around for land near Lake Okeechobee and thinks he'll buy some of it in a year or two.

He and his family have another 450 acres south of Lake Apopka in Orange County. He's doing a little repair work on these groves, but not much. After spending $80,000 to rehabilitate last year's damage, Chicone thinks he may just wait to see what nature does next year.

Mostly, he carries on a running discourse with himself. During a tour of his groves Tuesday morning, Chicone's statements included the following:

• "Handwriting's on the wall. It's just a matter of time."

• "They're tough, orange trees are really tough. In other words, we will see."

• "I would imagine that because this grove is located where it is, near the town, and because we have our equipment and everything, we will attempt to bring it back."

In many ways, Chicone is typical of the northern citrus grower.

His are family groves, begun by his 83-year-old father in the 1920s and intended for his 23-year-old son, a grower for only a couple of years. His groves are on land ill-suited for profits except through citrus and development. And his trees are so badly damaged that it will take a wad of money and a string of mild winters to bring them back to their condition before the freeze, plus the reserves to keep his family until the groves are again productive.

Groves south of I-4 have little history of freezes, although this week's weather made an exception. But their owners, for the most part, are wealthy people or corporations with large tracts and good enough odds with nature to make repairs with confidence.

In contrast, a great number of northern growers are in a quandary.

Mom-and-pop operations haven't the money to afford another plunge, nor can they find loan officers willing to bet on citrus anymore. Replacement trees are scarce and expensive because last year's outbreak of citrus canker, a bacterial tree-killing disease, has caused so many nurseries to be destroyed. Land prices are down and only a fraction of the groves are close enough to cities to attract would-be developers.

"The trouble with this grove is nobody wants to build a house out here," Chicone says.

Chicone has more room to maneuver than most northern growers.

With 500 acres, he is considered a large grower for the north. He isn't in debt, and he has done well enough in the past to have the choice of replanting, relocating, or sitting idle for a season. He even has a real estate license.

His uncertainty over what to do stems from many factors, but perhaps the one that tugs hardest is his heritage in citrus.

"You see, when people make that decision to sell, then we lose some of the atmosphere, the ambiance, we lose the romance of Orange County. That's what's sad," he says.

He wonders what will happen to his workers, Jody Berry and Walter Moore. Moore can't read or write, but Chicone admires him greatly. Moore called the grower four years ago insisting on a job. Chicone said no, then that he would think about it. He arrived next morning at the grove to find Moore, pruning like mad.

"He brought his own saw, brought his own ladder, he was *working* for me!" Chicone exclaimed. "And he'd done a good job. I said anyone who wants to work as much as that.... He's been with me ever since."

Chicone said he may purchase some southern land soon, but only as a hedge to make his long-held northern groves less of a risk. "It will not be like having groves in your own back yard where you see them every day," he said.

But citrus, when conditions are right, can be extremely profitable. Chicone is a successful grower who has been able to diversify, making outside investments and buying other properties. He is also a respected grower, serving as Orange County's representative on the Florida Citrus Mutual, the state's largest growers' organization.

Thus he is not without a practical side.

"See, many people think that we're in the business to grow orange juice," Chicone said. "We're not. We're in the business to make a profit."

Chicone, like all Florida growers, won't know the extent of his freeze losses for several days. But his streak of optimism may be returning.

Monday night, as a second straight night of record cold settled onto his groves, Chicone was as low as the temperatures. No, he told a caller from Cable News Network, I do not want to stand out in my grove at 1 a.m. for a live interview.

"I told them thank you very much, but I didn't want to go to a wake," he said.

Tuesday he surveyed the damage. Leaves were dying, curled into brittle green cones. That was bad. But the bark of the trees didn't appear to be split open by the cold. That was good.

Chicone called in a team of pickers to start salvaging his frozen oranges for quick transport to processing houses. As they arrived, Jody Berry was headed through a row of trees on his tractor, its disc harrow turning soil over fertilizer and undergrowth.

Off in another block, the buzz of Walter Moore's saw could be heard. Chicone drove by to watch the pruning. "Well, how's that saw running?" he asked.

Moore smiled. The chain saw was brand new.

Carl Schoettler
Baltimore Evening Sun
Finalist, Deadline Writing

Carl Schoettler, 53, was born and raised in Philadelphia. He was graduated with a B.S. in journalism from Temple University in 1959. He joined the Baltimore *Evening Sun* in 1959 and has written every imaginable kind of story there. He has won numerous writing awards and has taught journalism at the University of Maryland.

Schoettler writes long stories on short deadlines, including coverage of the Wheeling-Pittsburgh steel strike, reminiscenses of past strikes by retirees, Philadelphia's struggle without its two newspapers (reprinted here), and services for the victims of the Gander crash. He writes practically about hard and dirty subjects.

Philadelphia's main line: bring back our newspapers

SEPTEMBER 30, 1985

PHILADELPHIA—Sunday morning, and Philadelphians are grabbing out-of-town newspapers off Frank Carolei's stand on the northeast corner of Rittenhouse Square as if they're life preservers on the *Titanic*.

Philadelphia's daily newspapers—the *Inquirer* and the *Daily News*—have been on strike since Sept. 7 and this is the fourth Sunday the city has been without its own newspaper. People are getting a little stir crazy. They're tired of TV's Charlie Kuralt's Sunday morning tweetybird features about wildflowers in the Rocky Mountains.

There's a hot cop scandal under Billy Penn's hat down at City Hall. The Eagles bench Ron Jaworski for a rookie quarterback. The Phillies lose one in a row.

Philadelphians want to get a little printer's ink on their fingers that hasn't been imported from New York.

Bill Smith wants to know who's the new wrasslin' champeen, Hulk Hogan or Randy Macho Man Savage.

"Which paper's got last night's match at the Spectrum?" asks Smith, who is a very nicely turned out gentleman in a homburg hat, Oxford gray jacket, damask necktie, and doe-gray trousers. Rittenhouse Square once was the finest address in Philadelphia—and it's still pretty classy.

He looks for Macho Man and the Hulk in the the *Sunday Times* from Delaware County, the Camden *Courier* and the *Trenton Times*. The *Trenton Times*! Philadelphians are reading the *Trenton Times*!

"Nothin' in here," Smith says, unhappily. "I knew I shoulda went down there."

A city without its own newspaper loses a little of its personality, like a neurological patient with short-term memory loss. You remember what happened six years ago, but you don't know what happened last night.

"I miss the numbers," Smith says. "The daily numbers. The advertisements and the sales. Lots of people go for the sales, you know. Want ads."

"People want two things," says Jimmy Maxwell, who runs a newsstand about two blocks away at 19th and Chestnut streets. "Local TV and comics. My *TV Guide*s went up 500 percent. I went from 75 *TV Guide*s to 500.

"*USA Today* took off," Maxwell says. "I used to sell 12, now it's selling 125. People tend to like it. It's got a lot of pictures, graphs, McNugget-type news. It's addictive."

Maxwell started Sunday with about 500 *New York Times* lined up on the sidewalk against the wall of a luncheonette. By 10:30, half are gone. He sells them for $1.75.

Over on Rittenhouse Square, Frank Carolei sells *The New York Times* for two bucks.

"He's merciless," says Jimmy Maxwell.

Carolei says, "I got my price and I make 'em pay. I see you now. I never seen you before. I'll never see you again. Pay for the paper."

He deals, like Maxwell, out of a typical Philadelphia newsstand, a kind of oblong wooden box set on its end. Carolei's is in front of a boutique called Pegasus, which has a red-haired mannequin lying on her elbow in the window. Carolei sits inside, stuffing *New York Times*, while his son, Frank, who looks like he'd displace about 300 pounds in a hot tub, takes care of business. A guy named Larry Smullavitz helps out from underneath a blue University of Michigan cap.

"People want late sports," Frank Jr. says. "The Camden *Courier* and the *Trenton Times* got late sports."

They also cost a buck apiece on Sunday you want late sports.

"Three dollars for a *Washington Post!*" yelps a wounded customer.

"Go to Washington to get it," Smullavitz advises. "*The New York Times* at 42nd and Broadway, it's a dollar."

"Every time they complain about the price," the senior Carolei says, "it goes up."

On North Broad Street, the pickets who have shut down the papers look peaceful and drowsy in the warm, noontime autumn sun. The buildings the *Inquirer* and *Daily News* share spread out over a square block below an old-fashioned white stone clock tower topped with a cupola and ornamented with great marble urns. The papers are both published by Philadelphia Newspapers Inc., which is part of the Knight-Ridder chain. The circulation of the *Inquirer* is 525,000 during the week and a little more than a million on Sunday. The *Daily News* sells 295,000 papers daily—when they're publishing.

Nine unions negotiate with the newspaper management. On Friday, a settlement seemed close. A sticky problem about manning automatic machines was worked out between the newspapers and the mailers union, which represents the people who stuff coupons and those slick colorful ad pages inside the smudgy, inky news sections.

Talks about money were to begin Saturday. But management negotiators walked out almost instantly. They said the unions' demand for a $170 wage package was unrealistic. The company position remains unchanged from the $90 they offered before the strike began.

"They made a real tactical error," says Joe Rupertus, who sells ad space when he's not picketing. He's a member of the Newspaper Guild. "I think they lost any sympathy they had at all. That was a dumb thing to do. I got a feeling they all had dinner dates somewhere."

The Newspaper Guild and the paper settled non-economic demands three weeks ago.

"Basically we're out because of the mailers. The mailers have bad problems. They're becoming obsolete, like blacksmiths."

Rupertus pickets mostly from a plastic web lawn chair he's pulled up against a low brick wall in front of the *Inquirer* building. He's worked there 19 years. He thinks the publishers consolidated the anger of union members against their position by walking away from the meeting Saturday.

"We're very, very angry at the company," says Nancy Przybylinski, a Guild member who is an inside ad sales person. She wears her picket sign over a bold black-and-white check jacket.

Jean Malik, the picket captain, wears a union T-shirt and a Guild button that reads "A Woman's Place Is In Her Union."

"The president of the company keeps saying this is not their final offer," she says. "But they haven't changed since day one. He sends us letters at home."

"I've been through several strikes," Rupertus says. "Four. This is just now approaching being the worst. Next week, if we're still out, we'll break the record in recent times. Twenty-three days in 1977."

He watches the cars going by on Broad Street.

"People are really hungry for a newspaper," he says. "People riding by here yell at us because they don't have their paper."

At Rittenhouse Square, *The New York Times* is sold out. So are *The Washington Post* and the Camden *Courier* and the *Trenton Times* and the *Delaware County Times*. Late risers buy computer magazines and wonder where they can find real estate ads. And about 900,000 people don't read any newspaper at all Sunday.

Tom Teepen
Atlanta Constitution
Finalist, Commentary

Tom Teepen, 51, is a native of Nashville, Tennessee, and grew up in Mobile and Cincinnati. He was graduated with a degree in journalism from Ohio University in 1957 and became a Professional Journalism Fellow at Stanford University in 1967. He worked for two years at the Urbana (Ohio) *Daily Citizen*. He served for 14 years as editorial page editor of the *Dayton Daily News* and moved to the Atlanta *Constitution* as editorial page editor in 1982. He has won several writing awards from the AP and UPI.

Teepen demolishes the obtuseness of Reagan's advance team, laments the compromises in Sam Ervin's political career, suggests a proctologist for Frank Sinatra, beats up Ed Meese and even James Madison (reprinted here), and speculates on actresses as expert witnesses on farm policy. His fearless wit shows us the emperors are even more naked than we thought.

A Meese-Madison summit

NOVEMBER 28, 1985

Hello. Yes, this is Ed Meese. The attorney general, right. Yes, the constitutional fundamentalist—the very one. Yep, the guy who's been saying that whatever the framers said goes, and the courts can't make up new, modern wrinkles.

Who's this calling? *Really? The* James Madison? Where the heck you calling from, Jimmy? From 1787? Sept. 17. Fantastic! And the last of the delegates just signed off on the Constitution, huh?

Well, OK, "rendered the Constitution of the Federal government adequate to the exigencies of the union." But I have to tell you, Jimmy, we don't much talk like that any more, here in 1985. You get looked at funny if you do.

What? Well, you're right. I *have* been disturbed at the way trendy, liberal courts have been interpreting the Constitution.... You bet I'd appreciate your advice! Hey, you're the guy who really put it all together. A couple of things in particular have been bothering me and the president—some of this women's rights stuff, and civil rights.

I said, women's rights.... Well, yes, I know you never heard of them. But ever since the ladies got the vote and.... The vote.... Yeah, I know there's nothing in the Constitution about women being able to vote. Actually, there's nothing about them at all. You guys really aced 'em out. But now, whew, there's this abortion issue and here in this administration, we say fetuses are the ones with rights.

Well, it's true there isn't anything about fetuses in the Constitution, either. But the Constitution goes on about "persons," and the president and me, we figure fetuses are persons, and women aren't. That was your original intent, right?... Oh. Well, maybe we should get back just to the women's stuff.

It shouldn't be a problem? How's that, Jimmy?... Women are chattel? They belong to their husbands, just like any other property. Yes, yes, I know that was pretty generally the law back then, but....

I am *too* serious about sticking with you guys' original intent. But look, I have to tell you, Jimmy, it would be tough nowadays just, you know, *declaring* women to be chattel. A lot of them would get real upset. You know, maybe we better just move on to the civil rights things.

Well, when we talk about civil rights we usually really mean blacks.... Blacks, Jimmy.... The problem? Our administration doesn't see how busing could be constitutional.... Busing— you know, moving kids around in buses.

Well, they're these big, long machines, usually yellow, and we use them to carry people to and fro. See? That's just my point, you never heard of buses, so busing couldn't be constitutional, could it?... Aha, I thought not! Now we're really getting somewhere.

What? Well, yes, I know the Constitution says that blacks amount to only 3/5ths of a person each when we're counting up. Yes, I do know that the Constitution says fugitive slaves must be returned to their owners.

Well, yes, I realize your intent was not only to allow slavery but protect it, but—well, you see, Jimmy, we've, uh, heh-heh, freed the slaves, Jimmy.

Hey, don't get mad now. Look, *I* didn't free the slaves. It was another Republican.... So, if we want to get back to your original intent, what we really should do is go back to—Jimmy, I gotta tell you, I think bringing back slavery would be real awkward.

I know, I know it was your intent. Uh, look. I really appreciate your calling and all, but it's

Thanksgiving and.... Yeah, we still do Thanksgiving.... Yep, turkey, the works.... No, I don't have to go kill the turkey. See, these days, we freeze 'em, keep 'em in the fridge.... Refrigerator. It's this big, box-like thing, keeps stuff cold. Runs on electricity.... Electricity is— you remember Ben Franklin messing around with that kite in a storm?...

I am *not* making this up. Look, Madison, whether you like it or not, the world has changed in 200 years and....

Hello? Hello?

Les Payne
Newsday
Finalist, Commentary

Les Payne, 44, was born in Tuscaloosa, Alabama, and raised in Hartford, Connecticut. He was graduated from the University of Connecticut. He joined *Newsday* in 1969 and has worked as a beat reporter, copy editor, investigative writer, and national correspondent. He shared one Pulitzer Prize in 1974 for a series on the international traffic in heroin and was nominated again in 1978 for an 11-part series on South Africa. He has also won Columbia University's Tobenkin Award, the United Nations World Hunger Media Award, and the Howard University Journalism Prize and has served as a juror for the Emmy and Pulitzer prizes. He now serves as President of the National Association of Black Journalists.

Payne writes a series of columns calling attention to the racial nature of the Bernhard Goetz case and its coverage, Mayor Koch's turning with the winds of public opinion, the Jackson-Falwell television debate, and advice to young minority children (reprinted here).

Trying to tell children just a bit of the truth

JUNE 3, 1985

I recently spoke to a fifth-grade graduating class in Hempstead, one of the few commencements in Christendom not addressed by Gov. Mario Cuomo.

I had worked manfully to evade the engagement.

Though quite accustomed to public speaking, I am terrified of standing before an audience of youngsters and running on about matters that concern them in no discernible way.

My wife, Violet, reminded me that our son was 10 years old and likely held the same interests as the graduating class. My fears were not allayed. Going one-on-one with a 10-year-old of your own blood is not quite the same as rising up on your legs in front of a group of them who are strangers.

My son's expressed interests, for instance, have passed, in part, through his parents' filters. Youngsters his age feed on an alien diet of Van Halen, ice hockey, *Leave It to Beaver*, and God knows what else.

Interests aside, this graduating class was sure to be uncomfortable in their new clothes and fidgety during a dull graduating ceremony. And this acid-pen columnist would be pressed before them with index cards to inspire a "zeal for excellence." The thought made me queasy.

Cornered and desperate, I tried to explain this to Mrs. Griffith, a teacher at the Washington Street school. She was as formidable as a hanging judge.

"Oh, you'll do all right," she said in that fifth-grade teacher's voice, resonating with the finality of a governor refusing to grant a last-minute stay.

In the school yard, under a pleasant sun, I watched the fifth-graders march in. Each wore a white flower. The boys were immaculate in fresh suits, some with the jacket vents still stitched closed. They looked, though, like they'd rather be elsewhere. The girls were larger in every way and looked much more mature.

The program picked up for me when the salutatorian, Arami Portillo, read his one-page address. The diminutive Arami, in Churchillian understatement, cautioned his 10-year-old classmates that "this is only the beginning."

I could not imagine a sharper or better behaved class of 10-year-olds. I could not avoid noticing that the 51-member class was composed almost entirely of Hispanic and black students.

Such a racial pattern, common to most of the country, is not unusual on Long Island, which one magazine recently named as the best place to live in the nation. District lines are carefully drawn to ensure that tender white students are schooled in enclaves unto themselves to the fullest extent possible. Where Long Island housing patterns do not allow total segregation, school districts routinely track minority students to inferior classes where they can achieve a fair and equal education only by the most extraordinary means.

I could not bring myself to rain down this truth on the fifth-graders. They were too young and optimistic and wanted so much to believe that portion of the Pledge of Allegiance that speaks falsely of "liberty and justice for all."

But I did share with them my memory of the time my fifth-grade class was visited by Mary McLeod Bethune. Unlike Long Island, Tuscaloosa, Ala., made no claims of a desegregated public educational system.

The educator who founded Bethune-Cookman College told us that day how she had devoted her entire life to gaining one of the many precious benefits her country denied Afro-Americans—an education. She was the first free child born to her parents who had 16 others born in South Carolina slavery.

Religion and hard work in the cotton fields were taught to the Bethune children from the cradle, I remember her telling us. She also told of walking 10 miles to and from a religious school as a teen-ager. She later attended a seminary in North Carolina and taught for a while herself.

Not content simply to educate herself, Mary McLeod Bethune struggled to find a way to make higher education available for blacks in the South. In 1904, with but $1.50 in her pocket, she started a small Florida school which later grew to the Bethune-Cookman College.

I can still hear this stout, 75-year-old mahogany woman talk about how she nailed burlap sacks to the windows to keep out the winter winds. She brought tears to our eyes with her account of how she made ink out of berries, used charcoal for pencils, begged for lamps and kerosene, and looted trash heaps for dishes, chairs, and linen.

I told the fifth-graders that Mary McLeod Bethune, a forerunner of such leaders as Martin Luther King Jr., knew the dire consequences of a people denied an education. America withheld education from Afro-Americans in her day; conditions make it tougher for blacks than for others to acquire it these days.

I asked the fifth-graders to read about Mary McLeod Bethune this summer and adopt her zeal for education. I also charged them to resist the temptation of the street with its million vice-traps and snares.

And I closed by reading them Gwendolyn Brooks' brilliant poem warning black youngsters against falling for the lure of the streets:

"We real cool. / We left school. / We lurk late. / We strike straight. / We sing sin. / We thin gin. / We jazz June. / We die soon."

Daniel Henninger
The Wall Street Journal
Finalist, Editorial Writing

Daniel Henninger, 40, grew up in Cleveland and was graduated from Georgetown University with a B.S. in foreign service in 1968. He served as a staff writer on the *New Republic* magazine and *The National Observer*. In 1977, he joined *The Wall Street Journal* editorial staff and was promoted to assistant editor of the editorial page in 1983. He had a particularly good year in 1985, when he won the Gerald Loeb award for commentary and was runner-up in the ASNE Distinguished Writing Awards competition.

Henninger writes about the congressional pork barrel as a recipe for meat loaf, the supposed realities of Social Security, Leon Klinghoffer and the end of the PLO, TV commercials beating up on the Russians, and (reprinted here) how our dreams sustain the baseball industry. He writes neatly linked paragraphs full of information and clear explanation, with no trace of uncertainty.

Baseball dreams

AUGUST 8, 1985

It's a good thing they settled the baseball strike so quickly. Anything longer than a few days, and the American economy might have pitched into a depression. This horror became apparent to us when we saw Tuesday's hair-raising 21.73 drop in the Dow Jones Industrial Average. Life as we know it during the American summer was coming to an end, or at least a standstill. Carlton Fisk frozen at 29 homers. Dwight Gooden unplugged. Pete Rose tied down at 4,168 hits. America was at the brink!

So now the strike's over. But, as always, questions remain. Specifically, is there any way we can avoid working ourselves into a state of national anguish over these periodic major-league baseball strikes? There is. Stop dreaming. Our dreams are lining baseball's pockets.

This is how it works. We 30 million, the figure baseball commissioner Peter Ueberroth keeps citing as the number of baseball's fans, are the reason baseball players make so much money. Baseball holds the interest of 30 million fans in 26 teams each playing 162 games across six months. That fact is largely the reason local TV stations are paying the teams $117 million this year for broadcast rights. The national networks are paying another $161 million. That's a total of $278 million. There are 650 players in the major leagues. Simply dividing broadcasting revenue among the players would give each of them $427,000 this year, more than their current average annual salary of $360,000.

Baseball's finances and economics are, of course, more complicated than this; so complicated, it seems, that no one can completely figure them out. But baseball's broadcasting market is a handy way to understand how the players' salaries got so large. TV will recoup this huge outlay from its advertisers. NBC gets about $40,000 for 30 seconds of time on Saturday afternoons. The advertisers pay that price because they believe some of baseball's 30 million fans will buy the company's beer, car, or shaving cream. They are right.

But why are they right? None of us wants to spend too much time meditating over the fact that at bottom, these recurring battles between the players and owners are over dividing up a revenue stream whose size depends in no small part on how many of us are willing to drink Bud Lite. To us, baseball's all a dream. It's about Roy Hobbs.

Roy Hobbs is the mythical baseball player Robert Redford played in *The Natural.* That movie had every baseball cliche in the book. It was beautiful. Probably 10 million fathers took their 20 million sons (and more than a few daughters) to see it. Things happen after that movie is over. Back home, the 5-year-old pulls out a bat and says, "C'mon, Dad. Pitch to me. I'm Roy Hobbs. I'm gonna hit the clock." Dad pitches and, of course, he thinks to himself, against staggering odds, "Who knows, maybe the kid'll make it."

Most of baseball's 30 million fans persist in believing that Pete Rose and Reggie Jackson and Dwight Gooden aren't cut from the same cloth as the teams' owners; they're Roy Hobbs. The reason the fans persist in this dreamy image of baseball is that most of them played it once. Most of them got at least one good hit or made one great, lucky catch. And when they did, the rest of the team and maybe a small bleacher of fans cheered and screamed. Now they're "retired," and they sit home, by the millions, watching.

So what if the strike was about salary arbitrations, pension contributions, and concealed profits? That game the league's 650 dugout-spitting plutocrats play still looks like baseball to us. The strike's over. Hobbs! Get in there and hit!

Kenneth Ikenberry
The Washington Post
Finalist, Editorial Writing

Kenneth Ikenberry, 45, was born in Cedar Rapids, Iowa, and grew up in Washington, D.C. He was graduated from George Washington University in 1963 and worked for the *Washington Star* for 17 years as a reporter and editor. Since 1981, he has worked for *The Washington Post* editorial department.

Ikenberry's subjects include the tendency for unusable buildings to turn into Yuppie shops (reprinted here), New Coke and old pretensions, nostalgia for Greyhound buses and Art Deco, William Perry on the way up, and the perils of military specificity applied to fruitcake. The subjects tell it all: this writer sees our pretensions and demolishes them with irreverence.

Shops, theaters, and restaurants

One day the mayor of an East Coast city calls in a top aide and asks: "What do we do with the old slaughterhouse now that the sausage company's left town?"

"Well," says the aide, "I assume we turn it into shops, theaters, and restaurants."

"Of course," says the mayor, "just like the old rendering plant and the old sawmill."

In six months the place is opened as a complex of shops, theaters, and restaurants called The Abattoir, and thousands of people go there who wouldn't be caught dead in a slaughterhouse or a suburban mall.

After that the mayor doesn't have to call on his aides anymore. When the question comes up of what is to be done with the old trestle bridge, the old waterworks, or any other depressing old structure, he gets on the phone with the bankers, and together they say, "Shops, theaters, and restaurants!"

One morning the mayor's secretary bursts into his office: "The people down at The Old Concrete Sewer Pipe Factory say four new cookie shops have appeared there in the last 24 hours and two more are sprouting. They're displacing all the other shops—also the theaters and restaurants."

In fact, it soon becomes apparent that this is happening all up and down the East Coast, wherever cities have converted old steambaths, stables, railroad roundhouses, fish-packing plants, shipyards, smokestacks, shantytowns, and the sheltered areas under highway bridges into shops, theaters, and restaurants. All are discovering that the next stage is that everything turns into cookie shops.

A group of mayors assembles in Newark, which had been converted into a convention center, and a professor of urban entropy from Harvard explains the phenomenon:

"When you fill up grimy old structures that once served a useful purpose with shops, theaters, and restaurants, they tend to become absurdly over-specialized—like four stores each selling a different color of pasta, or a restaurant that serves only zucchini. These places are susceptible to being swept away by the slightest change in consumer taste, and when that happens the cookie shops, being rather hardy, move in and take over."

The end result, of course, is a chocolate chip cookie extending roughly from North Carolina to New England and from the Appalachians to the Atlantic. Don't say you weren't warned.

A selected bibliography

BOOKS ON WRITING, COACHING, AND EDITING

Best Newspaper Writing. Roy Peter Clark and Don Fry, eds. Published annually since 1979. St. Petersburg, FL: Poynter Institute for Media Studies (formerly Modern Media Institute).

Biagi, Shirley. *Interviews That Work: A Practical Guide for Journalists.* Belmont, CA: Wadsworth Pub. Co., 1985.

Brande, Dorothea. *Becoming a Writer.* Los Angeles: J.P. Tarcher; Boston: distributed by Houghton Mifflin, 1981. Reprint of 1934 Edition.

Elbow, Peter. *Writing with Power: Technique for Mastering the Writing Process.* New York: Oxford Univ. Press, 1981.

Elbow, Peter. *Writing Without Teachers.* New York: Oxford Univ. Press, 1973.

Hall, Donald. *Writing Well.* 5th ed. Boston: Little, Brown, 1985.

Improving Newswriting. Loren Ghiglione, ed. Washington, D.C.: ASNE, 1982.

The Literary Journalists. Norman Sims, ed. New York: Ballantine Books, 1984.

Mencher, Melvin. *News Reporting and Writing.* 3rd ed. Dubuque, IA: William C. Brown, 1984.

Murray, Donald M. *Learning By Teaching: Selected Articles on Writing and Teaching.* Upper Montclair, NJ: Boynton Cook, 1982.

Murray, Donald M. *A Writer Teaches Writing.* 2nd ed. New York: Houghton-Mifflin, 1984.

Murray, Donald M. *Writing for Your Readers: Notes on the Writer's Craft from The Boston Globe.* Chester, CT: Globe Pequot, 1983.

How I Wrote the Story. Christopher Scanlan, ed. Providence: Providence Journal Company, 1983.

Teel, Leonard Ray and Taylor, Ron. *Into the Newsroom: An Introduction to Journalism.* Englewood Cliffs, NJ: Prentice-Hall, 1983.

A Treasury of Great Reporting. 2nd ed. Louis L. Snyder and Richard B. Morris, eds. New York: Simon & Schuster, 1962.

Writers at Work: The Paris Review Interview Series. George Plimpton and Malcolm Cowley, eds. New York: Viking.

Writing in Style. Laura Babb, ed. New York: Houghton-Mifflin, 1975.

Zinsser, William K. *On Writing Well: An Informal Guide to Writing Nonfiction,* 3rd ed. New York: Harper & Row, 1985.

MAGAZINE AND JOURNAL ARTICLES

Berryhill, Michael. "The Lede and the Swan." *The Quill,* March 1983, pp. 13-16.

Clark, Roy Peter. "As Good As Their Words: Common Qualities of Superior Writers." *Washington Journalism Review,* Feb. 1985, pp. 46-47.

Clark, Roy Peter. "Making Hard Facts Easy Reading." *Washington Journalism Review,* Jan./Feb. 1984, pp. 24-26.

Clark, Roy Peter. "A New Shape for the News." *Washington Journalism Review,* March 1984, pp. 46-47.

Clark, Roy Peter. "Plotting the First Graph." *Washington Journalism Review,* Oct. 1982, pp. 48-50.

Clark, Roy Peter. "The Unoriginal Sin: How Plagiarism Poisons the Press." *Washington Journalism Review,* March 1983, pp. 43-47.

Fry, Don. "Excerpts Illustrate Four Varied Approaches to Good Writing." *ASNE Bulletin,* May 1985, pp. 24, 26.

Fry, Don. "The Presence of Richard Ben Cramer." *Style* 16 (1982): 437-443.

Jackson, Dennis. "Sportswriter Red Smith's 'Jousts with the Mother Tongue.' " *Style* 16 (1982): 414-435.

Jackson, Fleda Brown; Sloan, W. David; and Bennett, James R. "Journalism as Art: A Selective Bibliography." *Style* 16 (1982): 466-487.

Lanson, Gerald and Stephens, Mitchell. "Jell-O Journalism: Why Reporters Have Gone Soft in Their Leads." *Washington Journalism Review*, April 1982, pp. 21-23.

LaRocque, Paula. "Write for the Readers." *ASNE Bulletin*, Feb. 1983, p. 8.

Murray, Donald M. "Editors Must Find New Ways to Develop and Retain Writers." *ASNE Bulletin*, April 1981, pp. 4-7.

Nunberg, Geoffrey. "The Decline of Grammar." *Atlantic Monthly*, Dec. 1983, pp. 31-46.

Tobin, Richard L. "The Battle of Words Never Ceases." *ASNE Bulletin*, Feb. 1983, p. 16.

Westphal, David. "An Editor at a Writing Clinic: 'One Eye-Opener After Another.' " *ASNE Bulletin*, April 1981, pp. 11-12.

"Which Books on Writing and Editing Should be in the Newsroom?: Three Newsroom Writing Coaches Offer Their Lists." *ASNE Bulletin*, Sept. 1981, pp. 26-30.

"Writing: A Special Report from the APME Writing and Editing Committee." *APME News*, Sept. 1985, 24 pgs.

ENGLISH LANGUAGE, GRAMMAR, AND USAGE

Berner, R. Thomas. *Language Skills for Journalists*. 2nd. ed. Boston: Houghton-Mifflin, 1983.

Bernstein, Theodore M. *The Careful Writer: A Modern Guide to English Usage*. New York: Atheneum, 1965.

Kilpatrick, James J. *The Writer's Art.* Fairway, KS: Andrews, McMeel, Parker, 1984.

Safire, William. *I Stand Corrected: More on Language.* New York: Times Books, 1984.

Safire, William. *On Language.* New York: Times Books, 1980.

DICTIONARIES, GUIDES, HANDBOOKS, AND STYLEBOOKS

American Heritage Dictionary of the English Language. Boston: Houghton-Mifflin, 1984.

Associated Press Stylebook and Libel Manual. Reading, MA: Addison-Wesley, 1982.

Barzun, Jacques and Graff, Henry F. *The Modern Researcher.* 4th ed. New York: Harcourt, Brace, Jovanovich, 1985.

Bremner, John B. *Words on Words: A Dictionary for Writers and Others Who Care About Words.* New York: Columbia Univ. Press, 1980.

Cappon, Rene J. *The Associated Press Guide to Good Writing.* Reading, MA: Addison-Wesley, 1982.

Effective Writing and Editing: A Guidebook for Newspapers. Reston, VA: American Press Institute, 1985.

Strunk, William Jr. and White, E.B. *The Elements of Style,* 3rd ed. New York: Macmillan, 1979.

EXAMPLES OF GOOD WRITING

Didion, Joan. *Slouching Towards Bethlehem.* New York: Washington Square Press, 1981.

Kidder, Tracy. *Soul of a New Machine.* Boston: Little, Brown, 1981.

Kidder, Tracy. *House.* Boston: Houghton-Mifflin, 1985.

McPhee, John. *The John McPhee Reader.* William L. Howarth, ed. New York: Farrar, Straus, Giroux, 1976.

Orwell, George. *The Orwell Reader: Fiction, Essays and Reportage.* New York: Harcourt, Brace, Jovanovich, 1961.

Welty, Eudora. *One Writer's Beginnings.* Cambridge, MA: Harvard Univ. Press, 1984

Former ASNE Award Winners

1985

Deadline writing: Jonathan Bor, *The Post Standard,* Syracuse
Non-deadline writing: Greta Tilley, *Greensboro News & Record*
Commentary: Murray Kempton, *Newsday*
Editorial writing: Richard Aregood, *Philadelphia Daily News*

1984

Deadline writing: David Zucchino, *The Philadelphia Inquirer*
Non-deadline writing: James Kindall, *The Kansas City Star*
Commentary: Roger Simon, *The Chicago Sun-Times*
Business writing: Peter Rinearson, *The Seattle Times*

1983

Deadline writing: No awards made in this category.
Non-deadline writing: Greta Tilley, *Greensboro News & Record*
Commentary: Rheta Grimsley Johnson, *Memphis Commercial Appeal*
Business writing: Orland Dodson, *Shreveport Times*

1982

Deadline writing: Patrick Sloyan, *Newsday*
Non-deadline writing: William Blundell, *The Wall Street Journal*

Commentary: Theo Lippman Jr., *The Baltimore Sun*
Sports writing: Tom Archdeacon, *The Miami News*

1981

Deadline writing: Richard Zahler, *The Seattle Times*
Non-deadline writing: Saul Pett, Associated Press
Commentary: Paul Greenberg, *Pine Bluff Commercial*
Sports writing: Thomas Boswell, *The Washington Post*

1980

Deadline writing: Carol McCabe, *Providence Journal-Bulletin*
Non-deadline writing: Cynthia Gorney, *The Washington Post*
Commentary: Ellen Goodman, *The Boston Globe*

1979

Deadline writing: Richard Ben Cramer, *The Philadelphia Inquirer*
Non-deadline writing-News: Thomas Oliphant, *Boston Sunday Globe*
Non-deadline writing-Features: Mary Ellen Corbett, *Fort Wayne News Sentinel*
Grand Prize (Commentary): Everett S. Allen, *New Bedford Standard-Times*